Palgrave Texts in Econometrics

Series Editor
Michael P. Clements
Henley Business School
University of Reading
Reading, UK

Founding Editors
Kerry Patterson
Department of Economics
University of Reading
Reading, UK

Terence Mills
School of Business and Economics
Loughborough University
UK

This is a series of themed books in econometrics, where the subject is interpreted as including theoretical developments, applied econometrics and more specialized fields of application, for example financial econometrics, the econometrics of panel data sets, forecasting and so on. Each book in the series is directed to particular aspects of the underlying and unifying theme.

More information about this series at
http://www.palgrave.com/gp/series/14078

Jennifer L. Castle · David F. Hendry

Modelling our Changing World

palgrave
macmillan

Jennifer L. Castle
Magdalen College
University of Oxford
Oxford, UK

David F. Hendry
Nuffield College
University of Oxford
Oxford, UK

Additional material to this book can be downloaded from http://extras.springer.com.

Palgrave Texts in Econometrics
ISBN 978-3-030-21431-9   ISBN 978-3-030-21432-6 (eBook)
https://doi.org/10.1007/978-3-030-21432-6

© The Editor(s) if applicable and The Author(s) 2019. This book is an open access publication.
Open Access This book is licensed under the terms of the Creative Commons Attribution 4.0 International License (http://creativecommons.org/licenses/by/4.0/), which permits use, sharing, adaptation, distribution and reproduction in any medium or format, as long as you give appropriate credit to the original author(s) and the source, provide a link to the Creative Commons license and indicate if changes were made.
The images or other third party material in this book are included in the book's Creative Commons license, unless indicated otherwise in a credit line to the material. If material is not included in the book's Creative Commons license and your intended use is not permitted by statutory regulation or exceeds the permitted use, you will need to obtain permission directly from the copyright holder.
The use of general descriptive names, registered names, trademarks, service marks, etc. in this publication does not imply, even in the absence of a specific statement, that such names are exempt from the relevant protective laws and regulations and therefore free for general use.
The publisher, the authors and the editors are safe to assume that the advice and information in this book are believed to be true and accurate at the date of publication. Neither the publisher nor the authors or the editors give a warranty, expressed or implied, with respect to the material contained herein or for any errors or omissions that may have been made. The publisher remains neutral with regard to jurisdictional claims in published maps and institutional affiliations.

This Palgrave Pivot imprint is published by the registered company Springer Nature Switzerland AG
The registered company address is: Gewerbestrasse 11, 6330 Cham, Switzerland

Preface

This short introduction to *Modelling our Changing World* focuses on the concepts, tools and techniques needed to successfully model time series data. The basic framework draws on Hendry and Nielsen (2007), summarized in Hendry and Nielsen (2010) and Hendry and Mizon (2016). It emphasizes the need for general models to account for the complexities of the modern world and the magnitudes of the many changes that have occurred historically. The combination of evolutionary and abrupt changes poses a major challenge for empirical modelling and hence for developing appropriate methods for selecting models. Fortunately, many of the key concepts can be explained using simple examples. Moreover, computer software for automatic model selection can be used to undertake the more complicated empirical modelling studies.

Modelling our Changing World is aimed at general academic readers interested in a wide range of disciplines. The book is applicable to many areas within the sciences and social sciences, and the examples discussed cover our recent work on climate, volcanoes and economics. All disciplines using time series data should find the book of value. The level minimizes technicalities in favour of visual and textual descriptions, and provides a set of primers to introduce core concepts in an intuitive way. Any more technical discussion with mathematics occurs in boxed material and can be skipped without missing the key ideas and intuition. Undergraduates on environmental and economics courses including some statistics and econometrics should find it a useful complement to standard textbooks.

The book commences with some 'Primers' to elucidate the key concepts, then considers evolutionary and abrupt changes, represented by trends and shifts in a number of time series. Sometimes, we can use trends and breaks to our advantage, but first we must be able to find them in the data being modelled to avoid an incorrect representation. Once a good empirical model of changing series has been built combining our best theoretical understanding and most powerful selection methods, there remains the hazardous task of trying to see what the future might hold. Our approach uses *OxMetrics* (see Doornik 2018b) and *PcGive* (Doornik and Hendry 2018) as that is the only software that implements all the tools and techniques needed in the book. The software is available for download from www.timberlake.co.uk/software/oxmetrics.html. Most recently, XLModeler is an Excel add-in that provides much of the functionality of *PcGive*: see Doornik et al. 2019. More advanced Monte Carlo simulations also require *Ox* (see Doornik 2018a). The accompanying online appendix includes all files required to enable a full replication of the empirical example in Chapter 6, including data, algebra, and batch files using *OxMetrics*.

The references provide plenty of further reading for interested readers. For readers looking to follow up with a more technical treatment we recommend Hendry and Doornik (2014) for model selection, Clements and Hendry (1998, 1999) for forecasting, and Hendry (1995) for a comprehensive treatment of econometric modelling with time series data.

Oxford, UK   Jennifer L. Castle
                                                    David F. Hendry

References

Clements, M. P., and Hendry, D. F. (1998). *Forecasting Economic Time Series*. Cambridge: Cambridge University Press.

Clements, M. P., and Hendry, D. F. (1999). *Forecasting Non-stationary Economic Time Series*. Cambridge, MA: MIT Press.

Doornik, J. A. (2018a). *Object-Oriented Matrix Programming Using Ox*, 8th Edition. London: Timberlake Consultants Press.

Doornik, J. A. (2018b). *OxMetrics: An Interface to Empirical Modelling*, 8th Edition. London: Timberlake Consultants Press.

Doornik, J. A., and Hendry, D. F. (2018). *Empirical Econometric Modelling Using PcGive: Volume I*, 8th Edition. London: Timberlake Consultants Press.

Doornik, J. A., Hendry, D. F., and Laurent, L. (2019). XLModeler 1. https://xlmodeler.com/.

Hendry, D. F. (1995). *Dynamic Econometrics*. Oxford: Oxford University Press.

Hendry, D. F., and Doornik, J. A. (2014). *Empirical Model Discovery and Theory Evaluation*. Cambridge, MA: MIT Press.

Hendry, D. F., and Mizon, G. E. (2016). Improving the teaching of econometrics. *Cogent Economics and Finance*. https://doi.org/10.1080/23322039.2016.1170096. http://www.tandfonline.com/eprint/7dRymBhRtIQF2xtbvPMC/full.

Hendry, D. F., and Nielsen, B. (2007). *Econometric Modeling: A Likelihood Approach*. Princeton: Princeton University Press.

Hendry, D. F., and Nielsen, B. (2010). A modern approach to teaching econometrics. *European Journal of Pure and Applied Mathematics*, **3**, 347–369. https://ejpam.com/index.php/ejpam/article/view/796.

Acknowledgements

The background research was originally supported in part by grants from the Economic and Social Research Council, and more recently by the Open Society Foundations, the Oxford Martin School, the Institute for New Economic Thinking, the Robertson Foundation, and Statistics Norway. We are grateful to them all for the essential funding they provided, and to Jurgen A. Doornik, Neil R. Ericsson, Vivien L. Hendry, Andrew B. Martinez, Grayham E. Mizon, John N.J. Muellbauer, Bent Nielsen, Felix Pretis and Angela Wenham for helpful discussions and suggestions.

The book was prepared in *OxEdit* and initially typeset in LATEX using *MikTex*. Graphical illustrations, numerical computations and Monte Carlo experiments were done using *Ox*, *OxMetrics* and *PcGive*. The present release is *OxMetrics* 8.01 (November 2018).

Oxford
January 2019

Jennifer L. Castle
David F. Hendry

Contents

1	**Introduction**	1
	Reference	4
2	**Key Concepts: A Series of Primers**	5
	2.1 Time Series Data	6
	2.2 Stationarity and Non-stationarity	10
	2.3 Structural Breaks	18
	2.4 Model Selection	23
	References	31
3	**Why Is the World Always Changing?**	37
	3.1 Major Sources of Changes	38
	3.2 Problems if Incorrectly Modelling Non-stationarity	43
	References	46
4	**Making Trends and Breaks Work to Our Advantage**	47
	4.1 Potential Solutions to Stochastic Trend Non-stationarity	48
	4.2 Cointegration Between I(1) Processes	50

4.3	Location Shifts	53
4.4	Dynamic-Stochastic General Equilibrium (DSGE) Models	55
4.5	Handling Location Shifts	58
4.6	Some Benefits of Non-stationarity	60
References		63

5 Detectives of Change: Indicator Saturation — 67
- 5.1 Impulse-Indicator Saturation — 69
- 5.2 Step-Indicator Saturation — 75
- 5.3 Designing Indicator Saturation — 78
  - 5.3.1 Trend-Indicator Saturation — 79
  - 5.3.2 Multiplicative-Indicator Saturation — 80
  - 5.3.3 Designed-Break Indicator Saturation — 81
- 5.4 Outliers and Non-linearity — 82
- References — 83

6 The Polymath: Combining Theory and Data — 85
- 6.1 Theory Driven and Data Driven Models — 86
- 6.2 The Drawbacks of Using Each Approach in Isolation — 87
- 6.3 A Combined Approach — 89
- 6.4 Applying the Combined Approach to UK Inflation Data — 92
- References — 98

7 Seeing into the Future — 101
- 7.1 Forecasting Ignoring Outliers and Location Shifts — 103
- 7.2 Impacts of Stochastic Trends on Forecast Uncertainty — 105
- 7.3 Impacts of Location Shifts on Forecast Uncertainty — 106
- 7.4 Differencing Away Our Troubles — 107
- 7.5 Recommendations When Forecasting Facing Non-stationarity — 111
- References — 115

8 Conclusions: The Ever-Changing Way Forward	117
References	119
Author Index	121
Subject Index	125

About the Authors

Dr. Jennifer L. Castle is Tutorial Fellow in Economics at Magdalen College, Oxford University, and a Fellow at the Institute for New Economic Thinking in the Oxford Martin School.

She previously held a British Academy Postdoctoral Research Fellowship at Nuffield College, Oxford. She is a former director of the International Institute of Forecasters, and has contributed to the fields of Model Selection and Forecasting from both theoretical and practical approaches, publishing in leading journals and contributing to the development of several software packages.

Professor David F. Hendry, Kt is Director of the Program in Economic Modeling at the Institute for New Economic Thinking and co-director of Climate Econometrics at Nuffield College, Oxford University.

He was previously Professor of Econometrics, London School of Economics. He was knighted in 2009, and received a Lifetime Achievement Award from the Economic and Social Research Council in 2014. He is an Honorary Vice-President and a past President of the Royal Economic Society, a Fellow of the British Academy, the Royal Society of Edinburgh, the Econometric Society, the Academy of Social Sciences, the *Journal of Econometrics*, *Econometric Reviews*, International Association for Applied Econometrics and the International Institute of Forecasters. Sir David is a Foreign Honorary Member of the American Economic Association and American Academy of Arts and Sciences. He has been awarded eight Honorary Doctorates, is listed by the ISI as one of the world's 200 most cited economists, is a Thomson Reuters Citation Laureate, and has received the Guy Medal in Bronze from the Royal Statistical Society. He has published more than 200 papers and 25 books on econometric methods, theory, modelling, computing & history; numerical techniques; empirical economics; and forecasting, for which he was awarded the Isaac Kerstenetzky Scholarly Achievement Award in 2012.

List of Figures

Fig. 2.1	Panel (a) UK annual unemployment rate, 1860–2017; (b) a sequence of random numbers	8
Fig. 2.2	Correlations between successively futher apart observations: (a) UK unemployment rates; (b) random numbers	9
Fig. 2.3	Births and deaths per thousand of the UK population	11
Fig. 2.4	(a) US real per capita annual food expenditure in $000; (b) UK price inflation; (c) Real oil price in $ (log scale); (d) UK coal output (right-hand axis) and CO_2 emissions (left-hand axis), both in millions of tons (Mt) per annum	13
Fig. 2.5	(a) Time series of the cumulated random numbers; (b) correlations between successively futher apart observations	14
Fig. 2.6	(a) 'Explaining' global levels of atmospheric CO_2 by the UK retail price index (RPI); (b) no relation between their changes	15
Fig. 2.7	Two examples of structural breaks	19
Fig. 2.8	The impacts on the statistical distributions of the two examples of structural breaks	19
Fig. 2.9	Distributional shifts of total UK CO_2 emissions, Mt p.a.	20
Fig. 2.10	The impacts on statistical relationships of shifts in mean and slope parameters	20

Fig. 2.11	(a) The impact on the statistical distributions of selecting only significant parameters; (b) distributions after bias correction	30
Fig. 3.1	Global mean sea-level (GMSL) has risen by more than 20 cm since 1880 (*Source* CSIRO)	39
Fig. 3.2	Indexes of UK wages and prices (left-hand panel) and UK real wages and productivity (right-hand panel), both on log scales	41
Fig. 3.3	(a) UK wage inflation; and (b) changes in real national debt with major historical events shown	41
Fig. 3.4	Levels of atmospheric CO_2 in parts per million (ppm)	43
Fig. 4.1	Twenty successive serial correlations for (a) nominal wages; (b) real wages; (c) wage inflation; and (d) real wage growth	49
Fig. 4.2	Densities of the differences for: (a) nominal wages; (b) prices; (c) real wages and (d) productivity	50
Fig. 4.3	Time series for the wage share	51
Fig. 4.4	Pairs of artificial time series: (i) unrelated I(0); (ii) unrelated I(1); (iii) cointegrated	52
Fig. 4.5	Location shift in a normal or a fat-tailed distribution	54
Fig. 4.6	Partial co-breaking between wage and price inflation	59
Fig. 4.7	Histograms and densities of logs of UK real GDP in each of three 50-year epochs	62
Fig. 4.8	Histograms and densities of changes in UK CO_2 emissions in each of four 40-year epochs	63
Fig. 5.1	'Split-half' IIS search under null. (a) The data time series; (b) the first 5 impulse indicators included; (c) the other set of impulse indicators; (d) the outcome, as no indicators are selected	71
Fig. 5.2	(a) Perturbed data time series; (b) the first 5 impulse indicators included; (c) the other set of impulse indicators where the dashed line indicates retained; (d) the outcome with and without the selected indicator	73
Fig. 5.3	(a) The data time series; (b) the 4 step indicators included; (c) the other set of step indicators; (d) the outcome as no indicators are selected	77

List of Figures

Fig. 5.4	(a) The shifted time series; (b) the first 4 step indicators included where the thick solid line denotes selected; (c) the other 4 step indicators; (d) the outcome with the selected step indicator	78
Fig. 5.5	A location shift in the growth of UK real wages	79
Fig. 5.6	Several trend breaks in UK real wages detected by TIS	80
Fig. 6.1	(a) Time series of Δp_t and Δm_t; (b) scatter plot with the fitted regression of Δp_t on Δm_t and the deviations therefrom	93
Fig. 6.2	(a) Fitted, $\widehat{\Delta p_t}$, and actual values, Δp_t, from (6.2); (b) scaled residuals $\widehat{e}_t/\widehat{\sigma}$; (c) their density with a standard Normal for comparison] and (d) their residual correlogram	94
Fig. 7.1	1-step forecasts with and without the impulse indicator to model an outlier	103
Fig. 7.2	1-step forecasts with and without the step indicator	104
Fig. 7.3	Multi-period forecasts of log(GDP) using a non-stationary stochastic-trend model (dotted) and a trend-stationary model (dashed) with their associated 95% interval forecasts	105
Fig. 7.4	US real GDP with many successive 8-quarter ahead forecasts	107
Fig. 7.5	Successively differencing a trend break in (a) creates a step shift in (b) an impulse in (c) and a 'blip' in (d)	108
Fig. 7.6	Top panel: growth-rate forecasts; lower panel: implied forecasts of the levels	109
Fig. 7.7	Top panel: 1-step growth-rate forecasts from a 4-period moving average; lower panel: multi-period growth-rate forecasts with ± 2 standard errors from a random walk (bands) and a 4-period moving average of past growth rates (bars)	110
Fig. 7.8	Top panel: multi-period forecasts with ± 2 standard errors from the DGP of a random walk; lower panel: multi-period forecasts from a 2-period moving average with ± 2 calculated standard errors	111
Fig. 7.9	1-step ahead forecasts of the log of UK GDP over 2008–2012 by 'conventional' and robust methods	113

1
Introduction

Abstract The evolution of life on Earth—a tale of both slow and abrupt changes over time—emphasizes that change is pervasive and ever present. Change affects all disciplines using observational data, especially time series of observations. When the dates of events matter, so data are not ahistorical, they are called non-stationary denoting that some key properties like their means and variances change over time. There are several sources of non-stationarity and they have different implications for modelling and forecasting. This Chapter introduces the structure of our book which will explore how to model such observational data on an ever-changing world.

Keywords Change · Observational data · Stationarity · Non-stationarity · Forecast failure

Earth has undergone many remarkable events in its 4.5 billion years, from early forms of life through the evolution and extermination of enormous numbers of species, to the present day diversity of life. It has witnessed movements of continents, impacts from outer space, massive volcanism, and experienced changing climates from tropical through ice ages, and recent changes due to anthropogenic interventions following the development of homo sapiens, especially since the industrial revolution. The world is ever changing, both slowly over time and due to sudden shocks. This book explores how we can model observational data on such a world.

Many disciplines within the sciences and social sciences are confronted with data whose properties change over time. While at first sight, modelling volcanic eruptions, carbon dioxide emissions, sea levels, global temperatures, unemployment rates, wage inflation, or population growth seem to face very different problems, they share many commonalities. Measurements of such varied phenomena come in the form of time-series data. When observations on a given phenomenon, say CO_2 emissions, population growth or unemployment, come from a process whose properties remain constant over time—for example, having the same mean (average value) and variance (movements around that mean) at all points in time—they are said to be *stationary*. This is a technical use of that word, and does not entail 'unmoving' as in a traffic jam. Rather, such time series look essentially the same over different time intervals: indeed, a stationary time series is ahistoric in that the precise dates of observations should not matter greatly. However, almost all social, political, economic and environmental systems are non-stationary, with means, variances and other features, such as correlations between variables, changing over time. In the real world, whether an event under consideration happened in 1914, 1929, 1945 or 2008 usually matters, a clear sign that the data are *non-stationary*.

Much of economic analysis concerns equilibrium states although we all know that economies are buffeted by many more forces than those contained in such analyses. Sudden political changes, financial and oil crises, evolution of social mores, technological advances, wars and natural catastrophes all impinge on economic outcomes, yet are rarely part of theoretical economic analyses. Moreover, the intermittent but all too frequent occurrence of such events reveals that disequilibrium is the more natural state of economies. Indeed, forecast failures—where forecasts go badly wrong relative to their expected accuracy—reveal that such non-stationarities do happen, and have adverse effects both on economies and on the verisimilitude of empirical economic models. Castle et al. (2019) provide an introduction to forecasting models and methods and the properties of the resulting forecasts, explaining why forecasting mishaps are so common.

To set the scene, the book begins with a series of primers on non-stationary time-series data and their implications for empirical model selection. Two different sources of non-stationarity are delineated, the first coming from evolutionary changes and the second from abrupt, often unanticipated, shifts. Failing to account for either can produce misleading inferences, leading to models that do not adequately characterise the available evidence. We then go on to explore how features of non-stationary time-series data can be modelled, utilising both well-established and recent innovative techniques. Some of the proposed new techniques may surprise many readers. The solution is to include more variables than you have observations for, which is important to capture the ever changing nature of the data. Nevertheless, both theoretical analyses and computer simulations confirm that the approach is not only viable, but has excellent properties.

Various examples from different disciplines demonstrate not only the difficulties of working with such data, but also some advantages. We will gain insights into a range of phenomena by carefully modelling change in its many forms. The examples considered include the underlying causes and consequences of climate change, macroeconomic performance, various social phenomena and even detecting the impacts of volcanic eruptions on temperatures. However, valuable insights from theoretical subject-matter analyses must also be retained in an efficient approach and again recent developments can facilitate doing so. Forecasting will inevitably be hazardous in an ever-changing world, but we consider some ways in which systematic failure can be partly mitigated.

The structure of the book is as follows. In Chapter 2, primers outline the key concepts of time series, non-stationarity, structural breaks and model selection. Chapter 3 explores some explanations for change and briefly reviews the history of time-series modelling. Chapter 4 looks at how to use the ever changing data to your advantage: non-stationarity in some form is invaluable for identifying causal relationships and conducting policy. Chapter 5 shows how various forms of break can be detected and hence modelled. Chapter 6 examines an empirical example of combining theory and data to improve inference. Chapter 7 looks at forecasting non-stationary time series, with hints on how to handle structural breaks over the forecast horizon, and finally Chapter 8 concludes.

Reference

Castle, J. L., Clements, M. P., and Hendry, D. F. (2019). *Forecasting: An Essential Introduction.* New Haven, CT: Yale University Press.

Open Access This chapter is licensed under the terms of the Creative Commons Attribution 4.0 International License (http://creativecommons.org/licenses/by/4.0/), which permits use, sharing, adaptation, distribution and reproduction in any medium or format, as long as you give appropriate credit to the original author(s) and the source, provide a link to the Creative Commons license and indicate if changes were made.

The images or other third party material in this chapter are included in the chapter's Creative Commons license, unless indicated otherwise in a credit line to the material. If material is not included in the chapter's Creative Commons license and your intended use is not permitted by statutory regulation or exceeds the permitted use, you will need to obtain permission directly from the copyright holder.

2

Key Concepts: A Series of Primers

Abstract This chapter provides four primers. The first considers what a time series is and notes some of the major properties that time series might exhibit. The second extends that to distinguish stationary from non-stationary time series, where the latter are the prevalent form, and indeed provide the rationale for this book. The third describes a specific form of non-stationarity due to structural breaks, where the 'location' of a time series shifts abruptly. The fourth briefly introduces methods for selecting empirical models of non-stationary time series. Each primer notes at the start what key aspects will be addressed.

Keywords Time series · Persistence · Non-stationarity · Nonsense relations · Structural breaks · Location shifts · Model selection · Congruence · Encompassing

2.1 Time Series Data

What is a time series and what are its properties?

A time series orders observations
Time series can be measured at different frequencies
Time series exhibit different patterns of 'persistence'
Historical time can matter

A Time Series Orders Observations
A time series is any set of observations ordered by the passing of time. Table 2.1 shows an example. Each year, a different value arises. There are millions of recorded time series, in most social sciences like economics and politics, environmental sciences like climatology, and earth sciences like volcanology among other disciplines.

The most important property of a time series is the *ordering* of observations by 'time's arrow': the value in 2014 happened before that in 2015. We live in a world where we seem unable to go back into the past, to undo a car crash, or a bad investment decision, notwithstanding science-fiction stories of 'time-travellers'. That attribute will be crucial, as time-series analysis seeks to explain the present by the past, and forecast the future from the present. That last activity is needed as it also seems impossible to go into the future and return with knowledge of what happens there.

Time Series Occur at Different Frequencies
A second important feature is the *frequency* at which a time series is recorded, from nano-seconds in laser experiments, every second for electricity usage, through days for rainfall, weeks, months, quarters, years, decades and centuries to millenia in paleo-climate measures. It is relatively easy to combine higher frequencies to lower, as in adding up the economic

Table 2.1 A short annual time series

Date	2012	2013	2014	2015	2016	2017
Value	4	6	5	9	7	3

output of a country every quarter to produce an annual time series. An issue of concern to time-series analysts is whether important information is lost by such temporal aggregation. Using a somewhat stretched example, a quarterly time series that went 2, 5, 9, 4 then 3, 4, 8, 5 and so on, reveals marked changes with a pattern where the second 'half' is much larger than the 'first', whereas the annual series is always just a rather uninformative 20. The converse of creating a higher-frequency series from a lower is obviously more problematic unless there are one or more closely related variables measured at the higher frequency to draw on. For example, monthly measures of retail sales may help in creating a monthly series of total consumers' expenditure from its quarterly time series. In July 2018, the United Kingdom Office for National Statistics started producing monthly aggregate time series, using electronic information that has recently become available to it.

Time Series Exhibit Patterns of 'Persistence'

A third feature concerns whether or not a time series, whatever its frequency, exhibits *persistent patterns*. For example, are high values followed by lower, or are successive values closely related, so one sunny day is most likely to be succeeded by another? Monthly temperatures in Europe have a distinct seasonal pattern, whereas annual averages are less closely related with a slow upward trend over the past century.

Figure 2.1 illustrates two very different time series. The top panel records the annual unemployment rate in the United Kingdom from 1860–2017. The vertical axis records the rate (e.g., 0.15 is 15%), and the horizontal axis reports the time. As can be seen (we call this ocular econometrics), when unemployment is high, say above the long-run mean of 5% as from 1922–1939, it is more likely to be high in the next year, and similarly when it is low, as from 1945–1975, it tends to stay low. By way of contrast, the lower panel plots some computer generated random numbers between −2 and +2, where no persistence can be seen.

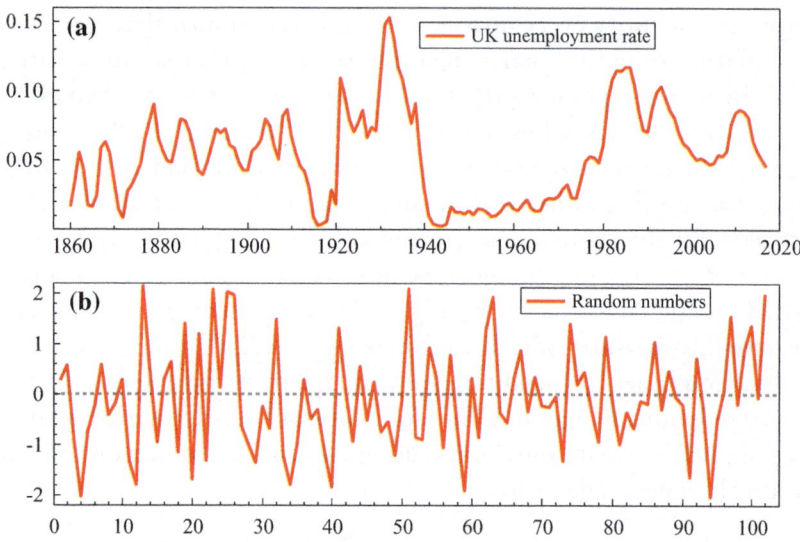

Fig. 2.1 Panel **(a)** UK annual unemployment rate, 1860–2017; **(b)** a sequence of random numbers

Many economic time series are very persistent, so correlations between values of the same variable many year's apart can often be remarkably high. Even for the unemployment series in Fig. 2.1(a), there is considerable persistence, which can be measured by the correlations between values increasingly far apart. Figure 2.2(a) plots the correlations between values r-years' apart for the UK unemployment rate, so the first vertical bar is the correlation between unemployment in the current year and that one year earlier, and so on going back 20 years. The dashed lines show an interval within which the correlations are not significantly different from zero. Note that sufficiently far apart correlations are negative, reflecting the 'long swings' between high and low unemployment visible in Fig. 2.1(a). Figure 2.2(b) again shows the contrast with the correlations between successively far apart random numbers, where all the bars lie in the interval shown by the dashed lines.

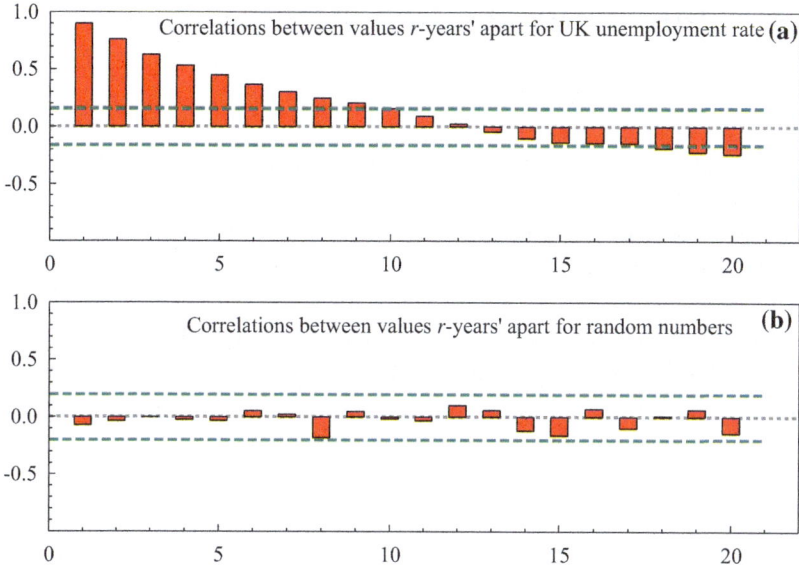

Fig. 2.2 Correlations between successively futher apart observations: (a) UK unemployment rates; (b) random numbers

Historical Time can Matter

Historical time is often an important attribute of a time series, so it matters that an event occurred in 1939 (say) rather than 1956. This leads to our second primer concerned with a very fundamental property of all time series: does it 'look essentially the same at different times', or does it evolve? Examples of relatively progressive evolution include technology, medicine, and longevity, where the average age of death in the western world has increased at about a weekend every week since around 1860. But major abrupt and often unexpected shifts can also occur, as with financial crises, earthquakes, volcanic eruptions or a sudden slow down in improving longevity as seen recently in the USA.

2.2 Stationarity and Non-stationarity

What is a non-stationary time series?

A time series is not stationary if historical time matters
Sources of non-stationarity
Historical review of understanding non-stationarity

A Time Series is Not Stationary if Historical Time Matters
We all know what it is like to be stationary when we would rather be moving: sometimes stuck in traffic jams, or still waiting at an airport long after the scheduled departure time of our flight. A feature of such unfortunate situations is that the setting 'looks the same at different times': we see the same trees beside our car until we start to move again, or the same chairs in the airport lounge. The word stationary is also used in a more technical sense in statistical analyses of time series: a stationary process is one where its mean and variance stay the same over time. Our solar system appears to be almost stationary, looking essentially the same over our lives (though perhaps not over very long time spans).

A time series is stationary when its first two moments, namely the mean and variance, are finite and constant over time.[1] In a stationary process, the influence of past shocks must die out, because if they cumulated, the variance could not be constant. Since past shocks do not accumulate (or integrate), such a stationary time series is said to be integrated of order zero, denoted I(0).[2] Observations on the process will center around the mean, with a spread determined by the magnitude of its constant variance. Consequently, any sample of a stationary process will 'look like' any other, making it *ahistorical*. The series of random numbers in Fig. 2.1(b) is an example. If an economy were stationary, we would not need to know the

---

[1] More precisely, this is weak stationarity, and occurs when for all values of t (denoted $\forall t$) the expected value $\mathsf{E}[\cdot]$ of a random variable y_t satisfies $\mathsf{E}[y_t] = \mu$, the variance, $\mathsf{E}[(y_t - \mu)^2] = \sigma^2$, and the covariances $\mathsf{E}[(y_t - \mu)(y_{t-s} - \mu)] = \gamma(s)$ $\forall s$, where μ, σ^2, and $\gamma(s)$ are finite and independent of t and $\gamma(s) \to 0$ quite quickly as s grows.
[2] When the moments depend on the initial conditions of the process, stationarity holds only asymptotically (see e.g., Spanos 1986), but we ignore that complication here.

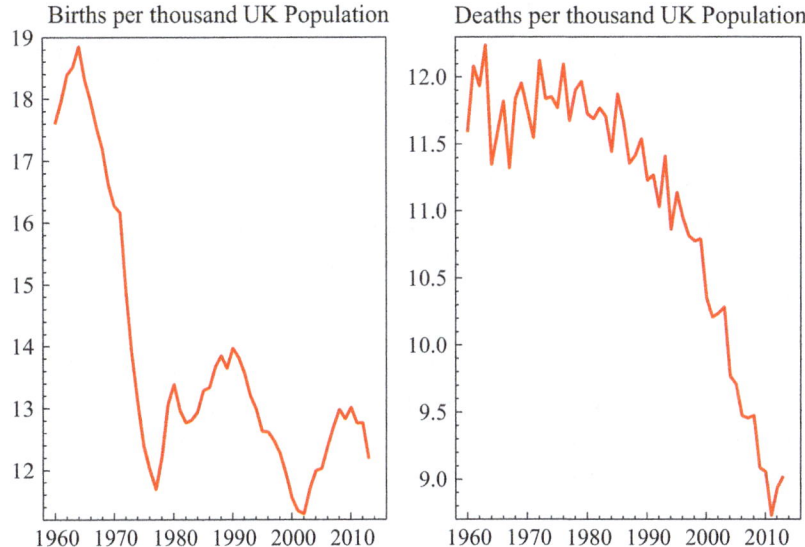

Fig. 2.3 Births and deaths per thousand of the UK population

historical dates of the observations: whether it was 1860–1895 or 1960–1995 would be essentially irrelevant.

As a corollary, a non-stationary process is one where the distribution of a variable does not stay the same at different points in time–the mean and/or variance changes–which can happen for many reasons. Stationarity is the exception and non-stationarity is the norm for most social science and environmental times series. Specific events can matter greatly, including major wars, pandemics, and massive volcanic eruptions; financial innovation; key discoveries like vaccination, antibiotics and birth control; inventions like the steam engine, dynamo and flight; etc. These can cause persistent shifts in the means and variances of the data, thereby violating stationarity. Figure 2.3 shows the large drop in UK birth rates following the introduction of oral contraception, and the large declines in death rates since 1960 due to increasing longevity. Comparing the two panels shows that births exceeded deaths at every date, so the UK population must have grown even before net immigration is taken into account.

Economies evolve and change over time in both real and nominal terms, sometimes dramatically as in major wars, the US Great Depression after 1929, the 'Oil Crises' of the mid 1970s, or the more recent 'Financial Crisis and Great Recession' over 2008–2012.

Sources of Non-stationarity
There are two important sources of non-stationarity often visible in time series: evolution and sudden shifts. The former reflects slower changes, such as knowledge accumulation and its embodiment in capital equipment, whereas the latter occurs from (e.g.) wars, major geological events, and policy regime changes. The first source is the cumulation of past shocks, somewhat akin to changes in DNA cumulating over time to permanently change later inherited characteristics. Evolution results from cumulated shocks, and that also applies to economic and other time series, making their means and variances change over time. The second source is the occurrence of sudden, often unanticipated, shifts in the level of a time series, called location shifts. The historical track record of economic forecasting is littered with forecasts that went badly wrong, an outcome that should occur infrequently in a stationary process, as then the future would be like the past. The four panels of Fig. 2.4 illustrate both such non-stationarities.

Panel (a) records US annual constant-price per capita food expenditure from 1929–2006 which has more than doubled, but at greatly varying rates manifested by the changing slopes of the line, with several major 'bumps'. Panel (b) reports the rates of price inflation workers faced: relatively stable till 1914, then rising and falling by around 20% per annum during and immediately after the First World War, peaking again during the oil crises of the 1970s before returning to a relatively stable trajectory. In Panel (c) real oil prices in constant price dollars fell for almost a century with intermittent temporary upturns before their dramatic revival in the Oil Crises that started the UK's 1970s inflation, with greatly increased volatility. Finally, Panel (d) records both the UK's coal output (dashed line) and its CO_2 emissions (solid line), both in Mt per annum: what goes up can come down. The fall in the former from 250 Mt per annum to near zero is as dramatic a non-stationarity as one could imagine, as is the behaviour of emissions, with huge 'outliers' in the 1920s and a similar '∩'

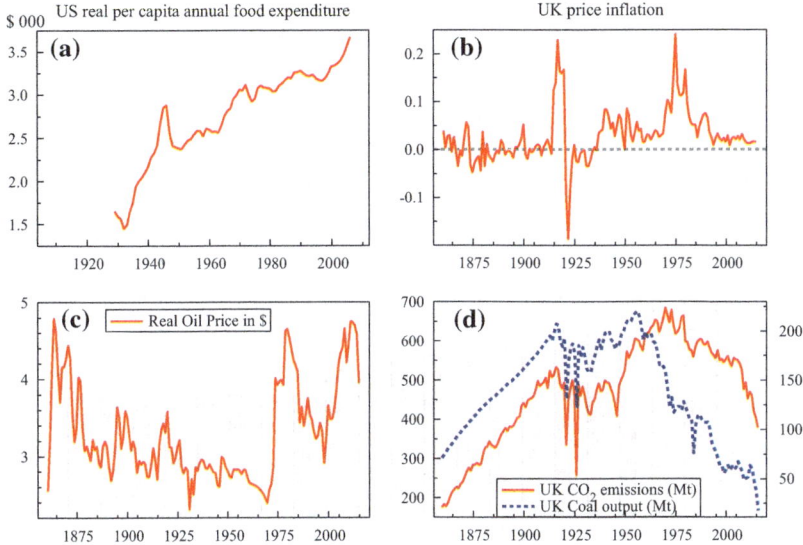

Fig. 2.4 (a) US real per capita annual food expenditure in $000; (b) UK price inflation; (c) Real oil price in $ (log scale); (d) UK coal output (right-hand axis) and CO_2 emissions (left-hand axis), both in millions of tons (Mt) per annum

shape. In per capita terms, the UK's CO_2 emissions are now below any level since 1860–when the UK was the workshop of the world.

An important source of non-stationarity is that due to what are called processes with unit roots. Such processes are highly persistent as they cumulate past shocks. Indeed, today's value of the time series equals the previous value plus the new shock: i.e., there is a unit parameter linking the successive values. Figure 2.5(a) shows the time series that results from cumulating the random numbers in Fig. 2.1(b), which evolves slowly downwards in this instance, but could 'wander' in any direction. Next, Fig. 2.5(b) records the resulting correlations between successive values, quite unlike that in Fig. 2.2(b). Even for observations 20 periods apart, the correlation is still large and positive.

Empirical modelling relating variables faces important difficulties when time series are non-stationary. If two *unrelated* time series are non-stationary because they evolve by accumulating past shocks, their cor-

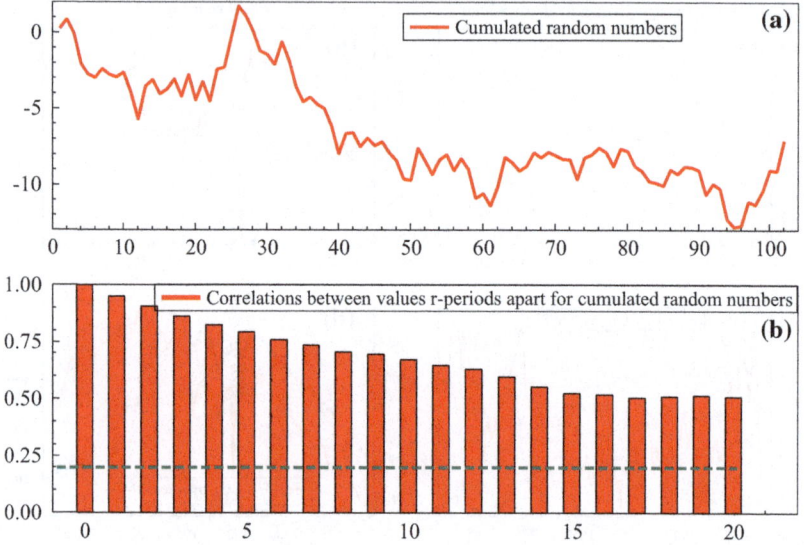

Fig. 2.5 (a) Time series of the cumulated random numbers; (b) correlations between successively futher apart observations

relation will nevertheless appear to be significant about 70% of the time using a conventional 5% decision rule.

Apocryphal examples during the Victorian era were the surprising high positive correlations between the numbers of human births and storks nesting in Stockholm, and between murders and membership of the Church of England. As a consequence, these are called nonsense relations. A silly example is shown in Fig. 2.6(a) where the global atmospheric concentrations of CO_2 are 'explained' by the monthly UK Retail Price Index (RPI), partly because both have increased over the sample, 1988(3) to 2011(6). However, Panel (b) shows that the changes in the two series are essentially unrelated.

The nonsense relations problem arises because uncertainty is seriously under-estimated if stationarity is wrongly assumed. During the 1980s, econometricians established solutions to this problem, and en-route also showed that the structure of economic behaviour virtually ensured that most economic data would be non-stationary. At first sight, this poses many difficulties for modelling economic data. But we can use it to

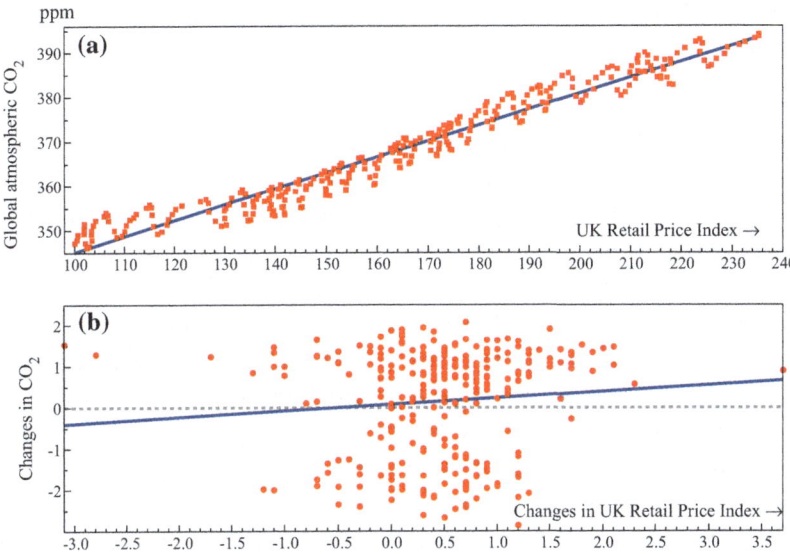

Fig. 2.6 (a) 'Explaining' global levels of atmospheric CO_2 by the UK retail price index (RPI); (b) no relation between their changes

our advantage as such non-stationarity is often accompanied by common trends. Most people make many more decisions (such as buying numerous items of shopping), than the small number of variables that guide their decisions (e.g., their income or bank balance). That non-stationary data often move closely together due to common variables driving economic decisions enables us to model the non-stationarities. Below, we will use the behaviour of UK wages, prices, productivity and unemployment over 1860–2016 to illustrate the discussion and explain empirical modelling methods that handle non-stationarities which arise from cumulating shocks.

Many economic models used in empirical research, forecasting or for guiding policy have been predicated on treating observed data as stationary. But policy decisions, empirical research and forecasting also must take the non-stationarity of the data into account if they are to deliver useful outcomes. We will offer guidance for policy makers and researchers on identifying what forms of non-stationarity are prevalent, what hazards each form implies for empirical modelling and forecasting, and for any resulting policy decisions, and what tools are available to overcome such hazards.

Historical Review of Understanding Non-stationarity

Developing a viable analysis of non-stationarity in economics really commenced with the discovery of the problem of 'nonsense correlations'. These high correlations are found between variables that should be unrelated: for example, that between the price level in the UK and cumulative annual rainfall shown in Hendry (1980).[3] Yule (1897) had considered the possibility that both variables in a correlation calculation might be related to a third variable (e.g., population growth), inducing a spuriously high correlation: this partly explains the close relation in Fig. 2.6. But by Yule (1926), he recognised the problem was indeed 'nonsense correlations'. He suspected that high correlations between successive values of variables, called serial, or auto, correlation as in Fig. 2.5(b), might affect the correlations between variables. He investigated that in a manual simulation experiment, randomly drawing from a hat pieces of paper with digits written on them. He calculated correlations between pairs of draws for many samples of those numbers and also between pairs after the numbers for each variable were cumulated once, and finally cumulated twice. For example, if the digits for the first variable went 5, 9, 1, 4, ..., the cumulative numbers would be 5, 14, 15, 19, ... and so on. Yule found that in the purely random case, the correlation coefficient was almost normally distributed around zero, but after the digits were cumulated once, he was surprised to find the correlation coefficient was nearly uniformly distributed, so almost all correlation values were equally likely despite there being no genuine relation between the variables. Thus, he found 'significant', though not very high, correlations far more often than for non-cumulated samples. Yule was even more startled to discover that the correlation coefficient had a U-shaped distribution when the numbers were doubly cumulated, so the correct hypothesis of no relation between the genuinely unrelated variables was virtually always rejected due to a near-perfect, yet nonsense, correlation of ± 1.

---

[3] Extensive histories of econometrics are provided by Morgan (1990), Qin (1993, 2013), and Hendry and Morgan (1995).

Granger and Newbold (1974) re-emphasized that an apparently 'significant relation' between variables, but where there remained substantial serial correlation in the residuals from that relation, was a symptom associated with nonsense regressions. Phillips (1986) provided a technical analysis of the sources and symptoms of nonsense regressions. Today, Yule's three types of time series are called integrated of order zero, one, and two respectively, usually denoted I(0), I(1), and I(2), as the number of times the series integrate (i.e., cumulate) past values. Conversely, differencing successive values of an I(1) series delivers an I(0) time series, etc., but loses any information connecting the levels. At the same time as Yule, Smith (1926) had already suggested that a solution was nesting models in levels and differences, but this great step forward was quickly forgotten (see Terence Mills 2011). Indeed, differencing is not the only way to reduce the order of integration of a group of related time series, as Granger (1981) demonstrated with the introduction of the concept of cointegration, extended by Engle and Granger (1987) and discussed in Sect. 4.2: see Hendry (2004) for a history of the development of cointegration.

The history of structural breaks–the topic of the next 'primer'–has been less studied, but major changes in variables and consequential shifts between relationships date back to at least the forecast failures that wrecked the embryonic US forecasting industry (see Friedman 2014). In considering forecasting the outcome for 1929–what a choice of year!–Smith (1929) foresaw the major difficulty as being unanticipated location shifts (although he used different terminology), but like his other important contribution just noted, this insight also got forgotten. Forecast failure has remained a recurrent theme in economics with notable disasters around the time of the oil crises (see e.g., Perron 1989) and the 'Great Recession' considered in Sect. 7.3.

What seems to have taken far longer to realize is that to every forecast failure there is an associated theory failure as emphasized by Hendry and Mizon (2014), an important issue we will return to in Sect. 4.4.[4] Meantime, we consider the other main form of non-stationarity, namely the many forms of 'structural breaks'.

---

[4] See http://www.voxeu.org/article/why-standard-macro-models-fail-crises for a less technical explanation.

2.3 Structural Breaks

What are structural breaks?

> Types of structural breaks
> Causes of structural breaks
> Consequences of structural breaks
> Tests for structural breaks
> Modelling facing structural breaks
> Forecasting in processes with structural breaks
> Regime-shift models

Types of Structural Breaks

A *structural break* denotes a shift in the behaviour of a variable over time, such as a jump in the money stock, or a change in a previous relationship between observable variables, such as between inflation and unemployment, or the balance of trade and the exchange rate. Many sudden changes, particularly when unanticipated, cause links between variables to shift. This is a problem that is especially prevalent in economics as many structural breaks are induced by events outside the purview of most economic analyses, but examples abound in the sciences and social sciences, e.g., volcanic eruptions, earthquakes, and the discovery of penicillin. The consequences of not taking breaks into account include poor models, large forecast errors after the break, mis-guided policy, and inappropriate tests of theories.

Such breaks can take many forms. The simplest to visualize is a shift in the mean of a variable as shown in the left-hand panel of Fig. 2.7. This is a 'location shift', from a mean of zero to 2. Forecasts based on the zero mean will be systematically badly wrong.

Next, a shift in the variance of a time series is shown in the right-hand graph of Fig. 2.7. The series is fairly 'flat' till about observation 19, then varies considerably more after.

Of course, both means and variances can shift, more than once and at different times. Such shifts in a variable can also be viewed through changes in its distribution as in Fig. 2.8. Both breaks have noticeable effects if the before–after distributions are plotted together as shown. For

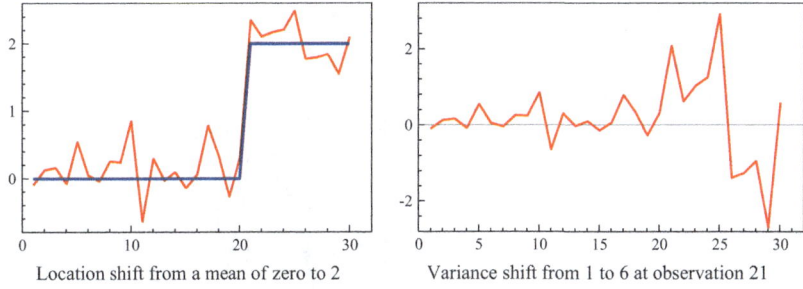

Fig. 2.7 Two examples of structural breaks

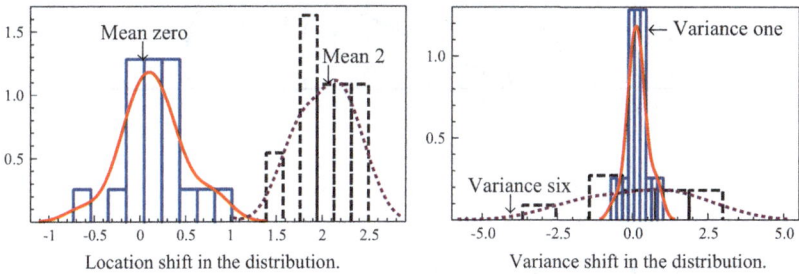

Fig. 2.8 The impacts on the statistical distributions of the two examples of structural breaks

a location shift, the entire distribution is moved to a new center; for a variance increase, it remains centered as before but much more spread.

Distributional shifts certainly occur in the real world, as Fig. 2.9 shows, plotting four sub-periods of annual UK CO_2 emissions in Mt. The first three sub-periods all show the centers of the distributions moving to higher values, but the fourth (1980–2016) jumps back below the previous sub-period distribution.

Shifts in just one variable in a relationship causes their link to break. In the left-hand graph of Fig. 2.10, the dependent variable has a location shift, but the explanatory variable does not: separate fits are quite unlike the overall fit. In the right-hand graph of Fig. 2.10, the regression slope parameter changes from 1 to 2. Combinations of breaks in means, variances, trends and slopes can also occur. Naturally, such combinations can be very difficult to unravel empirically.

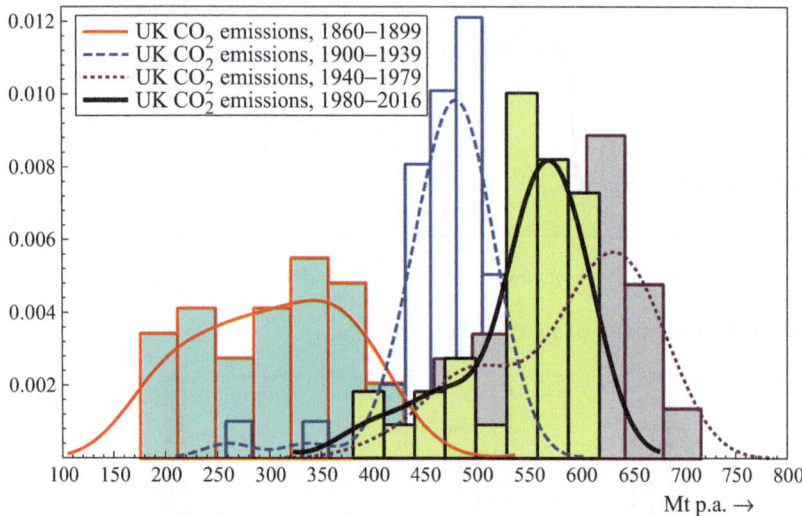

Fig. 2.9 Distributional shifts of total UK CO_2 emissions, Mt p.a.

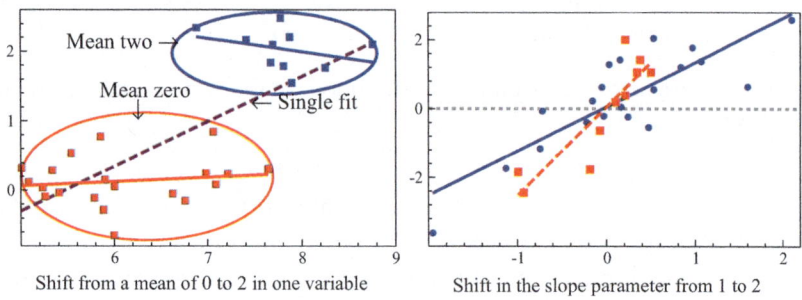

Fig. 2.10 The impacts on statistical relationships of shifts in mean and slope parameters

Causes of Structural Breaks

The world has changed enormously in almost every measurable way over the last few centuries, sometimes abruptly (for a large body of evidence, see the many time series in https://ourworldindata.org/). Of the numerous possible instances, dramatic shifts include World War I; the 1918–20 flu' epidemic; 1929 crash and ensuing Great Depression; World War II; the 1970s oil crises; 1997 Asian financial crisis; the 2000 'dot com' crash; and the 2008–2012 financial crisis and Great Recession (and maybe Brexit). Such large and sudden breaks usually lead to location shifts. More gradual changes can cause the parameters of relationships to 'drift': changes in technology, social mores, or legislation usually take time to work through.

Consequences of Structural Breaks

The impacts of structural breaks on empirical models naturally depend on their forms, magnitudes, and numbers, as well as on how well specified the model in question is. When large location shifts or major changes in the parameters linking variables in a relationship are not handled correctly, statistical estimates of relations will be distorted. As we discuss in Chapter 7, this often leads to forecast failure, and if the 'broken' relation is used for policy, the outcomes of policy interventions will not be as expected. Thus, viable relationships need to account for all the structural breaks that occurred, even though in practice, there will be an unknown number, most of which will have an unknown magnitude, form, and duration and may even have unknown starting and ending dates.

Tests for Structural Breaks

There are many tests for structural breaks in given relationships, but these often depend not only on knowing the correct relationship to be tested, but also on knowing a considerable amount about the types of breaks, and the properties of the time series being analyzed. Tests include those proposed by Brown et al. (1975), Chow (1960), Nyblom (1989), Hansen (1992a), Hansen (1992b) (for I(1) data), Jansen and Teräsvirta (1996), and Bai and Perron (1998, 2003). Perron (2006) provided a wide ranging survey of then available methods of estimation and testing in models with structural breaks, including their close links to processes with unit roots, which are non-stationary stochastic processes (discussed above) that can cause problems in statistical inference. To apply any test requires that the model is already specified, so while it is certainly wise to test if there are important structural breaks leading to parameter non-constancies, their discovery then reveals the model to be flawed, and how to 'repair' it is always unclear. Tests can reject because of other untreated problems than the one for which they were designed: for example, apparent non-constancy may be due to residual autocorrelation, or unmodelled persistence left in the unexplained component, which distorts the estimated standard errors (see e.g., Corsi et al. 1982). A break can occur because an omitted determinant shifts, or from a location shift in an irrelevant variable included inadvertently, and the 'remedy' naturally differs between such settings.

Modelling Facing Structural Breaks
Failing to model breaks will almost always lead to a badly-specified empirical model that will not usefully represent the data. Knowing of or having detected breaks, a common approach is to 'model' them by adding appropriate indicator variables, namely artificial variables that are zero for most of a sample period but unity over the time that needs to be indicated as having a shift: Fig. 2.7 illustrates a step indicator that takes the value 2 for observations 21–30. Indicators can be formulated to reflect any relevant aspect of a model, such as changing trends, or multiplied by variables to capture when parameters shift, and so on. It is possible to design *model selection* strategies that tackle structural breaks automatically as part of their algorithm, as advocated by Hendry and Doornik (2014). Even though such approaches, called indicator saturation methods (see Johansen and Nielsen 2009; Castle et al. 2015), lead to more candidate explanatory variables than there are available observations, it is possible for a model selection algorithm to include large blocks of indicators for any number of outliers and location shifts, and even parameter changes (see e.g., Ericsson 2012). Indicators relevant to the problem at hand can be designed in advance, as with the approach used to detect the impacts of volcanic eruptions on temperature in Pretis et al. (2016).

Forecasting in Processes with Structural Breaks
In the forecasting context, not all structural breaks matter equally, and indeed some have essentially no effect on forecast accuracy, but may change the precision of forecasts, or estimates of forecast-error variances. Clements and Hendry (1998) provide a taxonomy of sources of forecast errors which explains why location shifts—changes in the previous means, or levels, of variables in relationships—are the main cause of forecast failures. Ericsson (1992) provides a clear discussion. Figure 2.7 again illustrates why the previous mean provides a very poor forecast of the final 10 data points. Rapid detection of such shifts, or better still, forecasting them in advance, can reduce systematic forecast failure, as can a number of devices for

robustifying forecasts after location shifts, such as intercept corrections and additional differencing, the topic of Chapter 7.

Regime-Shift Models
An alternative approach models shifts, including recessions, as the outcome of stochastic shocks in non-linear dynamic processes, the large literature on which was partly surveyed by Hamilton (2016). Such models assume there is a probability at any point in time, conditional on the current regime and possibly several recent past regimes, that an economy might switch to a different state. A range of models have been proposed that could characterize such processes, which Hamilton describes as 'a rich set of tools and specifications on which to draw for interpreting data and building economic models for environments in which there may be changes in regime'. However, an important concern is which specification and which tools apply in any given instance, and how to choose between them when a given model formulation is not guaranteed to be fully appropriate. Consequently, important selection and evaluation issues must be addressed.

2.4 Model Selection

Why do we need model selection?

  What is model selection?
  Evaluating empirical models
  Objectives of model selection
  Model selection methods
  Concepts used in analyses of statistical model selection
  Consequences of statistical model selection

What is Model Selection?
Model selection concerns choosing a formal representation of a set of data from a range of possible specifications thereof. It is ubiquitous in observational-data studies because the processes generating the data are almost never known. How selection is undertaken is sometimes not

described, and may even give the impression that the final model reported was the first to be fitted. When the number of candidate variables needing analyzed is larger than the available sample, selection is inevitable as the complete model cannot be estimated. In general, the choice of selection method depends on the nature of the problem being addressed and the purpose for which a model is being sought, and can be seen as an aspect of testing multiple hypotheses: see Lehmann (1959). Purposes include understanding links between data series (especially how they evolved over the past), to test a theory, to forecast future outcomes, and (in e.g., economics and climatology) to conduct policy analyses.

It might be thought that a single 'best' model (on some criteria) should resolve all four purposes, but that transpires not to be the case, especially when observational data are not stationary. Indeed, the set of models from which one is to be selected may be implicit, as when the functional form of the relation under study is not known (linear, log-linear or non-linear), or when there may be an unknown number of outliers, or even shifts. Model selection can also apply to the design of experiments such that the data collected is well-suited to the problem. As Konishi and Kitagawa (2008, p. 75) state, 'The majority of the problems in statistical inference can be considered to be problems related to statistical modeling'. Relatedly, Sir David Cox (2006, p. 197) has said, 'How [the] translation from subject-matter problem to statistical model is done is often the most critical part of an analysis'.

Evaluating Empirical Models
Irrespective of how models are selected, it is always feasible to evaluate any chosen model against the available empirical evidence. There are two main criteria for doing so in our approach, *congruence* and *encompassing*.

The first concerns how well the model fits the data, the theory and any constraints imposed by the nature of the observations. Fitting the data requires that the unexplained components, or residuals, match the properties assumed for the errors in the model formulation. These usually entail no systematic behaviour, such as successive residuals being correlated (serial or autocorrelation), that the residuals are relatively homogeneous in their variability (called homoscedastic), and that all parameters which are assumed to be constant over time actually are. Matching the theory requires that the model formulation is consistent with the analysis from which it is derived, but does not require that the theory model is imposed on the data, both because abstract theory may not reflect the underlying behaviour, and because little would be learned if empirical results merely put ragged cloth on a sketchy theory skeleton. Matching intrinsic data properties may involve taking logarithms to ensure an inherently positive variable is modelled as such, or that flows cumulate correctly to stocks, and that outcomes satisfy accounting constraints.

Although satisfying all of these requirements may seem demanding, there are settings in which they are all trivially satisfied. For example, if the data are all orthogonal, and independent identically distributed (IID)—such as independent draws from a Normal distribution with a constant mean and variance and no data constraints—all models would appear to be congruent with whatever theory was used in their formulation. Thus, an additional criterion is whether a model can encompass, or explain the results of, rival explanations of the same variables. There is a large literature on alternative approaches, but the simplest is parsimonious encompassing in which an empirical model is embedded within the most general formulation (often the union of all the contending models) and loses no significant information relative to that general model. In the orthogonal IID setting just noted, a congruent model may be found wanting because some variables it excluded are highly significant statistically when included. That example also emphasizes that congruence is not definitive, and most certainly is not 'truth', in that a sequence of successively encompassing congruent empirical models can be developed in a progressive research strategy: see Mizon (1984, 2008), Hendry (1988, 1995), Govaerts et al. (1994), Hoover and Perez (1999), Bontemps and Mizon (2003, 2008), and Doornik (2008).

Objectives of Model Selection

At base, selection is an attempt to find all the relevant determinants of a phenomenon usually represented by measurements on a variable, or set of variables, of interest, while eliminating all the influences that are irrelevant for the problem at hand. This is most easily understood for relationships between variables where some are to be 'explained' as functions of others, but it is not known which of the potential 'explaining' variables really matter. A simple strategy to ensure all relevant variables are retained is to always keep every candidate variable; whereas to ensure no irrelevant variables are retained, keep no variables at all. Manifestly these strategies conflict, but highlight the 'trade-off' that affects all selection approaches: the more likely a method is to retain relevant influences by some criterion (such as statistical significance) the more likely some irrelevant influences will chance to be retained. The costs and benefits of that trade-off depend on the context, the approach adopted, the sample size, the numbers of irrelevant and relevant variables—which are unknown—how substantive the latter are, as well as on the purpose of the analysis.

For reliably testing a theory, the model must certainly include all the theory-relevant variables, but also all the variables that in fact affect the outcomes being modelled, whereas little damage may be done by also including some variables that are not actually relevant. However, for forecasting, even estimating the in-sample process that generated the data need not produce the forecasts with the smallest mean-square errors (see e.g., Clements and Hendry 1998). Finally, for policy interventions, it is essential that the relation between target and instrument is causal, and that the parameters of the model in use are also invariant to the intervention if the policy change is to have the anticipated effect. Here the key concept is of invariance under changes, so shifts in the policy variable, say a price rise intended to increase revenue from sales, does not alter consumers' attitudes to the company in question, thereby shifting their demand functions and so leading to the unintended consequence of a more than proportionate fall in sales.

Model Selection Methods

Most empirical models are selected by some process, varying from imposing a theory-model on the data evidence (having 'selected' the theory), through manual choice, which may be to suit an investigator's preferences, to when a computer algorithm such as machine learning is used. Even in this last case, there is a large range of possible approaches, as well as many choices as to how each algorithm functions, and the different settings in which each algorithm is likely to work well or badly—as many are likely to do for non-stationary data. The earliest selection approaches were manual as no other methods were on offer, but most of the decisions made during selection were then undocumented (see the critique in Leamer 1978), making replication difficult. In economics, early selection criteria were based on the 'goodness-of-fit' of models, pejoratively called 'data mining', but Gilbert (1986) highlighted that a greater danger of selection was its being used to suppress conflicting evidence. Statistical analyses of selection methods have provided many insights: e.g., Anderson (1962) established the dominance of testing from the most general specification and eliminating irrelevant variables relative to starting from the simplest and retaining significant ones. The long list of possible methods includes, but is not restricted to, the following, most of which use parsimony (in the sense of penalizing larger models) as part of their choice criteria.

Information criteria have a long history as a method of choosing between alternative models. Various information criteria have been proposed, all of which aim to choose between competing models by selecting the model with the smallest information loss. The trade-off between information loss and model 'complexity' is captured by the penalty, which differs between information criteria. For example, the AIC proposed by Akaike (1973), sought to balance the costs when forecasting from a stationary infinite autoregression of estimation variance from retaining small effects against the squared bias of omitting them. Schwarz (1978) SIC (also called BIC, for Bayesian information criterion), aimed to consistently estimate the parameters of a fixed, finite-dimensional model as the sample size increased to infinity. HQ, from Hannan and Quinn (1979), established the smallest penalty function that will deliver the same outcome as SIC in very large samples. Other variants of information criteria include focused criteria (see Claeskens and Hjort 2003), and the posterior information criterion in Phillips and Ploberger (1996).

Variants of **selection by goodness of fit** include choosing by the maximum multiple correlation coefficient (criticised by Lovell 1983); Mallows (1973) C_p criterion; step-wise regression (see e.g., Derksen and Keselman 1992, which Leamer called 'unwise'), which is a class of single-path search procedures for (usually) adding variables one at a time to a regression (e.g., including the next variable with the highest remaining correlation), only retaining significant estimated parameters, or dropping the least significant remaining variables in turn.

Penalised-fit approaches like shrinkage estimators, as in James and Stein (1961), and the Lasso (least absolute shrinkage and selection operator) proposed by Tibshirani (1996) and Efron et al. (2004). These are like step-wise with an additional penalty for each extra parameter.

Bayesian selection methods which often lead to model averaging: see Raftery (1995), Phillips (1995), Buckland et al. (1997), Burnham and Anderson (2002), and Hoeting et al. (1999), and Bayesian structural time series (BSTS: Scott and Varian 2014).

Automated general-to-specific (Gets) approaches as in Hoover and Perez (1999), Hendry and Krolzig (2001), Doornik (2009), and Hendry and Doornik (2014). This approach will be the one mainly used in this book when we need to explicitly select a model from a larger set of candidates, especially when there are more such candidates than the number of observations.

Model selection also has many different designations, such as subset selection (Miller 2002), and may include computer learning algorithms.

Concepts for analyses of statistical model selection

There are also many different concepts employed in the analyses of statistical methods of model selection. Retention of irrelevant variables is often measured by the 'false-positives rate' or 'false-discovery rate' namely, how often irrelevant variables are incorrectly selected by a test adventitiously rejecting the null hypothesis of irrelevance. If a test is correctly calibrated (which unfortunately is often not the case for many methods of model selection, such as step-wise), and has a nominal significance level of (say) 1%, it should reject the null hypothesis incorrectly 1% of the time (Type-I error). Thus, if 100 such tests are conducted under the null, 1 should reject by chance on average (i.e., 100×0.01). Hendry and Doornik (2014) refer to the actual retention rate of irrelevant variables during selection as the empirical gauge and seek to calibrate their algorithm such that the gauge is close to the nominal significance level. Johansen and Nielsen (2016) investigate the distribution of estimates of the gauge. Bayesian approaches often focus on the concept of 'model uncertainty', essentially the probability of selecting closely similar models that nevertheless lead to different conclusions. With 100 candidate variables, there are $2^{100} \approx 10^{30}$ possible models generated by every combination of the 100 variables, creating great scope for such model uncertainty. Nevertheless, when all variables are irrelevant, on average 1 variable would be retained at 1%, so model uncertainty has been hugely reduced from a gigantic set of possibilities to a tiny number. Although different irrelevant variables will be selected adventitiously in different draws, this is hardly a useful concept of 'model uncertainty'.

The more pertinent difficulty is finding and retaining relevant variables, which depends on how substantive their influence is. If a variable would not be retained by the criterion in use even when it was the known sole relevant variable, it will usually not be retained by selection from a larger set. Crucially, a relevant variable can only be retained if it is in the candidate set being considered, so indicators for outliers and shifts will never be found unless they are considered. One strategy is to always retain the set of variables entailed by the theory that motivated the analysis while selecting from other potential determinants, shift effects etc., allowing model discovery jointly with evaluating the theory (see Hendry and Doornik 2014).

Consequences of Statistical Model Selection
Selection of course affects the statistical properties of the resulting estimated model, usually because only effects that are 'significant' at the pre-specified level are retained. Thus, which variables are selected varies in different samples and on average, estimated coefficients of retained relevant variables are biased away from the origin. Retained irrelevant variables are those that chanced to have estimated coefficients far from zero in the particular data sample. The former are often called 'pre-test biases' as in Judge and Bock (1978). The top panel in Fig. 2.11 illustrates when $\widehat{b}$ denotes the distribution without selection, and $\widetilde{b}$ with selection requiring

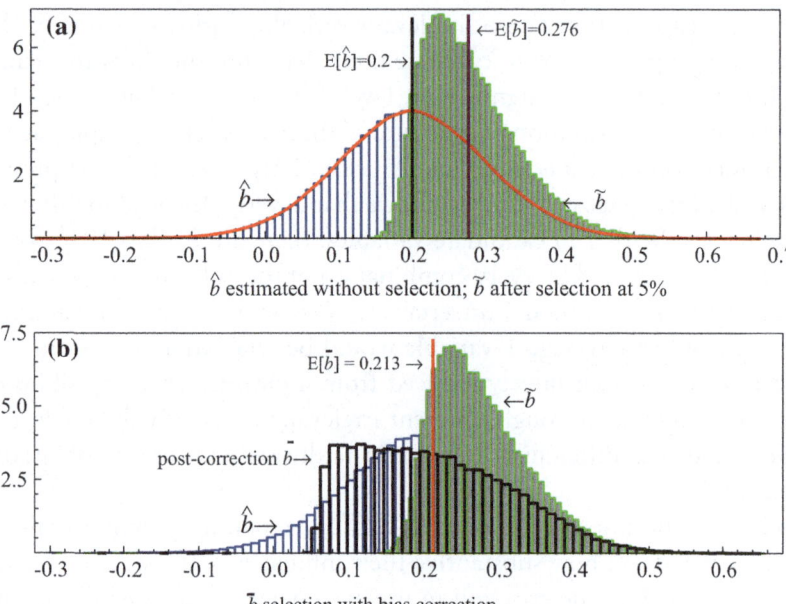

Fig. 2.11 (a) The impact on the statistical distributions of selecting only significant parameters; (b) distributions after bias correction

significance at 5%. The latter distribution is shifted to the right and has a mean $\mathsf{E}[\widetilde{b}]$ of 0.276 when the unselected mean $\mathsf{E}[\widehat{b}]$ is 0.2, leading to an upward bias of 38%.

However, if coefficients of relevant variables are highly significant, such selection biases are small. In some settings, such biases can be corrected after selection in well-structured algorithms, as shown by Hendry and Krolzig (2005). The lower panel in Fig. 2.11 illustrates the effect of bias correction on the distribution of $\widetilde{b}$ to $\overline{b}$. There is a strong shift back to the left, and the corrected mean is 0.213, so now is only slightly biased. The same bias corrections applied to the coefficients of irrelevant variables that are retained by chance can considerably reduce their mean-square errors.

A more important issue is that omitting relevant variables will bias the remaining retained coefficients (except if all variables are mutually orthogonal), and that effect will often be far larger than selection biases, and cannot be corrected as it is not known which omitted variables are relevant.

Of course, simply asserting a relation and estimating it without selection is likely to be even more prone to such biases unless an investigator is omniscient. In almost every observational discipline, especially those facing non-stationary data, selection is inevitable. Consequently, the least-worst route is to allow for as many potentially relevant explanatory variables as feasible to avoid omitted-variables biases, and use an automatic selection approach, aka a machine-learning algorithm, balancing the costs of over and under inclusion. Hence, Campos et al. (2005) focus on methods that commence from the most general feasible specification and conduct simplification searches leading to three generations of automatic selection algorithms in the sequence Hoover and Perez (1999), *PcGets* by Hendry and Krolzig (2001) and *Autometrics* by Doornik (2009), embedded in the approach to model discovery by Hendry and Doornik (2014). We now consider the prevalence of non-stationarity in observational data.

References

Akaike, H. (1973). Information theory and an extension of the maximum likelihood principle. In Petrov, B. N., and Csaki, F. (eds.), *Second International Symposion on Information Theory*, pp. 267–281. Budapest: Akademia Kiado.

Anderson, T. W. (1962). The choice of the degree of a polynomial regression as a multiple-decision problem. *Annals of Mathematical Statistics*, **33**, 255–265.

Bai, J., and Perron, P. (1998). Estimating and testing linear models with multiple structural changes. *Econometrica*, **66**, 47–78.

Bai, J., and Perron, P. (2003). Computation and analysis of multiple structural change models. *Journal of Applied Econometrics*, **18**, 1–22.

Bontemps, C., and Mizon, G. E. (2003). Congruence and encompassing. In Stigum, B. P. (ed.), *Econometrics and the Philosophy of Economics*, pp. 354–378. Princeton: Princeton University Press.

Bontemps, C., and Mizon, G. E. (2008). Encompassing: Concepts and implementation. *Oxford Bulletin of Economics and Statistics*, **70**, 721–750.

Brown, R. L., Durbin, J., and Evans, J. M. (1975). Techniques for testing the constancy of regression relationships over time (with discussion). *Journal of the Royal Statistical Society B*, **37**, 149–192.

Buckland, S. T., Burnham, K. P., and Augustin, N. H. (1997). Model selection: An integral part of inference. *Biometrics*, **53**, 603–618.

Burnham, K. P., and Anderson, D. R. (2002). *Model Selection and Multimodel Inference: A Practical Information-Theoretic Approach*, 2nd Edition. New York: Springer.

Campos, J., Ericsson, N. R., and Hendry, D. F. (2005). Editors' introduction. In Campos, J., Ericsson, N. R., and Hendry, D. F. (eds.), *Readings on General-to-Specific Modeling*, pp. 1–81. Cheltenham: Edward Elgar.

Castle, J. L., Doornik, J. A., Hendry, D. F., and Pretis, F. (2015). Detecting location shifts during model selection by step-indicator saturation. *Econometrics*, **3(2)**, 240–264. http://www.mdpi.com/2225-1146/3/2/240.

Chow, G. C. (1960). Tests of equality between sets of coefficients in two linear regressions. *Econometrica*, **28**, 591–605.

Claeskens, G., and Hjort, N. L. (2003). The focussed information criterion (with discussion). *Journal of the American Statistical Association*, **98**, 879–945.

Clements, M. P., and Hendry, D. F. (1998). *Forecasting Economic Time Series*. Cambridge: Cambridge University Press.

Corsi, P., Pollock, R. E., and Prakken, J. C. (1982). The Chow test in the presence of serially correlated errors. In Chow, G. C., and Corsi, P. (eds.), *Evaluating the Reliability of Macro-economic Models*. New York: Wiley.

Cox, D. R. (2006). *Principles of Statistical Inference*. Cambridge: Cambridge University Press.

Derksen, S., and Keselman, H. J. (1992). Backward, forward and stepwise automated subset selection algorithms: Frequency of obtaining authentic and noise variables. *British Journal of Mathematical and Statistical Psychology*, **45**, 265–282.

Doornik, J. A. (2008). Encompassing and automatic model selection. *Oxford Bulletin of Economics and Statistics*, **70**, 915–925.

Doornik, J. A. (2009). Autometrics. In Castle, J. L., and Shephard, N. (eds.), *The Methodology and Practice of Econometrics*, pp. 88–121. Oxford: Oxford University Press.

Efron, B., Hastie, T., Johnstone, I., and Tibshirani, R. (2004). Least angle regression. *The Annals of Statistics*, **32**, 407–499.

Engle, R. F., and Granger, C. W. J. (1987). Cointegration and error correction: Representation, estimation and testing. *Econometrica*, **55**, 251–276.

Ericsson, N. R. (1992). Parameter constancy, mean square forecast errors, and measuring forecast performance: An exposition, extensions, and illustration. *Journal of Policy Modeling*, **14**, 465–495.

Ericsson, N. R. (2012). Detecting crises, jumps, and changes in regime. Working paper, Federal Reserve Board of Governors, Washington, DC.

Friedman, W. A. (2014). *Fortune Tellers: The Story of America's First Economic Forecasters*. Princeton: Princeton University Press.

Gilbert, C. L. (1986). Professor Hendry's econometric methodology. *Oxford Bulletin of Economics and Statistics*, **48**, 283–307. Reprinted in Granger, C. W. J. (ed.) (1990). *Modelling Economic Series*. Oxford: Clarendon Press.

Govaerts, B., Hendry, D. F., and Richard, J.-F. (1994). Encompassing in stationary linear dynamic models. *Journal of Econometrics*, **63**, 245–270.

Granger, C. W. J. (1981). Some properties of time series data and their use in econometric model specification. *Journal of Econometrics*, **16**, 121–130.

Granger, C. W. J., and Newbold, P. (1974). Spurious regressions in econometrics. *Journal of Econometrics*, **2**, 111–120.

Hamilton, J. D. (2016). Macroeconomic regimes and regime shifts. In Taylor, J. B., and Uhlig, H. (eds.), *Handbook of Macroeconomics*, Vol. 2, pp. 163–201. Amsterdam: Elsevier.

Hannan, E. J., and Quinn, B. G. (1979). The determination of the order of an autoregression. *Journal of the Royal Statistical Society B*, **41**, 190–195.

Hansen, B. E. (1992a). Testing for parameter instability in linear models. *Journal of Policy Modeling*, **14**, 517–533.

Hansen, B. E. (1992b). Tests for parameter instability in regressions with I(1) processes. *Journal of Business and Economic Statistics*, **10**, 321–335.

Hendry, D. F. (1980). Econometrics: Alchemy or science? *Economica*, **47**, 387–406.

Hendry, D. F. (1988). Encompassing. *National Institute Economic Review*, **125**, 88–92.

Hendry, D. F. (1995). *Dynamic Econometrics*. Oxford: Oxford University Press.

Hendry, D. F. (2004). The Nobel Memorial Prize for Clive W.J. Granger. *Scandinavian Journal of Economics*, **106**, 187–213.

Hendry, D. F., and Doornik, J. A. (2014). *Empirical Model Discovery and Theory Evaluation*. Cambridge, MA: MIT Press.

Hendry, D. F., and Krolzig, H.-M. (2001). *Automatic Econometric Model Selection*. London: Timberlake Consultants Press.

Hendry, D. F., and Krolzig, H.-M. (2005). The properties of automatic Gets modelling. *Economic Journal*, **115**, C32–C61.

Hendry, D. F., and Mizon, G. E. (2014). Unpredictability in economic analysis, econometric modeling and forecasting. *Journal of Econometrics*, **182**, 186–195.

Hendry, D. F., and Morgan, M. S. (eds.) (1995). *The Foundations of Econometric Analysis*. Cambridge: Cambridge University Press.

Hoeting, J., Madigan, D., Raftery, A., and Volinsky, C. (1999). Bayesian Model Averaging: A Tutorial. *Statistical Science*, **14(4)**, 382–417.

Hoover, K. D., and Perez, S. J. (1999). Data mining reconsidered: Encompassing and the general-to-specific approach to specification search. *Econometrics Journal*, **2**, 167–191.

James, W., and Stein, C. (1961). Estimation with quadratic loss. In Neyman, J. (ed.), *Proceedings of the Fourth Berkeley Symposium on Mathematical Statistics and Probability*, pp. 361–379. Berkeley: University of California Press.

Jansen, E. S., and Teräsvirta, T. (1996). Testing parameter constancy and super exogeneity in econometric equations. *Oxford Bulletin of Economics and Statistics*, **58**, 735–763.

Johansen, S., and Nielsen, B. (2009). An analysis of the indicator saturation estimator as a robust regression estimator. In Castle, J. L., and Shephard, N. (eds.), *The Methodology and Practice of Econometrics*, pp. 1–36. Oxford: Oxford University Press.

Johansen, S., and Nielsen, B. (2016). Asymptotic theory of outlier detection algorithms for linear time series regression models. *Scandinavian Journal of Statistics*, **43**, 321–348.

Judge, G. G., and Bock, M. E. (1978). *The Statistical Implications of Pre-test and Stein-Rule Estimators in Econometrics*. Amsterdam: North Holland Publishing Company.

Konishi, S., and Kitagawa, G. (2008). *Information Criteria and Statistical Modeling*. New York: Springer.

Leamer, E. E. (1978). *Specification Searches: Ad Hoc Inference with Non-Experimental Data*. New York: Wiley.

Lehmann, E. L. (1959). *Testing Statistical Hypotheses*. New York: Wiley.

Lovell, M. C. (1983). Data mining. *Review of Economics and Statistics*, **65**, 1–12.

Mallows, C. L. (1973). Some comments on c_p. *Technometrics*, **15**, 661–675.

Miller, A. J. (ed.) (2002). *Subset Selection in Regression*, 2nd Edition. London: Chapman & Hall (1st, 1990).

Mills, T. C. (2011). Bradford Smith: An econometrician decades ahead of his time. *Oxford Bulletin of Economics and Statistics*, **73**, 276–285.

Mizon, G. E. (1984). The encompassing approach in econometrics. In Hendry, D. F., and Wallis, K. F. (eds.), *Econometrics and Quantitative Economics*, pp. 135–172. Oxford: Basil Blackwell.

Mizon, G. E. (2008). Encompassing. In Durlauf, S., and Blume, L. (eds.), *New Palgrave Dictionary of Economics*, 2nd Edition. London: Palgrave Macmillan. https://doi.org/10.1057/9780230226203.0470.

Morgan, M. S. (1990). *The History of Econometric Ideas*. Cambridge: Cambridge University Press.

Nyblom, J. (1989). Testing for the constancy of parameters over time. *Journal of the American Statistical Association*, **84**, 223–230.

Perron, P. (1989). The Great Crash, the oil price shock and the unit root hypothesis. *Econometrica*, **57**, 1361–1401.

Perron, P. (2006). Dealing with structural breaks. In Hassani, H., Mills, T. C., and Patterson, K. D. (eds.), *Palgrave Handbook of Econometrics*, pp. 278–352. Basingstoke: Palgrave MacMillan.

Phillips, P. C. B. (1986). Understanding spurious regressions in econometrics. *Journal of Econometrics*, **33**, 311–340.

Phillips, P. C. B. (1995). Bayesian model selection and prediction with empirical applications. *Journal of Econometrics*, **69**, 289–331.

Phillips, P. C. B., and Ploberger, W. (1996). An asymptotic theory of Bayesian inference for time series. *Econometrica*, **64**, 381–412.

Pretis, F., Schneider, L., Smerdon, J. E., and Hendry, D. F. (2016). Detecting volcanic eruptions in temperature reconstructions by designed break-indicator saturation. *Journal of Economic Surveys*, **30**, 403–429.

Qin, D. (1993). *The Formation of Econometrics: A Historical Perspective*. Oxford: Clarendon Press.

Qin, D. (2013). *A History of Econometrics: The Reformation from the 1970s*. Oxford: Clarendon Press.

Raftery, A. (1995). Bayesian model selection in social research. *Sociological Methodology*, **25**, 111–196.

Schwarz, G. (1978). Estimating the dimension of a model. *Annals of Statistics*, **6**, 461–464.

Scott, S. L., and Varian, H. R. (2014). Predicting the present with Bayesian structural time series. *International Journal of Mathematical Modelling and Numerical Optimisation*, **5(102)**, 4–23.

Smith, B. B. (1926). Combining the advantages of first-difference and deviation-from-trend methods of correlating time series. *Journal of the American Statistical Association*, **21**, 55–59.

Smith, B. B. (1929). Judging the forecast for 1929. *Journal of the American Statistical Association*, **24**, 94–98.

Spanos, A. (1986). *Statistical Foundations of Econometric Modelling*. Cambridge: Cambridge University Press.

Tibshirani, R. (1996). Regression shrinkage and selection via the lasso. *Journal of the Royal Statistical Society B*, **58**, 267–288.

Yule, G. U. (1897). On the theory of correlation. *Journal of the Royal Statistical Society*, **60**, 812–838.

Yule, G. U. (1926). Why do we sometimes get nonsense-correlations between time-series? A study in sampling and the nature of time series (with discussion). *Journal of the Royal Statistical Society*, **89**, 1–64. Reprinted in Hendry, D. F., and Morgan, M. S. (1995), *The Foundations of Econometric Analysis*. Cambridge: Cambridge University Press.

Open Access This chapter is licensed under the terms of the Creative Commons Attribution 4.0 International License (http://creativecommons.org/licenses/by/4.0/), which permits use, sharing, adaptation, distribution and reproduction in any medium or format, as long as you give appropriate credit to the original author(s) and the source, provide a link to the Creative Commons license and indicate if changes were made.

The images or other third party material in this chapter are included in the chapter's Creative Commons license, unless indicated otherwise in a credit line to the material. If material is not included in the chapter's Creative Commons license and your intended use is not permitted by statutory regulation or exceeds the permitted use, you will need to obtain permission directly from the copyright holder.

3

Why Is the World Always Changing?

Abstract Empirical models used in disciplines as diverse as economics through to climatology analyze data assuming observations are from stationary processes even though the means and variances of most 'real world' time series change. We discuss some key sources of non-stationarity in demography, economics, politics and the environment, noting that (say) non-stationarity in economic data will 'infect' variables that are influenced by economics. Theory derivations, empirical models, forecasts and policy will go awry if the two forms of non-stationarity introduced above are not tackled. We illustrate non-stationary time series in a range of disciplines and discuss how to address the important difficulties that non-stationarity creates, as well as some potential benefits.

Keywords Sources of change · Wages, prices and productivity · Modelling non-stationarity

Many empirical models used in research and to guide policy in disciplines as diverse as economics to climate change analyze data by methods that assume observations come from stationary processes. However, most 'real world' time series are not stationary in that the means and variances of outcomes change over time. Present levels of knowledge, living standards, average age of death etc., are not highly unlikely draws from their distributions in medieval times, but come from distributions with very different means and variances. For example, the average age of death in London in the 1860s was around 45, whereas today it is closer to 80—a huge change in the mean. Moreover, some individuals in the 1860s lived twice the average, namely into their 90s, whereas today, no one lives twice the average age, so the relative variance has also changed.

3.1 Major Sources of Changes

As well as the two World Wars causing huge disruption, loss of life, and massive damage to infrastructure, there have been numerous smaller conflicts, which are still devastating for those caught up in such conflict. In addition to those dramatic shifts noted above as causes of structural breaks, we could also include for the UK the post World War I crash; the 1926 general strike; and the creation of the European Union with the UK joining the EU (but now threatening to leave). There were many policy regime shifts, including periods on then off the Gold Standard; the Bretton Woods agreement in 1945; floating exchange rates from 1973; in and out of the Exchange Rate Mechanism (ERM) till October 1992; Keynesian fiscal policies; then Monetarist; followed by inflation targeting policies; and the start of the Euro zone. All that against a background of numerous important and evolving changes: globalization and development worldwide with huge increases in living standards and reductions in extreme poverty; changes in inequality, demography, health, longevity, and migration; legal reforms and different social mores; huge technology advances in electricity, refrigeration, transport, communications (including telephones, radio, television, and now mobiles), flight, nuclear power, medicine, new materials, computers, and containerization, with major industrial decline from cotton, coal, steel, and shipbuilding industries virtually vanishing, but being replaced by businesses based on new technologies and services.

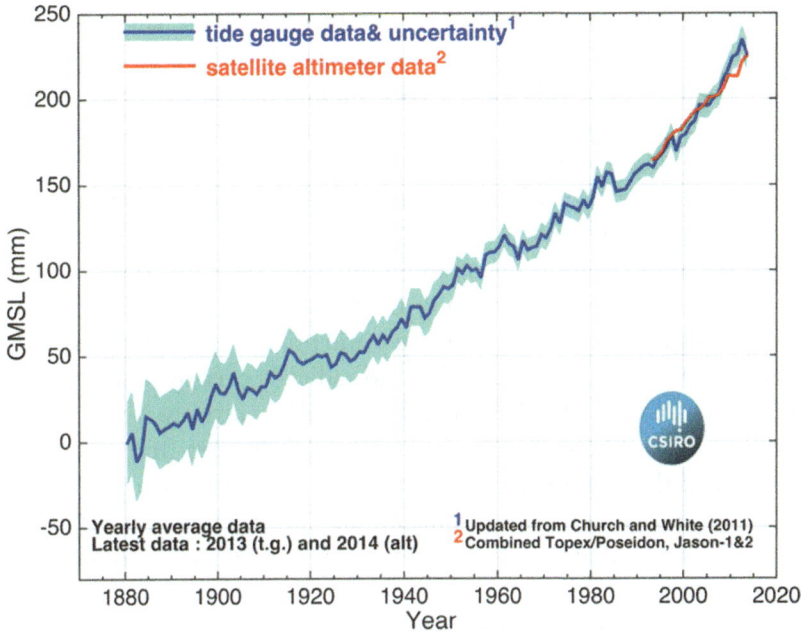

Fig. 3.1 Global mean sea-level (GMSL) has risen by more than 20 cm since 1880 (*Source* CSIRO)

Because economic data are non-stationary, that will 'infect' other variables which are influenced by economics (e.g., CO_2 emissions), and so spread like a pandemic to most socio-economic and related variables, and probably will feed back onto economics. Many theories, most empirical models of time series, and all forecasts will go awry when both forms of non-stationarity introduced above are not tackled. A key feature of processes where the distributions of outcomes shift over time is that probabilities of events calculated in one time period need not apply in another: 'once in a hundred years' can become 'once a decade'. Flooding by storm surges becomes more likely with sea-levels rising from climate change. Figure 3.1 shows that global mean sea-level has risen over 20 cm since 1880, and is now rising at 3.4 mm p.a. versus 1.3 mm p.a. over 1850–1992 (see e.g., Jevrejeva et al. 2016).[1]

---

[1] See https://www.cmar.csiro.au/sealevel/sl_data_cmar.html.

More generally, an important source of changes are environmental, perhaps precipitated by social and economic behaviour like CO_2 emissions and their consequences, but also occurring naturally as with earthquakes, volcanic eruptions and phenomena like El Niño. Policy decisions have to take non-stationarities into account: as another obvious example, with increasing longevity, pension payments and life insurance commitments and contracts are affected.

We first provide more illustrations of non-stationary time series to emphasize how dramatically many have changed. Figure 3.2, left-hand panel graphs UK annual nominal wages and prices over the long historical period 1860–2014. These have changed radically over the last 150 years, rising by more than **70,000%** and **10,000%** respectively. Their rates of growth have also changed intermittently, as can be seen from the changing slopes of the graph lines. The magnitude of a 25% change is marked to clarify the scale. It is hard to imagine any 'revamping' of the statistical assumptions such that these outcomes could be construed as coming from stationary processes.[2]

Figure 3.2, right-hand panel, records productivity, measured as output per person per year, with real wages (i.e., in constant prices), namely the difference between the two (log) time series in the left-hand panel. Both trend strongly, but move closely together, albeit with distinct slope changes and 'bumps' en route. The 'flat-lining' after the 'Great Recession' of 2008–2012 is highlighted by the ellipse. The wider 25% change marker highlights the reduced scale. Nevertheless, both productivity and real wages have increased by about sevenfold over the period, a huge rise in living standards. This reflects a second key group of causes of the changing world: increased knowledge inducing technical and medical progress, embodied in the latest vintage of capital equipment used by an increasingly educated workforce.

Figure 3.3(a) plots annual wage inflation (price inflation is similar as Fig. 2.4(b) showed) to emphasize that changes, or growth rates, also can be non-stationary, here from both major shifts in means (the thicker black line in Panel (a)), as well as in variances. Compare the quiescent 50-year

---

[2] It is sometimes argued that economic time series could be stationary around a deterministic trend, but it seems unlikely that GDP would continue trending upwards if nobody worked.

3 Why Is the World Always Changing?   41

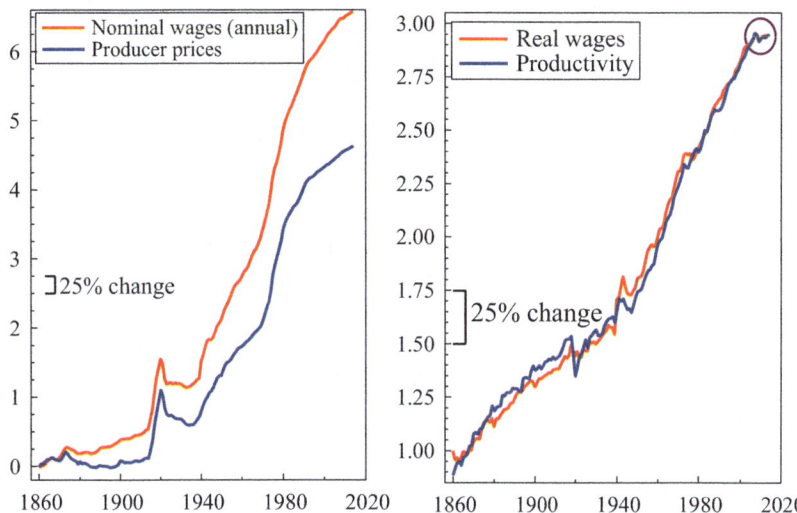

Fig. 3.2 Indexes of UK wages and prices (left-hand panel) and UK real wages and productivity (right-hand panel), both on log scales

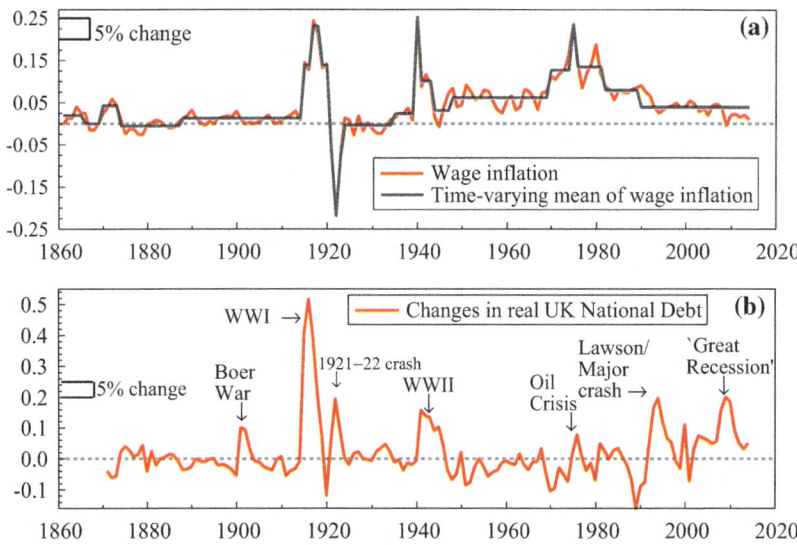

Fig. 3.3 (a) UK wage inflation; and (b) changes in real national debt with major historical events shown

period before 1914 with the following 50 years, noting the scale of 5% in (a). Historically, wages have fallen (and risen) more than 20% in a year.

Figure 3.3(b) records changes in real UK National Debt, with the associated events. In any empirical, observationally-based discipline, 'causes' can never be 'proved', merely attributed as overwhelmingly likely. The events shown on Fig. 3.3(b) nevertheless seem to be the proximate causes: real National Debt rises sharply in crises, including wars and major recessions. Even in constant prices, National Debt has on occasion risen by 50% in a year—and that despite inflation then being above 20%—although here the 5% scale is somewhat narrower than in (a). Wars and major recessions are the third set of reasons why the world is ever changing, although at a deeper level of explanation one might seek to understand their causes.

None of the above real-world time series has a constant mean or variance, so cannot be stationary. The two distinct features of stochastic trends and sudden shifts are exhibited, namely 'wandering' widely, most apparent in Fig. 3.2, and suddenly shifting as in Fig. 3.3, features that will recur. Such phenomena are not limited to economic data, but were seen above in demographic and climatological time series.

Figure 3.4 illustrates the non-stationary nature of recent climate time series compared to ice-age cycles for global concentrations of atmospheric CO_2 relative to recent rapid annual increases (see e.g., Sundquist and Keeling 2009). The observations in the left-hand panel are at 1000 year intervals, over almost 800,000 years, whereas those in the right-hand panel are monthly, so at dramatically different frequencies.

Given the almost universal absence of stationarity in real-world time series, Hendry and Juselius (2000) delineated four issues with important consequences for empirical modelling, restated here as:

(A) the key role of stationarity assumptions in empirical modelling and inference in many studies, despite its absence in data;
(B) the potentially hazardous impacts on theory analyses, empirical modelling, forecasting and policy of incorrectly assuming stationarity;
(C) the many sources of the two main forms of non-stationarity (evolution and abrupt shifts), that need to be considered when modelling;
(D) yet fortunately, statistical analyses can often be undertaken to eliminate many of the most adverse effects of non-stationarity.

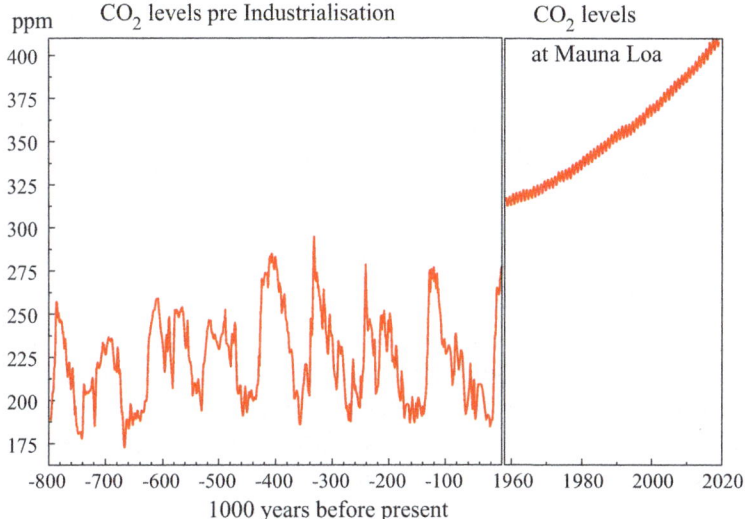

Fig. 3.4 Levels of atmospheric CO_2 in parts per million (ppm)

We now consider issues (A), (B) and (D) in turn: the sources referred to in (C) have been discussed immediately above.

3.2 Problems if Incorrectly Modelling Non-stationarity

(A) Theories and models of human behaviour that assume stationarity, so do not account for the non-stationarity in their data, will continually fail to explain outcomes. In a stationary world, the best predictor of what we expect an event to be like tomorrow should be based on all the information available today. This is the conditional expectation given all the relevant information. In elementary econometrics and statistics textbooks, such a conditional expectation is proved to provide the smallest variance of all unbiased predictors of the mean of the distribution. An implicit, and never stated, assumption is that the distributions over which such conditional expectations are calculated are constant over time. But if the mean of its distribution shifts, a conditional expectation today can predict a value that is far from tomorrow's outcome. This will create a 'disequilibrium', where individuals who formed such expectations will need to adjust to their mistakes.

(B) In fact, the mathematical basis of much of 'modern' macroeconomics requires stationarity to be valid, and fails when distributions shift in unanticipated ways. As an analogy, continuing to use such mathematical tools in non-stationary worlds is akin to insisting on using Euclidean geometry to measure angles of triangles on a globe: then navigation can go seriously adrift. We return to this aspect in the next chapter.

In turn, the accuracy and precision of forecasts are affected by non-stationarity. Its presence leads to far larger interval forecasts (the range within which a forecaster anticipates the future values should lie) than would occur in stationary processes, so if a stationary model is incorrectly fitted, its calculated uncertainty can dramatically under-estimate the true uncertainty. This is part of the explanation for the nonsense-regressions issue we noted above. Worse still, unexpected location shifts usually lead to forecast failure, where forecast errors are systematically much larger than would be expected in the absence of shifts, as happened during the Financial Crisis and Great Recession over 2008–2012. Consequently, the uncertainty of forecasts can be much greater than that calculated from past data, both because the sources of evolution in data cumulate over time, and also because 'unknown unknowns' can occur, especially unanticipated location shifts.

Scenarios based on outcomes produced by simulating empirical models are often used in economic policy, for example, by the Bank of England in deciding its interest-rate decisions. When the model is a poor representation of the non-stationarities prevalent in the economy, policy changes (such as interest-rate increases) can actually cause location shifts that then lead to forecast failure, so after the event, what had seemed a good decision is seen to be badly based.

Thus, all four arenas of theory, modelling, forecasting and policy face serious hazards from non-stationarity unless it is appropriately handled. Fortunately, in each setting some actions can be taken, albeit providing palliative, rather than complete, solutions. Concerning theory derivations, there is an urgent need to develop approaches that allow for economic agents always facing disequilibrium settings, and needing error-correction strategies after suffering unanticipated location shifts. Empirical modelling can detect and remove location shifts that have happened: for example, statistical tools for dealing with shifts enabled Statistics Norway to revise their economic forecasts within two weeks of the shock induced by the Lehmann Brothers bankruptcy in 2008. Modelling can also avoid the 'nonsense relation' problem by checking for genuine long-run connections between variables (called cointegration, the development of which led to a Nobel Prize for Sir Clive Granger), as well as embody feedbacks that help correct previous mistakes. Forecasting devices can allow for the ever-growing uncertainty arising from cumulating shocks. There are also methods for helping to robustify forecasts against systematic failure after unanticipated location shifts. Tests have been formulated to check for policy changes having caused location shifts in the available data, and if found, warn against the use of those models for making future policy decisions.

(D) Finally, although non-stationary time series data are harder to model and forecast, there are some important benefits deriving from non-stationarity. Long-run relationships are difficult to isolate with stationary data: since all connections between variables persist unchanged over time, it is not easy to determine genuine causal links. However, cumulated shocks help reveal what relationships stay together (i.e., cointegrate) for long time periods. This is even more true of location shifts, where only connected variables will move together after a shift (called co-breaking). Such shifts also alter the correlations between variables, facilitating more accurate estimates of empirical models, and revealing what variables are not consistently connected. Strong trends and location shifts can also highlight genuine connections, such as cointegration, through a fog of measurement errors in data series. Lastly, past location shifts allow the tests noted in the previous paragraph to be implemented before a wrong policy is adopted. The next chapter considers how to model trends and shifts and the potential benefits of doing so.

References

Hendry, D. F., and Juselius, K. (2000). Explaining cointegration analysis: Part I. *Energy Journal,* **21**, 1–42.

Jevrejeva, S., Jackson, L. P., Riva, R. E. M., Grinsted, A., and Moore, J. C. (2016). Coastal sea level rise with warming above 2°C. *Proceedings of the National Academy of Sciences,* **113(47)**, 13342–13347.

Sundquist, E. T., and Keeling, R. F. (2009). The Mauna Loa carbon dioxide record: Lessons for long-term earth observations. *Geophysical Monograph Series,* **183**, 27–35.

Open Access This chapter is licensed under the terms of the Creative Commons Attribution 4.0 International License (http://creativecommons.org/licenses/by/4.0/), which permits use, sharing, adaptation, distribution and reproduction in any medium or format, as long as you give appropriate credit to the original author(s) and the source, provide a link to the Creative Commons license and indicate if changes were made.

The images or other third party material in this chapter are included in the chapter's Creative Commons license, unless indicated otherwise in a credit line to the material. If material is not included in the chapter's Creative Commons license and your intended use is not permitted by statutory regulation or exceeds the permitted use, you will need to obtain permission directly from the copyright holder.

4

Making Trends and Breaks Work to Our Advantage

Abstract The previous Chapter noted there are benefits of non-stationarity, so we now consider that aspect in detail. Non-stationarity can be caused by stochastic trends and shifts of data distributions. The simplest example of the first is a random walk of the kind created by Yule, where the current observation equals the previous one perturbed by a random shock. This form of integrated process occurs in economics, demography and climatology. Combinations of I(1) processes are also usually I(1), but in some situations stochastic trends can cancel to an I(0) outcome, called cointegration. Distributions can shift in many ways, but location shifts are the most pernicious forms for theory, empirical modelling, forecasting and policy. We discuss how they too can be handled, with the potential benefit of highlighting when variables are not related as assumed.

Keywords Integrated processes · Serial correlation · Stochastic trends · Cointegration · Location shifts · Co-breaking · Dynamic stochastic general equilibrium models (DSGEs)

4.1 Potential Solutions to Stochastic Trend Non-stationarity

As described in Sect. 2.2, Yule created integrated processes deliberately, but there are many economic, social and natural mechanisms that induce integratedness in data. Perhaps the best known example of an I(1) process is a random walk, where the current value is equal to the previous value plus a random error. Thus the change in a random walk is just a random error. Such a process can wander widely, and was first proposed by Bachelier (1900) to describe the behaviour of prices in speculative markets. However, such processes also occur in demography (see Lee and Carter 1992) as well as economics, because the stock of a variable, like population or inventories, cumulates the net inflow as discussed for Fig. 2.3. A natural integrated process is the concentration of atmospheric CO_2, as emissions cumulate due to CO_2's long atmospheric lifetime, as in the right-hand panel of Fig. 3.4. Such emissions have been mainly anthropogenic since the industrial revolution. When the inflows to an integrated process are random, the variance will grow over time by cumulating past perturbations, violating stationarity. Thus, unlike an I(0) process which varies around a constant mean with a constant variance, an I(1) process has an increasing variance, usually called a stochastic trend, and may also 'drift' in a general direction over time to induce a trend in the level.

Cumulating past random shocks should make the resulting time series relatively smooth since successive observations share a large number of past inputs. Also the correlations between successive values will be high, and only decline slowly as their distance apart increases–the persistence discussed in Sect. 2.1. Figure 4.1(a), (b) illustrates for the logs of wages and real wages, where the sequence of successive correlations shown is called a correlogram. Taking wages in the top-left panel (a) as an example, the outcome in any year is still correlated 0.97 with the outcome 20 years previously, and similar high correlations between variables 20 years apart hold for real wages. Values outside the dashed lines are significantly different from zero at 5%.

Differencing is the opposite of integration, so an I(1) process has first differences that are I(0). Thus, despite its non-stationarity, an I(1) process can be reduced to I(0) by differencing, an idea that underlies the

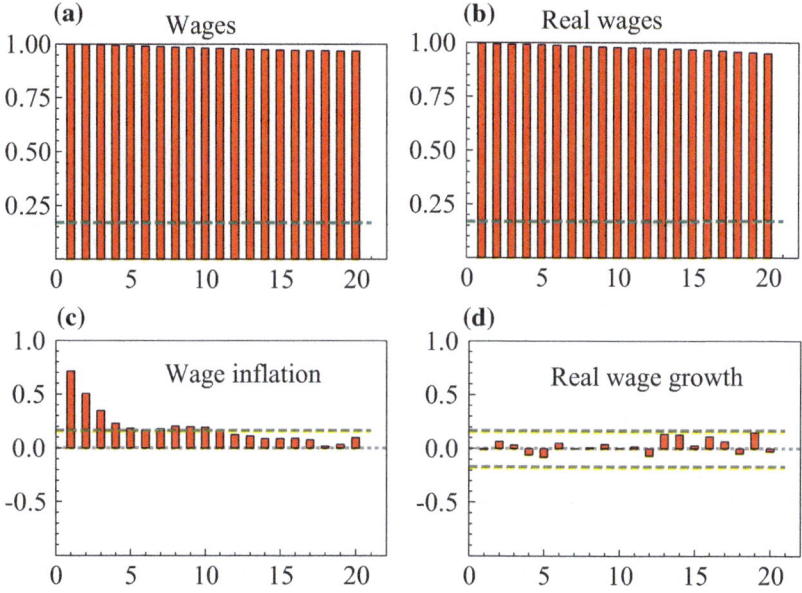

Fig. 4.1 Twenty successive serial correlations for (a) nominal wages; (b) real wages; (c) wage inflation; and (d) real wage growth

empirical modelling and forecasting approach in Box and Jenkins (1976). Now successive values in the correlogram should decline quite quickly, as Figs. 4.1(c) and (d) show for the differences of these two time series. Wage inflation is quite highly correlated with its values one and two periods earlier, but there are much smaller correlations further back, although even as far back as 20 years, all the correlations are positive. However, the growth of real wages seems essentially random in terms of its correlogram. As a warning, such evidence does not imply that real wage growth cannot be modelled empirically, merely that the preceeding value by itself does not explain the current outcome.

Differences of I(1) time series should also be approximately Normally distributed when the shocks are nearly Normal. Such outcomes implicitly suppose there are no additional 'abnormal' shocks such as location shifts. Figure 4.2 illustrates for wage and price inflation, and the growth in real wages and productivity. None of the four distributions is Normal, with all

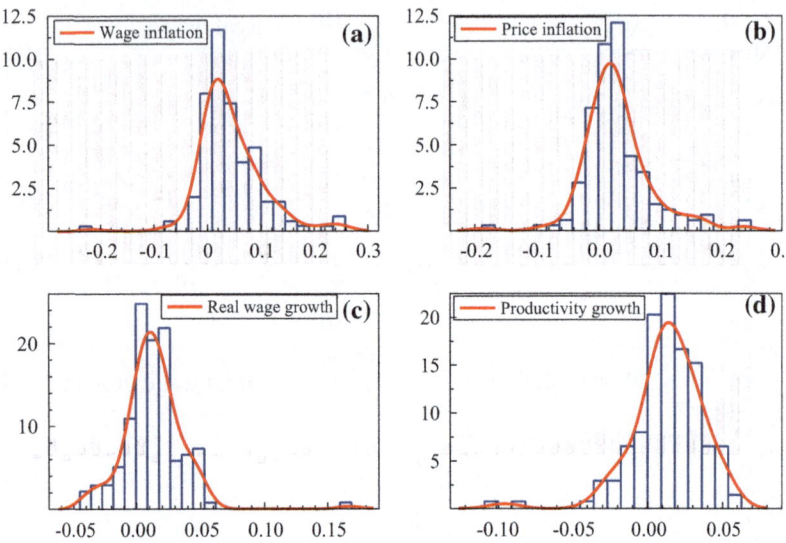

Fig. 4.2 Densities of the differences for: **(a)** nominal wages; **(b)** prices; **(c)** real wages and **(d)** productivity

revealing large outliers, which cannot be a surprise given their time series graphs in Fig. 3.2.

To summarise, both the mean and the variance of I(1) processes change over time, and successive values are highly interdependent. As Yule (1926) showed, this can lead to nonsense regression problems. Moreover, the conventional forms of distributions assumed for estimates of parameters in empirical models under stationarity no longer hold, so statistical inference becomes hazardous unless the non-stationarity is taken into account.

4.2 Cointegration Between I(1) Processes

Linear combinations of several I(1) processes are usually I(1) as well. However, stochastic trends can cancel between series to yield an I(0) outcome. This is called cointegration. Cointegrated relationships define a 'long-run equilibrium trajectory', departures from which induce 'equilibrium correc-

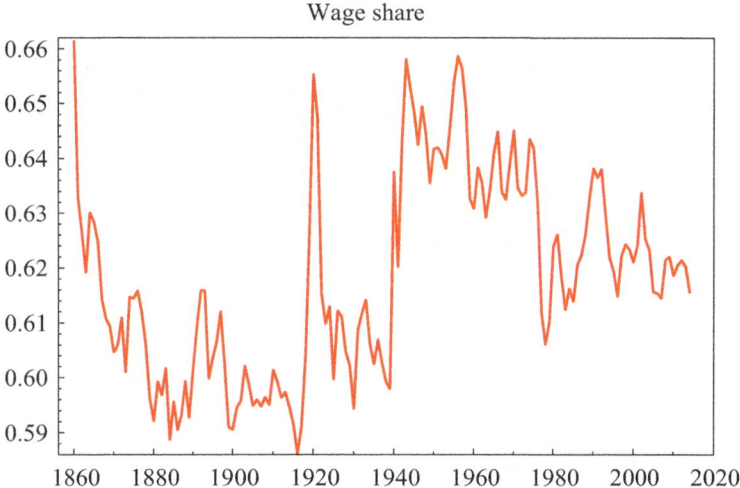

Fig. 4.3 Time series for the wage share

tion' that moves the relevant system back towards that path.[1] Equilibrium-correction mechanisms are a very large class of models that coincide with cointegrated relations when data are I(1), but also apply to I(0) processes which are implicitly always cointegrated in that all linear combinations are I(0). When the data are I(2) there is a generalized form of cointegration leading to I(0) combinations. Equilibrium-correction mechanisms (EqCMs) can be written in a representation in which changes in variables are inter-related, but also include lagged values of the I(0) combinations. EqCMs have the key property that they converge back to the long-run equilibrium of the data being modelled. This is invaluable when that equilibrium is constant, but as we will see, can be problematic if there are shifts in equilibria.

Real wages and productivity, shown in Fig. 3.2, are each I(1), but their differential, which is the wage share shown in Fig. 4.3, could be I(0). The wage share cancels the separate stochastic trends in real wages and productivity to create a possible cointegrating relation where the stochastic

---

[1] Davidson et al. (1978), and much of the subsequent literature, call these 'error correction'.

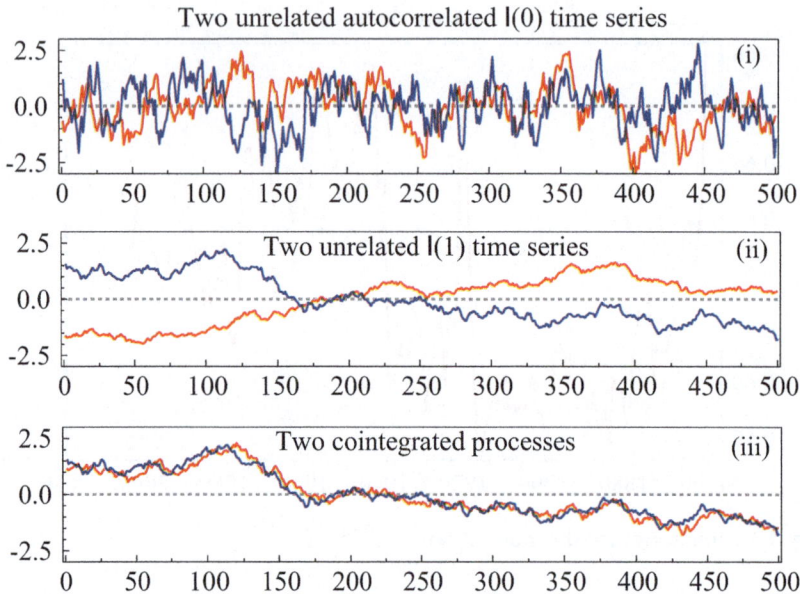

Fig. 4.4 Pairs of artificial time series: (i) unrelated I(0); (ii) unrelated I(1); (iii) cointegrated

trends have been removed, but there also seem to be long swings and perhaps location shifts, an issue we consider in Sect. 4.3.

To illustrate pairs of variables that are (i) unrelated I(0) but autocorrelated, (ii) unrelated I(1), and (iii) cointegrated, Fig. 4.4 shows 500 observations on computer-generated data. The very different behaviours are marked, and although rarely so obvious in practice, the close trajectories of real wages and productivity in Fig. 3.3 over 150 years resembles the bottom panel.

In economics, integrated-cointegrated data seem almost inevitable because of the Granger (1981) Representation Theorem, for which he received the Sveriges Riksbank Prize in Economic Science in Memory of Alfred Nobel in 2003. His result shows that cointegration between variables must occur if there are fewer decision variables (e.g., your income and bank account balance) than the number of decisions (e.g., hundreds of shopping items: see Hendry 2004, for an explanation). If that setting was the only source of non-stationarity, there would be two ways of bringing an analysis involving integrated processes back to I(0): differencing to remove cumulative inputs (which always achieves that aim), or finding linear combinations that form cointegrating relations. There must always be fewer cointegrating relations than the total number of variables, as otherwise the system would be stationary, so some variables must still be differenced to represent the entire system as I(0).

Cointegration is not exclusive to economic time series. The radiative forcing of greenhouse gases and other variables affecting global climate cointegrate with surface temperatures, consistent with models from physics (see Kaufmann et al. 2013; Pretis 2019). Thus, cointegration occurs naturally, and is consistent with many existing theories in the natural sciences where interacting systems of differential equations in non-stationary time series can be written as a cointegrating model.

Other sources of non-stationarity also matter, however, especially shifts in the means of data distributions of I(0) variables, including equilibrium correction means, and growth rate averages, so we turn to this second main source of non-stationarity. There is a tendency in the econometrics literature to identify 'non-stationarity' purely with integrated data (time series with unit roots), and so incorrectly claim that differencing a time series induces stationarity. Certainly, a unit root is removed by considering the difference, but there are other sources of non-stationarity, so for clarity we refer to the general case as wide-sense non-stationarity.

4.3 Location Shifts

Location shifts are changes from the previous mean of an I(0) variable. There have been enormous historical changes since 1860 in hours of work, real incomes, disease prevalence, sanitation, infant mortality, and average age of death among many other facets of life: see http://ourworldindata.org/ for comprehensive coverage. Figure 3.2 showed how greatly log wages and prices had increased over 1860–2014 with real wages rising sevenfold. Such huge increases could not have been envisaged in 1860. Uncertainty abounds, both in the real world and in our knowledge thereof. However, some events are so uncertain that probabilities of their happening cannot be sensibly assigned. We call such irreducible uncertainty 'extrinsic unpredictability', corresponding to unknown unknowns: see Hendry and Mizon (2014). A pernicious form of extrinsic unpredictability affecting inter-temporal analyses, empirical modelling, forecasting and policy interventions is that of unanticipated location shifts, namely shifts that occur at unanticipated times, changing by unexpected magnitudes and directions.

Figure 4.5 illustrates a hypothetical setting. The initial distribution is either a standard Normal (solid line) with mean zero and variance unity, or a 'fat-tailed' distribution (dashed line), which has a high probability of generating 'outliers' at unknown times and of unknown magnitudes and signs (sometimes called anomalous 'black swan events' as in Taleb 2007). As I(1) time series can be transformed back to I(0) by differencing or cointegration, the Normal distribution often remains the basis for calculating probabilities for statistical inference, as in random sampling from a known distribution. Hendry and Mizon (2014) call this 'intrinsic unpredictability', because the uncertainty in the outcome is intrinsic to the properties of the random variables. Large outliers provide examples of 'instance unpredictability' since their timings, magnitudes and signs are uncertain, even when they are expected to occur in general, as in speculative asset markets.

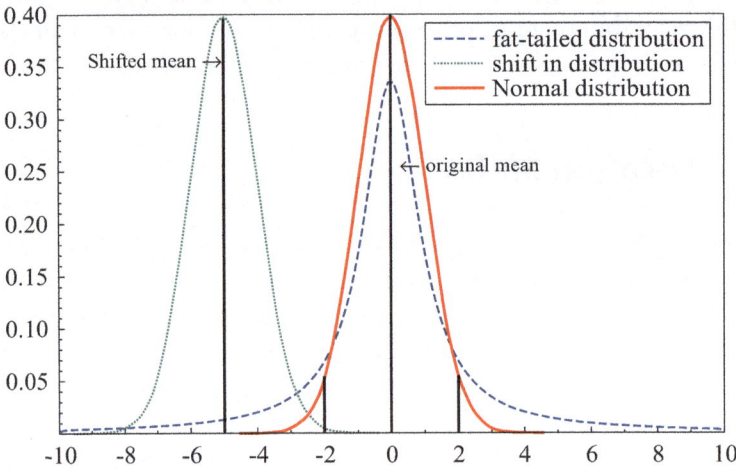

Fig. 4.5 Location shift in a normal or a fat-tailed distribution

However, in Fig. 4.5 the baseline distribution experiences a location shift to a new Normal distribution (dotted line) with a mean of -5. As we have already seen, there are many causes for such shifts, and many shifts have occurred historically, precipitated by changes in legislation, wars, financial innovation, science and technology, medical advances, climate change, social mores, evolving beliefs, and different political and economic regimes. Extrinsically unpredictable location shifts can make the new ordinary seem highly unusual relative to the past. In Fig. 4.5, after the shift, outcomes will now usually lie between 3 and 7 standard deviations away from the *previous* mean, generating an apparent 'flock' of black swans, which could never happen with independent sampling from the baseline distribution, even when fat-tails are possible. During the Financial Crisis in 2008, the possibility of location shifts generating many extremely unlikely bad draws does not seem to have been included in risk models. But extrinsic unpredictability happens in the real world (see e.g., Soros 2008): as we have remarked, current outcomes are not highly discrepant draws from the distributions prevalent in the Middle Ages, but 'normal' draws from present distributions that have shifted greatly. Moreover, the distributions of many data differences are not stationary: for example, real growth per capita in the UK has increased intermittently since the Industrial Revolution as seen in Fig. 3.2, and most nominal differences have experienced location shifts, illustrated by Fig. 3.3. Hendry (2015) provides dozens of other examples.

4.4 Dynamic-Stochastic General Equilibrium (DSGE) Models

Everyone has to take decisions at some point in time that will affect their future in important ways: marrying, purchasing a house with a mortgage, making an investment in a risky asset, starting a pension or life insurance, and so on. The information available at the time reflects the past and present but obviously does not include knowledge of the future. Consequently, a view has to be taken about possible futures that might affect the outcomes.

All too often, such views are predicated on there being no unanticipated future changes relevant to that decision, namely the environment is assumed to be relatively stationary. Certainly, there are periods of reasonable stability when observing how past events unfolded can assist in planning for the future. But as this book has stressed, unexpected events occur, especially unpredicted shifts in the distributions of relevant variables at unanticipated times. Hendry and Mizon (2014) show that the intermittent occurrence of 'extrinsic unpredictability' has dramatic consequences for any theory analyses of time-dependent behaviour, empirical modelling of time series, forecasting, and policy interventions. In particular, the mathematical basis of the class of models widely used by central banks, namely DSGE models, ceases to be valid as DSGEs are based on an inter-temporal optimization calculus that requires the absence of distributional shifts.

This is not an 'academic' critique: the supposedly 'structural' Bank of England Quarterly Model (BEQM) broke down during the Financial Crisis, and has since been replaced by another DSGE called COMPASS, which may be pointing in the wrong direction: see Hendry and Muellbauer (2018).

> **DSGE Models**
> Many of the theoretical equations in DSGE models take a form in which a variable today, denoted y_t, depends on its 'expected future value' often written as $\mathsf{E}_t[y_{t+1}|\mathcal{I}_t]$, where $\mathsf{E}_t[\cdot]$ indicates the date at which the expectation is formed about the variable in the [ ]. Such expectations are conditional on what information is available, which we denoted by $\mathcal{I}_t$, so are naturally called conditional expectations, and are defined to be the average over the relevant conditional distribution. If the relation between y_{t+1} and $\mathcal{I}_t$ shifts as in Fig. 4.5, y_{t+1} could be far from what was expected.

As we noted above, in a stationary world, a 'classic' proof in elementary statistics courses is that the conditional expectation has the smallest variance of all unbiased predictors of the mean of their distribution. By basing their expectations for tomorrow on today's distribution, DSGE formulations assume stationarity, possibly after 'removing' stochastic trends by some method of de-trending. From Fig. 4.5 it is rather obvious that the previous mean, and hence the previous conditional expectation, is not an unbiased predictor of the outcome after a location shift.

As we have emphasized, underlying distributions can and do shift unexpectedly. Of course, we are all affected to some extent by unanticipated shifts of the distributions relevant to our lives, such as unexpectedly being made redundant, sudden increases in mortgage costs or tax rates, or reduced pension values after a stock market crash. However, we then usually change our plans, and perhaps also our views of the future. The first unfortunate outcome for DSGE models is that their parameters shift after a location shift. The second is that their mathematical derivations usually assume that the agents in their model do not change their behaviour from what would be the optimum in a stationary world. However, as ordinary people seem unlikely to be better at forecasting breaks than professional economists, or even quickly learning their implications after they have occurred, most of us are forced to adapt our plans after such shifts.

By ignoring the possibility of distributional shifts, conditional expectations can certainly be 'proved' to be unbiased, but that does not imply they will be in practice. Some econometric models of inflation, such as the so-called new-Keynesian Phillips curve, involve expectations of the unknown future value written as $\mathsf{E}[y_{t+1}|\mathcal{I}_t]$. A common procedure is to replace that conditional expectation by the actual future outcome y_{t+1}, arguing that the conditional expectation is unbiased for the actual outcome, so will only differ from it by unpredictable random shocks with a mean of zero. That implication only holds if there have been no shifts in the distributions of the variables, and otherwise will entail mis-specified empirical models that can seriously mislead in their policy implications as Castle et al. (2014) demonstrate.

There is an intimate link between forecast failure, the biasedness of conditional expectations and the inappropriate application of inter-temporal optimization analysis: when the first is due to an unanticipated location shift, the other two follow. Worse, a key statistical theorem in modern macroeconomics, called the law of iterated expectations, no longer holds when the distributions from which conditional expectations are formed change over time. The law of iterated expectations implies that today's expectation of tomorrow's outcome, given what we know today, is equal to tomorrow's expectation. Thus, one can 'iterate' expectations over time.

The theorem is not too hard to prove when all the distributions involved are the same, but it need not hold when any of the distributions shift between today and tomorrow for exactly the same reasons as Fig. 2.8 reveals: that shift entails forecast failure, a violation of today's expectation being unbiased for tomorrow, and the failure of the law of iterated expectations.

As a consequence, dynamic stochastic general equilibrium models are inherently non-structural; their mathematical basis fails when substantive distributional shifts occur and their parameters will be changed. This adverse property of all DSGEs explains the 'break down' of BEQM facing the Financial Crisis and Great Recession as many distributions shifted markedly, including that of interest rates (to unprecedently low levels from Quantitative Easing) and consequently the distributions of endowments across individuals and families. Unanticipated changes in underlying probability distributions, especially location shifts, have detrimental impacts on all economic analyses involving conditional expectations and hence intertemporal derivations as well as causing forecast failure. What we now show is that with appropriate tools, the impacts of outliers and location shifts on empirical modelling can be taken into account.

4.5 Handling Location Shifts

At first sight, location shifts seem highly problematic for econometric modelling, but as with stochastic trends, there are several potential solutions. Differencing a time series will also inadvertently convert a location shift to an impulse (an impulse in the first difference is equivalent to a step-shift in the level). Secondly, time series can co-break, analogous to cointegration, in that location shifts can cancel between series.

Thus, time series can be combined to remove some or all of the individual shifts. Individual series may exhibit multiple shifts, but when modelling one series by another, co-breaking implies that fewer shifts will be detected when the series break together. Figure 3.2 showed the divergent strong but changing trends in nominal wages and prices, and Fig. 3.3 recorded the many shifts in wage inflation. Nevertheless, as shown by the time series of real wage growth in Fig. 4.6, almost all the shifts in wage inflation and price inflation cancelled over 1860–2014. The only one not

4 Making Trends and Breaks Work to Our Advantage

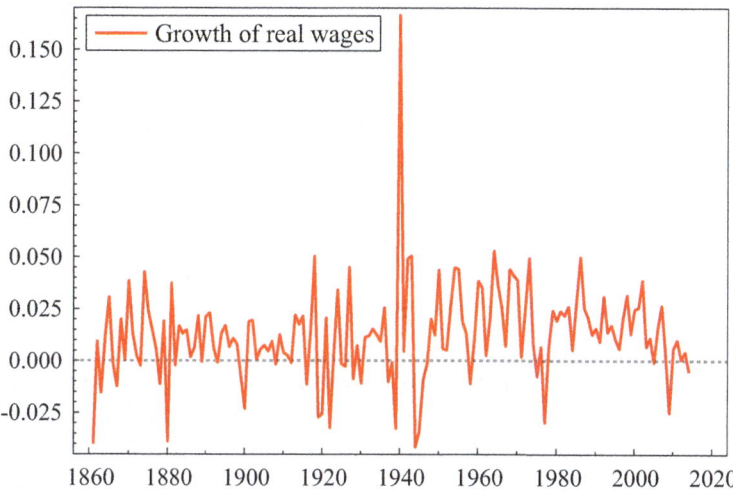

Fig. 4.6 Partial co-breaking between wage and price inflation

to is the huge 'spike' in 1940, which was a key step in the UK's war effort, to encourage new workers to replace army recruits.

The third possible solution is to find all the location shifts and outliers whatever their magnitudes and signs then include indicators for them in the model. To do so requires us to solve the apparently impossible problem of selecting from more candidate variables in a model than observations. Hendry (1999) accidently stumbled over a solution. Most contributors to Magnus and Morgan (1999) had found that models of US real per capita annual food demand were non-constant over the sample 1929–1952, so dropped that earlier data from their empirical modelling. Figure 2.4(a) indeed suggests very different behaviour pre and post 1952, but by itself that does not entail that econometric models which include explanatory variables like food prices and real incomes must shift. To investigate why, yet replicate others' models, Hendry added impulse indicators (which are 'dummy variables' that are zero everywhere except for unity at one data point) for all observations pre-1952, which revealed three large outliers corresponding to a US Great Depression food programme and post-war de-rationing. To check that his model was constant from 1953 onwards, he later added impulse indicators for that period, thereby including more variables plus indicators than observations, but only entered in his model in two large blocks, each much smaller than the number of observations. This has led to a statistical theory for modelling multiple outliers and location shifts (see e.g., Johansen and Nielsen 2009; Castle et al. 2015), available in our computational tool *Autometrics* (Doornik 2009) and in the package *Gets* (Pretis et al. 2018) in the statistical software environment *R*. This approach, called indicator saturation, considers a possible outlier or shift at every point in time, but only retains significant indicators. That is how the location-shift lines drawn on Fig. 3.3 were chosen, and is the subject of Chapter 5.

Location shifts are of particular importance in policy, because a policy change inevitably creates a location shift in the system of which it is a part. Consequently, a necessary condition for the policy to have its intended effect is that the parameters in the agency's empirical models of the target variables must remain invariant to that policy shift. Thus, prior to implementing a policy, invariance should be tested, and that can be done automatically as described in Hendry and Santos (2010) and Castle et al. (2017).

4.6 Some Benefits of Non-stationarity

Non-stationarity is pervasive, and as we have documented, needs to be handled carefully to produce viable empirical models, but its occurrence is not all bad news. When time series are I(1), their variance grows over time, which can help establish long-run relationships. Some economists believe that so-called 'observational equivalence'—where several different theories look alike on all data—is an important problem. While that worry could be true in a stationary world, cointegration can only hold between I(1) variables that are genuinely linked. 'Observational equivalence' is also unlikely facing location shifts: no matter how many co-breaking relations exist, there must always be fewer than the number of variables, as some must shift to change others, separating the sheep from the goats.

When I(1) variables also trend, or drift, that can reveal the underlying links between variables even when measurement errors are quite large (see Duffy and Hendry 2017). Those authors also establish the benefits of location shifts that co-break in identifying links between mis-measured variables: intuitively, simultaneous jumps in both variables clarify their connection despite any 'fog' from measurement errors surrounding their relationship. Thus, large shifts can help reveal the linkages between variables, as well as the absence thereof.

Moreover, empirical economics is plagued by very high correlations between variables (as well as over time), but location shifts can substantively reduce such collinearity. In particular, as demonstrated by White and Kennedy (2009), location shifts can play a positive role in clarifying causality. Also, White (2006) uses large location shifts to estimate the effects of natural experiments.

Finally, location shifts also enable powerful tests of the invariance of the parameters of policy models to policy interventions before new policies are implemented, potentially avoiding poor policy outcomes (see Hendry and Santos 2010). Thus, while wide-sense non-stationarity poses problems for economic theories, empirical modelling and forecasting, there are benefits to be gained as well.

Non-stationary time series are the norm in many disciplines including economics, climatology, and demography as illustrated in Figs. 2.3–3.2: the world changes, often in unanticipated ways. Research, and especially policy, must acknowledge the hazards of modelling what we have called wide-sense non-stationary time series, where distributions of outcomes change, as illustrated in Fig. 4.5. Individually and together when stochastic trends and location shifts are not addressed, they can distort in-sample inferences, lead to systematic forecast failure out-of-sample, and substantively increase forecast uncertainty as we will discuss in Chapter 7. However, both forms can be tamed in part using the methods of cointegration and modelling location shifts respectively, as Fig. 4.6 showed.

A key feature of every non-stationary process is that the distribution of outcomes shifts over time, illustrated in Fig. 4.7 for histograms and densities of logs of UK real GDP in each of three 50-year epochs. Consequently, probabilities of events calculated in one time period do not apply in another: recent examples include increasing longevity affecting pension costs, and changes in frequencies of flooding vitiating flood-defence systems.

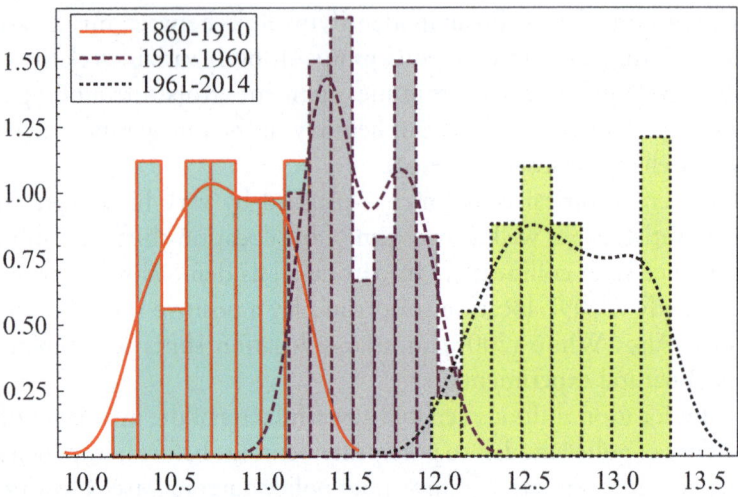

Fig. 4.7 Histograms and densities of logs of UK real GDP in each of three 50-year epochs

The problem of shifts in distributions is not restricted to the levels of variables: distributions of changes can also shift albeit that is more difficult to see in plots like Fig. 4.7. Consequently, Fig. 4.8 shows histograms and densities of changes in UK CO_2 emissions in each of four 40-year epochs in four separate graphs but on common scales for both axes. The shifts are now relatively obvious at least between the top two plots and between pre and post World War II, although the wide horizontal axis makes any shifts between the last two periods less obvious.

Conversely, we noted some benefits of stochastic trends and location shifts as they help reveal genuine links between variables, and also highlight non-constant links, both of which are invaluable knowledge in a policy context.

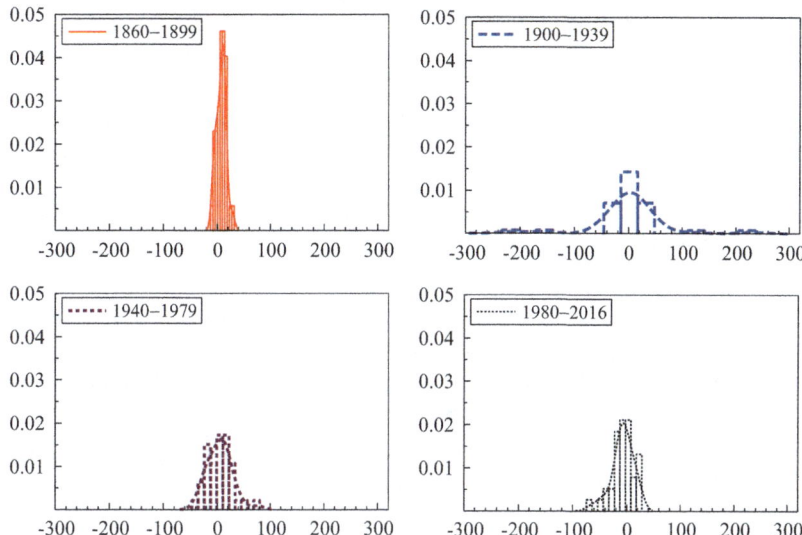

Fig. 4.8 Histograms and densities of changes in UK CO_2 emissions in each of four 40-year epochs

References

Bachelier, L. (1900). Théorie de la spéculation. *Annales Scientifiques de l'École Normale Supérieure*, **3**, 21–86.

Box, G. E. P., and Jenkins, G. M. (1976). *Time Series Analysis, Forecasting and Control*. San Francisco: Holden-Day. First published, 1970.

Castle, J. L., Hendry, D. F., and Martinez, A. B. (2017). Evaluating forecasts, narratives and policy using a test of invariance. *Econometrics*, **5(39)**. https://doi.org/10.3390/econometrics5030039.

Castle, J. L., Doornik, J. A., Hendry, D. F., and Nymoen, R. (2014). Misspecification testing: Non-invariance of expectations models of inflation. *Econometric Reviews*, **33**, 553–574.

Castle, J. L., Doornik, J. A., Hendry, D. F., and Pretis, F. (2015). Detecting location shifts during model selection by step-indicator saturation. *Econometrics*, **3(2)**, 240–264. http://www.mdpi.com/2225-1146/3/2/240.

Davidson, J. E. H., Hendry, D. F., Srba, F., and Yeo, J. S. (1978). Econometric modelling of the aggregate time-series relationship between consumers' expenditure and income in the United Kingdom. *Economic Journal*, **88**, 661–692.

Doornik, J. A. (2009). Autometrics. In Castle, J. L., and Shephard, N. (eds.), *The Methodology and Practice of Econometrics*, pp. 88–121. Oxford: Oxford University Press.

Duffy, J. A., and Hendry, D. F. (2017). The impact of near-integrated measurement errors on modelling long-run macroeconomic time series. *Econometric Reviews*, **36**, 568–587.

Granger, C. W. J. (1981). Some properties of time series data and their use in econometric model specification. *Journal of Econometrics*, **16**, 121–130.

Hendry, D. F. (1999). An econometric analysis of US food expenditure, 1931–1989. In Magnus, J. R., and Morgan, M. S. (eds.), *Methodology and Tacit Knowledge: Two Experiments in Econometrics*, pp. 341–361. Chichester: Wiley.

Hendry, D. F. (2004). The Nobel Memorial Prize for Clive W.J. Granger. *Scandinavian Journal of Economics*, **106**, 187–213.

Hendry, D. F. (2015). *Introductory Macro-econometrics: A New Approach*. London: Timberlake Consultants. http://www.timberlake.co.uk/macroeconometrics.html.

Hendry, D. F., and Mizon, G. E. (2014). Unpredictability in economic analysis, econometric modeling and forecasting. *Journal of Econometrics*, **182**, 186–195.

Hendry, D. F., and Muellbauer, J. N. J. (2018). The future of macroeconomics: Macro theory and models at the Bank of England. *Oxford Review of Economic Policy*, **34**, 287–328. https://academic.oup.com/oxrep/article/34/1-2/287/4781814.

Hendry, D. F., and Santos, C. (2010). An automatic test of super exogeneity. In Watson, M. W., Bollerslev, T., and Russell, J.(eds.), *Volatility and Time Series Econometrics*, pp. 164–193. Oxford: Oxford University Press.

Johansen, S., and Nielsen, B. (2009). An analysis of the indicator saturation estimator as a robust regression estimator. In Castle, J. L., and Shephard, N. (eds.), *The Methodology and Practice of Econometrics*, pp. 1–36. Oxford: Oxford University Press.

Kaufmann, R. K., Kauppi, H., Mann, M. L., and Stock, J. H. (2013). Does temperature contain a stochastic trend: Linking statistical results to physical mechanisms. *Climatic Change*, **118(3–4)**, 729–743.

Lee, R. D., and Carter, L. R. (1992). Modeling and forecasting U.S. mortality. *Journal of the American Statistical Association*, **87**, 659–671.

Magnus, J. R., and Morgan, M. S. (eds.) (1999). *Methodology and Tacit Knowledge: Two Experiments in Econometrics*. Chichester: Wiley.

Pretis, F. (2019). Econometric models of climate systems: The equivalence of two-component energy balance models and cointegrated VARs. *Journal of Econometrics*. https://doi.org/10.1016/j.jeconom.2019.05.013.

Pretis, F., Reade, J. J., and Sucarrat, G. (2018). Automated general-to-specific (GETS) regression modeling and indicator saturation for outliers and structural breaks. *Journal of Statistical Software*, **68**, 4. https://www.jstatsoft.org/article/view/v086i03.

Soros, G. (2008). *The New Paradigm for Financial Markets*. London: Perseus Books.

Taleb, N. N. (2007). *The Black Swan*. New York: Random House.

White, H. (2006). Time series estimation of the effects of natural experiments. *Journal of Econometrics*, **135**, 527–566.

White, H., and Kennedy, P. (2009). Retrospective estimation of causal effects through time. In Castle, J. L., and Shephard, N. (eds.), *The Methodology and Practice of Econometrics*, pp. 59–87. Oxford: Oxford University Press.

Yule, G. U. (1926). Why do we sometimes get nonsense-correlations between time-series? A study in sampling and the nature of time series (with discussion). *Journal of the Royal Statistical Society*, **89**, 1–64. Reprinted in Hendry, D. F., and Morgan, M. S. (1995). *The Foundations of Econometric Analysis*. Cambridge: Cambridge University Press.

Open Access This chapter is licensed under the terms of the Creative Commons Attribution 4.0 International License (http://creativecommons.org/licenses/by/4.0/), which permits use, sharing, adaptation, distribution and reproduction in any medium or format, as long as you give appropriate credit to the original author(s) and the source, provide a link to the Creative Commons license and indicate if changes were made.

The images or other third party material in this chapter are included in the chapter's Creative Commons license, unless indicated otherwise in a credit line to the material. If material is not included in the chapter's Creative Commons license and your intended use is not permitted by statutory regulation or exceeds the permitted use, you will need to obtain permission directly from the copyright holder.

5

Detectives of Change: Indicator Saturation

Abstract Structural changes are pervasive from innovations affecting many disciplines. These can shift distributions, altering relationships and causing forecast failure. Many empirical models also have outliers: both can distort inference. When the dates of shifts are not known, they need to be detected to be handled, usually by creating an indicator variable that matches the event. The basic example is an impulse indicator equal to unity for the date of an outlier and zero elsewhere. We discuss an approach to finding multiple outliers and shifts called saturation estimation. For finding outliers, an impulse indicator is created for every observation and the computer program searches to see which, if any, match an outlier. Similarly for location shifts: a step indicator equal to unity till time t is created for every t and searched over. We explain how and why this approach works.

Keywords Detecting shifts · Indicator saturation methods · Impulse-indicator saturation (IIS) · Step-indicator saturation (SIS) · Outliers · Non-linearity

Shifting distributions are indicative of structural change, but that can take many forms, from sudden location shifts, changes in trend rates of growth, or in estimated parameters reflecting changes over time in relationships between variables. Further, outliers that could be attributed to specific events, but are not modelled, can lead to seemingly fat-tailed distributions when in fact the underlying process generating the data is thin tailed. Incorrect or changing distributions pose severe problems for modelling any phenomena, and need to be correctly dealt with for viable estimation and inference on parameters of interest. Empirical modelling that does not account for shifts in the distributions of the variables under analysis risks reaching potentially misleading conclusions by wrongly attributing explanations from such contamination to chance correlations with other included variables, as well as having non-constant parameters.

While the dates of some major events like the Great Depression, oil and financial crises, and major wars are known *ex post*, those of many other events are not. Moreover, the durations and magnitudes of the impacts on economies of shifts are almost never known. Consequently, it behoves any investigator of economic (and indeed many other) time series to find and neutralize the impacts of all the in-sample outliers and shifts on the estimates of their parameters of interest. Shifts come at unanticipated times with many different shapes, durations and magnitudes, so general methods to detect them are needed. 'Ocular' approaches to spotting outliers in a model are insufficient: an apparent outlier may be captured by one of the explanatory variables, and the absence of any obvious outliers does not entail that large residuals will not appear after fitting.

It may be thought that the considerable number of tests required to check for outliers and shifts everywhere in a sample might itself be distorting, and hence adversely affect statistical inference. In particular, will one find too many non-existent perturbations by chance? That worry may be exacerbated by the notion of using an indicator saturation approach, where an indicator for a possible outlier or shift at every observation is included in the set of explanatory variables to be searched over. Even if there are just 100 observations, there will be a hundred indicators plus variables, so there are many trillions of combinations of models created by including or omitting each variable and every indicator, be they for outliers or for shifts starting and ending at different times.

Despite the apparent problems, indicator saturation methods can address all of these forms of mis-specification. First developed to detect unknown numbers of outliers of unknown magnitudes at unknown points in the sample, including at the beginning and end of a sample, the method can be generalized to detect all forms of deterministic structural change. We begin by outlining the method of impulse-indicator saturation (IIS) to detect outliers, before demonstrating how the approach can be generalized to include step, trend, multiplicative and designer saturation. We then briefly discuss how to distinguish between non-linearity and structural change.

Saturation methods can detect multiple breaks, and have the additional benefit that they can be undertaken conjointly with all other aspects of model selection. Explanatory variables, dynamics and non-linearities can be selected jointly with indicators for unknown breaks and outliers. Such a 'portmanteau' approach to detecting breaks while also selecting over many candidate variables is essential when the underlying DGP is unknown and has to be discovered from the available evidence. Most other break detection methods rely on assuming the model is somehow correctly specified other than the breaks, and such methods can lack power to detect breaks if the model is far from 'correct', an event that will occur with high probability in non-stationary time series.

5.1 Impulse-Indicator Saturation

IIS creates a complete set of indicator variables. Each indicator takes the value 1 for a single observation, and 0 for all other observations. As many indicators as there are observations are created, each with a different observation corresponding to the value 1. So for a sample of T observations, T indicators are then included in the set of candidate variables. However, all those indicators are most certainly **not** included together in the regression, as otherwise a perfect fit would always result and nothing would be learned. Although saturation creates T additional variables when there are T observations, *Autometrics* provides an expanding and contracting block search algorithm to undertake model selection when there are more variables than observations, as discussed in the model selection primer in Chapter 2. To aid exposition, we shall outline the 'split-half' approach analyzed in Hendry et al. (2008), which is just the simplest way to explain and analyze IIS, so bear in mind that such an approach can be generalized to a larger number of possibly unequal 'splits', and that the software explores many paths.

> **Defining Indicators**
> Impulse indicators are defined as $\{1_{\{j=t\}}\}$ where $1_{\{j=t\}}$ is equal to unity when $j = t$ and equal to zero otherwise for $j = 1, \ldots, T$.

Including an impulse indicator for a particular observation in a static regression delivers the same estimate of the model's parameters as if that observation had been left out. Consequently, the coefficient of that indicator is equal to the residual of the associated observation when predicted from a model based on the other observations. In dynamic relations, omitting an observation can distort autocorrelations, but an impulse indicator will simply deliver a zero residual at that observation. Thus, in both cases, including $T/2$ indicators provides estimates of the model based on the other half of the observations. Moreover, we get an estimate of any discrepancies in that half of the observations relative to the other half. Those indicators can then be tested for significance using the estimated error variance from the other half as the baseline, and any significant indicators are recorded. Importantly, under the null, each half's estimates of parameters and error variance are unbiased.

To understand the 'split-half' approach, consider a linear regression that only includes an intercept, to which we add the first $T/2$ impulse indicators, although there are in fact no outliers. Doing so has the same effect as dummying out the first half of the observations such that unbiased estimates of the mean and variance are obtained from the remaining data. Any observations in the first half that are discrepant relative to those estimates at the chosen significance level, α, say 1%, will result in selected indicators. The locations of any significant indicators are recorded, then the first $T/2$ indicators are replaced by the second $T/2$, and the procedure repeated. The two sets of sub-sample significant indicators (if any) are added to the model for selection of the finally significant indicators. This step is not superfluous: when there is a location shift, for example, some

5 Detectives of Change: Indicator Saturation

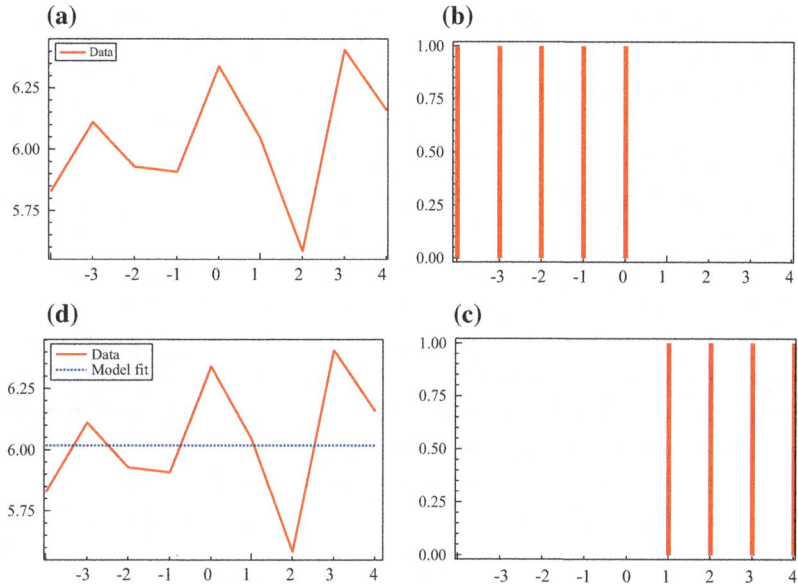

Fig. 5.1 'Split-half' IIS search under null. (**a**) The data time series; (**b**) the first 5 impulse indicators included; (**c**) the other set of impulse indicators; (**d**) the outcome, as no indicators are selected

indicators may be significant as approximations to the shift, but become insignificant when the correct indicators are included.

Figure 5.1 illustrates the 'split-half' approach when $T = 9$ for an independent, identically distributed (IID) Normal random variable with a mean of 6.0 and a variance of 0.33. Impulse indicators will be selected at the significance level $\alpha = 0.05$.

> **Computer Generated Data**
> The IID Normal variable is denoted by $y_t \sim \mathsf{IN}[\mu, \sigma_y^2]$, where μ is the mean and σ_y^2 is the variance. A random number generator on a computer creates an $\mathsf{IN}[0, 1]$ series which is then scaled appropriately.

Figure 5.1(a) shows the data time series, where the dating relates to periods before and after a shift described below. Then panels (b) and (c) record which of the 9 impulse indicators were included in turn, then panel

(d) shows the outcome, where the fitted model is just a constant as no indicators are selected. Since $\alpha T = 0.05 \times 9 = 0.45$, that is the average null retention rate, where α is called the theoretical gauge, which measures a key property of the procedure. This implies that we expect about one irrelevant indicator to be retained every *second* time IIS is applied to $T = 9$ observations using $\alpha = 0.05$ when the null is true, so finding none is not a surprise.

Hendry et al. (2008) establish a feasible algorithm for IIS, and derive its null distribution for an IID process. Johansen and Nielsen (2009) extend those findings to general dynamic regression models (possibly with trends or unit roots), and show that the distributions of regression parameter estimates remain almost unaltered, despite investigating the potential relevance of T additional indicators, with a small efficiency loss under the null of no breaks when αT is small. For a stationary process, with a correct null of no outliers and a symmetric error distribution, under relatively weak assumptions, the limiting distribution of the estimators of the regression parameters of interest converges to the population parameters at the usual rate (namely $\sqrt{T}$) despite using IIS. Moreover, that is still a Normal distribution, where the variance is somewhat larger than the conventional form, determined by the stringency of the significance level used for retaining impulse indicators. For example, using a 1% significance level, the estimator variance will be around 1% larger.

If the significance level is set to the inverse of the sample size, $1/T$, only one irrelevant indicator will be retained on average by chance, entailing that just one observation will be 'dummied out'. Think of it: IIS allows us to examine T impulse indicators for their significance almost costlessly when they are not needed. Yet IIS has also checked for the possibility of an unknown number of outliers, of unknown magnitudes and unknown signs, not knowing in advance where in the data set they occurred!

The empirical gauge g is the fraction of incorrectly retained variables, so here is the number of indicators retained under the null divided by T. More generally, if on average one irrelevant variable in a hundred is adventitiously retained in the final selection, the empirical gauge is $g = 0.01$. Johansen and Nielsen (2016) derive its distribution, and show g is close to α for small α. IIS has a close affinity to robust statistics, which is not surprising as it seeks to prevent outliers from contaminating estimates of parameters of interest. Thus, they also demonstrate that IIS is a member of the class of robust estimators, being a special case of a 1-step Huber-skip estimator when the model specification is known.

> **Illustrating IIS for an Outlier**
> We generate an outlier of size λ at observation k by
> $y_t = \mu + \lambda 1_{\{t=k\}} + \varepsilon_t$ where $\varepsilon_t \sim \text{IN}\left[0, \sigma_\varepsilon^2\right]$ and $\lambda \neq 0$.

To illustrate 'split-half' IIS search under the alternative (i.e., when there is an outlier as in the box), Fig. 5.2 records the behaviour of IIS for an outlier of $\lambda = -1.0$ at observation $k = 1$, so earlier dates are shown as negative. Selecting at $\alpha = 0.05$, no first-half indicators are retained (Fig. 5.2 panel (b)), as the discrepancy between the first-half and second-half means is not large relative to the resulting variance. When those indicators are

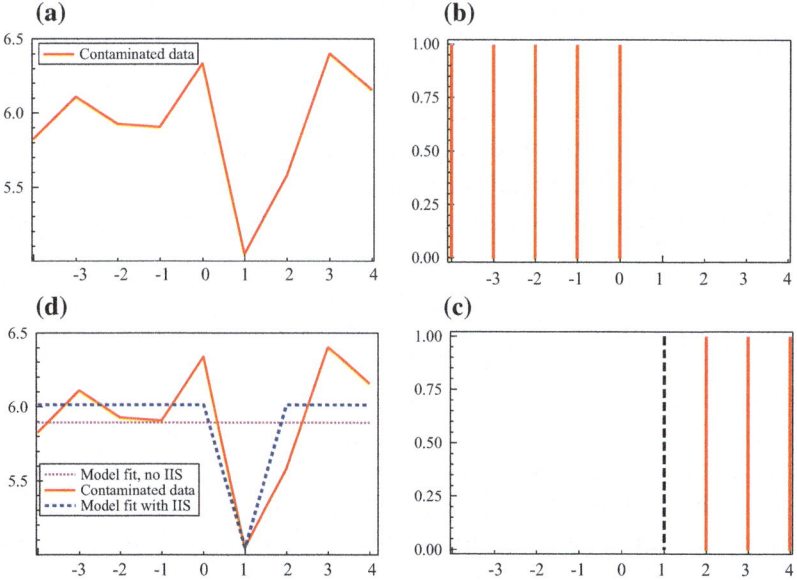

Fig. 5.2 (a) Perturbed data time series; (b) the first 5 impulse indicators included; (c) the other set of impulse indicators where the dashed line indicates retained; (d) the outcome with and without the selected indicator

dropped and the second set entered, the first for the period after the outlier is now retained: note that the first-half variance is very small.

Here the combined set is also just the second selection. When the null of no outliers or breaks is true, any indicator that is significant on a sub-sample would remain so overall, but for many alternatives, sub-sample significance can be transient, due to an unmodelled feature that occurs elsewhere in the data set.

Despite its apparently arcane formulation involving more variables plus indicators than available observations, the properties of which we discussed above, IIS is closely related to a number of other well-known statistical approaches. First, consider recursive estimation, where a model is fitted to a small initial subset of the data, say $K > N$ values when there are N variables, then observations are added one at a time to check for changes in parameter estimates. In IIS terms, this is equivalent to starting with impulse indicators for the last $T - K$ observations, then dropping those indicators one at a time as each next observation is included in the recursion.

Second, rolling regressions, where a fixed sample length is used, so earlier observations are dropped as later ones are added, is a further special case, equivalent to sequentially adding impulse indicators to eliminate earlier observations and dropping those for later.

Third, investigators sometimes drop observations or truncate their sample for what they view as discrepant periods such as wars. Again, this is a special case of IIS, namely including impulse indicators for the observations to be eliminated, precisely as we discussed above for modelling US food demand from 1929 to 1952. A key lack in all these methods is not inspecting the indicators for their significance or information content. However, because the variation in such apparently 'discrepant' periods can be invaluable in breaking collinearities and enhancing estimation precision, much can be learned by applying IIS instead, and checking which, if any, observations are actually problematic, perhaps using archival research to find out why.

Fourth, the Chow test for parameter constancy can be implemented by adding impulse indicators for the subsample to be tested, clearly a special case of IIS. Thus, IIS nests all of these settings. There is a large literature on testing for a known number of breaks, but indicator saturation is applicable when there is an unknown number of outliers or shifts, and can be implemented jointly with selecting over other regressors. Instrumental variables variants follow naturally, with the added possibility of checking the instrument equations for outliers and shifts, leading to being able to test the specification of the equation of interest for invariance to shifts in the instruments.

IIS is **designed** to detect outliers rather than location shifts, but split-half can also be used to illustrate indicator saturation when there is a single location shift which lies entirely within one of the halves. For a single location shift, Hendry and Santos (2010) show that the detection power, or potency, of IIS is determined by the magnitude of the shift; the length of the break interval, which determines how many indicators need to be found; the error variance of the equation; and the significance level, α, as a Normal-distribution critical value, c_α, is used by the IIS selection algorithm. Castle et al. (2012) establish the ability of IIS in *Autometrics* to detect multiple location shifts and outliers, including breaks close to the start and end of the sample, as well as correcting for non-Normality. Nevertheless, we next consider step-indicator saturation, which is explicitly designed for detecting location shifts.

5.2 Step-Indicator Saturation

A step shift is just a block of contiguous impulses of the same signs and magnitudes. Although IIS is applicable to detecting these, then the retained indicators could be combined into one dummy variable taking the average value of the shift over the break period and 0 elsewhere, perhaps after conducting a joint F-test on the *ex post* equality of the retained IIS coefficients, there is a more efficient method for detecting step shifts. We can instead generate a saturating set of $T - 1$ step-shift indicators which take the value 1 from the beginning of the sample up to a given observation, and 0 thereafter, with each step switching from 1 to 0 at a different observation. Step indicators are the cumulation of impulse indicators up to each next observation. The 'T'th step would just be the intercept. The $T - 1$ steps are included in the set of candidate regressors.

The split-half algorithm is conducted in exactly the same way, but there are some differences.

> **Defining Step Indicators**
> Step indicators are defined by $1_{\{t \leq j\}}$, $j = 1, \ldots, T$, where $1_{\{t \leq j\}} = 1$ for observations up to j, and zero otherwise.

First, while impulse indicators are mutually orthogonal, step indicators overlap increasingly as their second index increases. Second, for a location shift that is not at either end, say from T_1 to T_2, two indicators are required to characterize it: $1_{\{t \leq T_2\}} - 1_{\{t < T_1\}}$. Third, for a split-half analysis, the ease of detection is affected by whether or not T_1 and T_2 lie in the same split, and whether location shifts occur in both halves with similar signs and magnitudes. Castle et al. (2015) derive the null retention frequency of SIS and demonstrate the improved potency relative to IIS for longer location shifts.

We now consider 'split-sample' SIS for the same data as used for IIS above. As it happens, the second half coincides with the break period, so rather than use the first and second halves, we illustrate 'half-sample' SIS, where some indicators are chosen from each half as shown in Fig. 5.3 under the null. As *Autometrics* software uses multi-path block searches, this choice is potentially one of many paths explored, so has no specific advantage, but hopefully avoids the impression that the method is successful because the shift neatly coincides with the second half.

Figure 5.3 panel (a) records the time series; panels (b) and (c) the first and second choices of the 9 step indicators where now solid, dotted, dashed and long dashed clarify the steps, and panel (d) reports the same outcome as for IIS, as no indicators are selected.

> **Illustrating SIS for a Location Shift**
> Here we generate a location shift of magnitude λ at observation k by $y_t = \mu + \lambda 1_{\{t \geq k\}} + \varepsilon_t$ where $\varepsilon_t \sim \text{IN}\left[0, \sigma_\varepsilon^2\right]$ and $\lambda \neq 0$.

Next, we modify the process that generated an outlier to instead generate a location shift of $\lambda = -1$ at $k = 0$, but with the same half selections of step indicators. Figure 5.4 illustrates the outcome. Panel (a) records the shifted data, (b) shows the first selection of step indicators and (c) the remainder

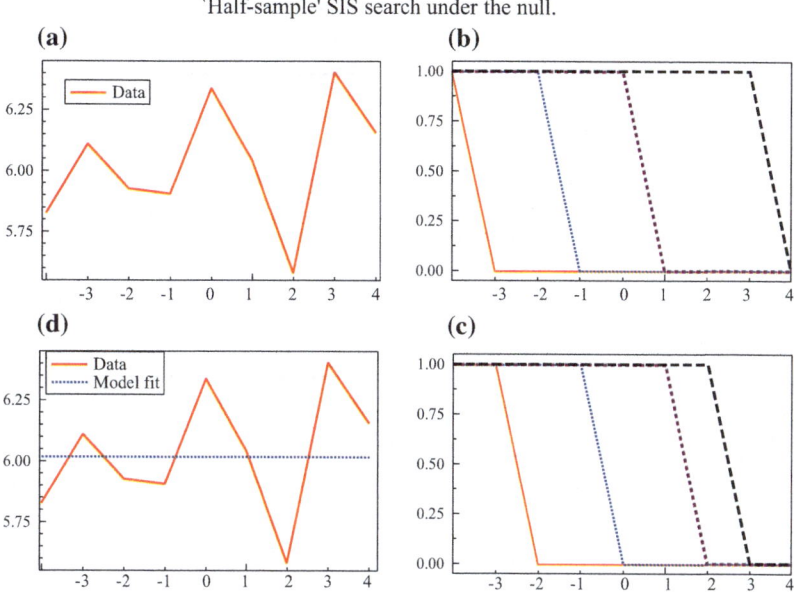

Fig. 5.3 (a) The data time series; (b) the 4 step indicators included; (c) the other set of step indicators; (d) the outcome as no indicators are selected

where now the thick solid line denotes the selected indicator, with (d) showing the outcome with and without that selected step indicator.

Notice how the fit without handling the shift produces 'spurious' residual autocorrelation, as all the residuals are first positive, then all become negative after observation 1. 'Treating' the residual autocorrelation by a conventional recipe would not be a good solution (see Mizon 1995) as the location shift is not correctly modelled. Finally, a more parsimonious and less 'overfitted' outcome results than would be found using IIS which would produce a perfect fit to the last 4 data points.

Figure 4.6 for the growth of real wages was used to illustrate co-breaking between wage growth and inflation, both of which experienced myriad shifts. However, the graph hides that the latter half of the twentieth century had a substantively higher mean real-wage growth at 1.8% p.a. post-1945 versus 0.7% p.a. pre, and 1.3% overall. Real wages would have increased 16-fold at 1.8% p.a. from 1860, rather than just threefold at 0.7% p.a.,

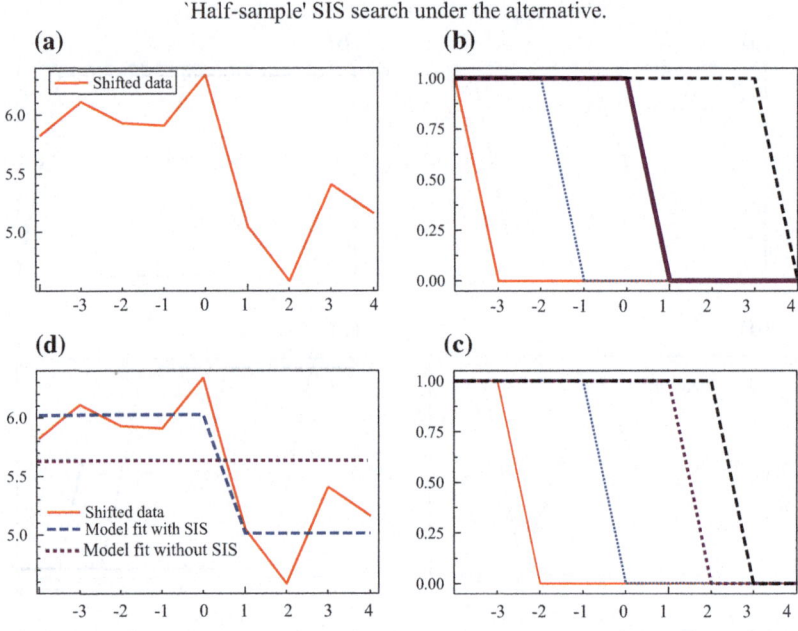

Fig. 5.4 (a) The shifted time series; (b) the first 4 step indicators included where the thick solid line denotes selected; (c) the other 4 step indicators; (d) the outcome with the selected step indicator

and sevenfold in practice: 'small' changes in growth rates can dramatically alter living standards. The location shifts shown on the graph were selected by SIS at $\alpha = 0.005$, and were not noticed, or included, in earlier models, but helped clarify the many influences on real wages (see Castle and Hendry 2014).

5.3 Designing Indicator Saturation

But why stop at step-indicator saturation? A location shift in the growth rate of a variable must imply that there is a change in the trend of the variable itself.

5.3.1 Trend-Indicator Saturation

Thus, one way of capturing a trend break would be to saturate the model with a series of trend indicators, which generate a trend up to a given observation and 0 thereafter for every observation. However, trend breaks can be difficult to detect as small changes in trends can take time to accumulate, even if they eventually lead to very substantial differences.

> **Defining Trend Indicators**
> Trend indicators are defined as $\mathsf{T}_{jt} = t - j + 1$ for $t \geq j$, $j = 1, \ldots, T$ and 0 otherwise.

Figure 5.5 also illustrated the issue that although the long-run effect of the step shift detected by SIS starting in 1945 was dramatic, that would not have been clear at the time. The average growth of 1.4% p.a. over the first 15 years, 1945–1960, after SIS detects the shift, is little different from the 1.2% p.a. near the start of data period over the 15 years 1864–1879. Indeed, fitting SIS to the sample up to 1960, it finds a location shift from 1944 of 1.1% which could be the end of a World War II effect rather than the start of the prolonged higher growth to come.

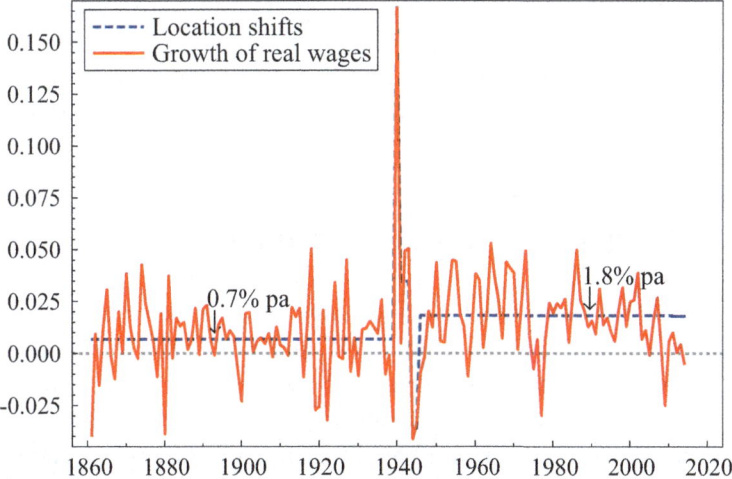

Fig. 5.5 A location shift in the growth of UK real wages

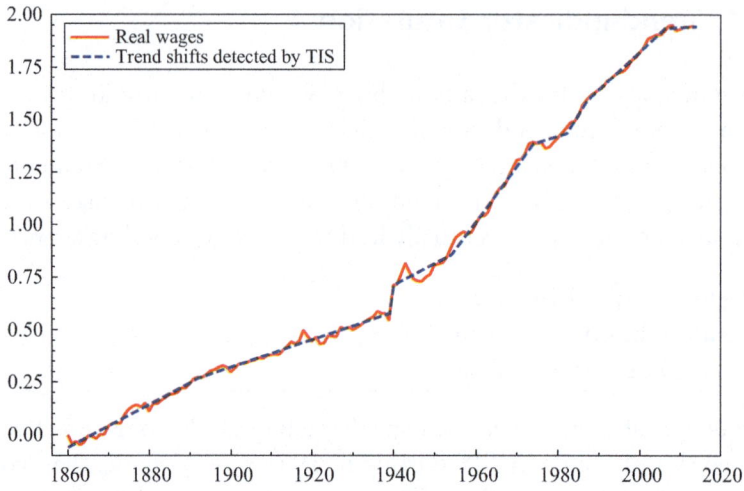

Fig. 5.6 Several trend breaks in UK real wages detected by TIS

We illustrate trend-indicator saturation (TIS) for the level of real wages as shown in Fig. 5.6. Selection was undertaken at $\alpha = 0.001$, using such a tight significance level because the variable is I(1) with shifts, so considerable residual serial correlation seemed likely. An overall trend was retained without selection, so deviations therefrom were being detected. Even at such a tight significance level, nine trend indicators were retained, several acting for short periods, as with the jump between 1939 and 1940 (matching the spike in Fig. 5.5), and the flattening over 1973–1981, and again at the end of the period.

5.3.2 Multiplicative-Indicator Saturation

Ericsson (2012) considered a wide range of possible indicator saturation methods, including combining IIS and SIS (super saturation) and multiplicative-indicator saturation (MIS) where every variable in a candidate set is multiplied by every step indicator. For example, with 100 observations and four regressor variables there will be 400 candidates to select from. Kitov and Tabor (2015) have investigated the properties of

MIS by simulation, and found it can detect shifts in regression parameters despite the huge number of candidate variables. This prompted Castle et al. (2017) to apply the approach to successfully detect induced shifts in estimated models following a policy intervention. They offer an explanation for the surprisingly good performance of MIS as follows. Imagine knowing where a shift occurred, so you split your data sample at that point and fit the now correctly specified model separately to the two sub-samples. You would be deservedly surprised if those appropriate sub-sample estimates did not reflect the parameter shifts. Choosing the split by MIS will add variability, but the correct indicator, or one close to it, should be selected as that is where the parameters changed. Of course, as ever with model selection, 'unlucky' draws from the error distribution may make the shift appear to happen slightly earlier or later than actually occurred. We consider an application of MIS in the next Chapter.

5.3.3 Designed-Break Indicator Saturation

If the breaks under investigation have a relatively regular shape, saturation techniques can be 'designed' appropriately, denoted DIS. This idea has been used by Pretis et al. (2016) to detect the impacts of volcanic eruptions on temperature records. When a volcano erupts, it spews material into the atmosphere and above, which can 'block' sunlight, or more accurately, reduce received solar radiation. The larger the eruption, the more solar radiation is reduced. Thus, the eruption of Tambora in 1816 created the 'year without a summer' in the Northern Hemisphere, adding to the difficulties people confronted just after the end of the Napoleonic wars. More generally, atmospheric temperatures drop rapidly during and immediately after an eruption, then as the ejected material is removed from the atmosphere, temperature slowly recovers, like a 'v'. Thus, a saturating set of indicators with such a shape can be created and applied to the relevant time series, selecting rather like we described above for SIS. The follow up in Schneider et al. (2017) demonstrates the success of DIS for detecting the impacts of volcanic eruptions to improve dendrochronological temperature reconstructions.

5.4 Outliers and Non-linearity

The methods discussed above were designed to detect unknown outliers (IIS), location shifts (SIS), trend breaks (TIS), parameter changes (MIS) and volcanic eruptions (DIS) that actually happened, at a pre-set significance level. An alternative explanation for what appears to be structural change is that the data generating process is non-linear. Possible examples include Markov switching models (see e.g., Hamilton 1989), threshold (see e.g., Priestley 1981) and smooth transition models (see e.g., Granger Teräsvirta 1993), where the non-linearity is 'regular' in some way. Distinguishing between the two explanations can be difficult. Indeed, non-linearities and deterministic structural breaks can often be closely similar. But a key advantage of *Autometrics* is that it operates as a variable selection algorithm, allowing selection over non-linear functions as well as potential outliers and breaks, so both explanations can be tested jointly, and both explanations could well play a role in explaining the phenomena of interest.

The *Autometrics*-based approach in Castle and Hendry (2014) creates a class of non-linear functions from transformations of the original data variables to approximate a wide range of potential non-linearities in a low-dimensional way. The problem with including, say, a general cubic function of all the (non-indicator) candidate variables is the explosion in the number of terms that need to be considered. For example, with 20 candidates, there are 1539 cubic terms. However, their simplification adds only 60 terms, at the possible risk of not capturing all the non-linearity in some settings. When an investigator has a specific non-linear function as a preferred explanation, that can be tested against the selected model by encompassing to see if (a) the proposed function is significant, and if so (b) whether it eliminates all the other non-linear terms.

References

Castle, J. L., Doornik, J. A., and Hendry, D. F. (2012). Model selection when there are multiple breaks. *Journal of Econometrics*, **169**, 239–246.

Castle, J. L., Doornik, J. A., Hendry, D. F., and Pretis, F. (2015). Detecting location shifts during model selection by step-indicator saturation. *Econometrics*, **3(2)**, 240–264. http://www.mdpi.com/2225-1146/3/2/240.

Castle, J. L., and Hendry, D. F. (2014). Semi-automatic non-linear model selection. In Haldrup, N., Meitz, M., and Saikkonen, P. (eds.), *Essays in Nonlinear Time Series Econometrics*, pp. 163–197. Oxford: Oxford University Press.

Castle, J. L., Hendry, D. F., and Martinez, A. B. (2017). Evaluating forecasts, narratives and policy using a test of invariance. *Econometrics*, **5(39)**. https://doi.org/10.3390/econometrics5030039.

Ericsson, N. R. (2012). Detecting crises, jumps, and changes in regime. Working paper, Federal Reserve Board of Governors, Washington, DC.

Granger, C. W. J., and Teräsvirta, T. (1993). *Modelling Nonlinear Economic Relationships*. Oxford: Oxford University Press.

Hamilton, J. D. (1989). A new approach to economic analysis of nonstationary time series. *Econometrica*, **57**, 357–384.

Hendry, D. F., Johansen, S., and Santos, C. (2008). Automatic selection of indicators in a fully saturated regression. *Computational Statistics*, **33**, 317–335. Erratum, 337–339.

Hendry, D. F., and Santos, C. (2010). An automatic test of super exogeneity. In Watson, M. W., Bollerslev, T., and Russell, J. (eds.), *Volatility and Time Series Econometrics*, pp. 164–193. Oxford: Oxford University Press.

Johansen, S., and Nielsen, B. (2009). An analysis of the indicator saturation estimator as a robust regression estimator. In Castle, J. L., and Shephard, N. (eds.), *The Methodology and Practice of Econometrics*, pp. 1–36. Oxford: Oxford University Press.

Johansen, S., and Nielsen, B. (2016). Asymptotic theory of outlier detection algorithms for linear time series regression models. *Scandinavian Journal of Statistics*, **43**, 321–348.

Kitov, O. I., and Tabor, M. N. (2015). Detecting structural changes in linear models: A variable selection approach using multiplicative indicator saturation. Unpublished paper, University of Oxford.

Mizon, G. E. (1995). A simple message for autocorrelation correctors: Don't. *Journal of Econometrics*, **69**, 267–288.

Pretis, F., Schneider, L., Smerdon, J. E., and Hendry, D. F. (2016). Detecting volcanic eruptions in temperature reconstructions by designed break-indicator saturation. *Journal of Economic Surveys*, **30**, 403–429.

Priestley, M. B. (1981). *Spectral Analysis and Time Series.* New York: Academic Press.

Schneider, L., Smerdon, J. E., Pretis, F., Hartl-Meier, C., and Esper, J. (2017). A new archive of large volcanic events over the past millennium derived from reconstructed summer temperatures. *Environmental Research Letters*, **12(9)**. https://doi.org/10.1088/1748-9326/aa7a1b/meta.

Open Access This chapter is licensed under the terms of the Creative Commons Attribution 4.0 International License (http://creativecommons.org/licenses/by/4.0/), which permits use, sharing, adaptation, distribution and reproduction in any medium or format, as long as you give appropriate credit to the original author(s) and the source, provide a link to the Creative Commons license and indicate if changes were made.

The images or other third party material in this chapter are included in the chapter's Creative Commons license, unless indicated otherwise in a credit line to the material. If material is not included in the chapter's Creative Commons license and your intended use is not permitted by statutory regulation or exceeds the permitted use, you will need to obtain permission directly from the copyright holder.

6

The Polymath: Combining Theory and Data

Abstract There are numerous possible approaches to building a model of a given data set, whether it be time series, cross section or panel. In economics, imposing a 'theory model' on the data, by simply estimating its parameters, is common. In 'big data' analyses, various methods of selecting relationships are used (aka 'data mining'), but in practice, modellers often select equations from data using theory-based guidelines. We discuss an approach that can retain all available theory information unaffected by selecting over additional candidate variables, lags (for time series), and non-linear functions, taking account of both potential outliers and shifts, yet can deliver an improved model when the theory specification is incomplete, incorrect, or changes over time.

Keywords Theory driven · Data driven · Evaluation · Discovery · Modelling inflation

6.1 Theory Driven and Data Driven Models

Two main approaches to empirically modelling a relationship are purely theory driven and purely data driven. In the former, common in economics, the putative relation is derived from a theoretical analysis claimed to represent the relevant situation, then its parameters are estimated by imposing that 'theory model' on the data.

> **Theory Driven Modelling**
> Let y_t denote the variable to be modelled by a set of n explanatory variables $\mathbf{z}_t$ when the theory relation is $y_t = f(\mathbf{z}_t)$,
> then the parameters of the known function $f(\cdot)$ are estimated from a sample of data over $t = 1, \ldots, T$.

In what follows, we will use a simple aggregate example based on the theory-model that monetary expansion causes inflation, reflecting Friedman's claim: 'inflation is always and everywhere a monetary phenomenon'. While it is certainly true that sufficiently large money growth can cause inflation (as in the Hungarian hyperinflation of 1945–1946), it need not do so, as the vast increase in the US monetary base from Quantitative Easing has shown, with the Federal Reserve System balances expanding by several $trillion. Thus, our dependent variable (y_t) is the rate of inflation, related by a linear function ($f(\cdot)$), in the simplest setting to the growth rate of the money stock together with lagged values of inflation and money growth ($\mathbf{z}_t$) to reflect non-instantaneous adjustments. Previous research has established that 'narrow money' (technically called M1 for currency in circulation plus chequing accounts) does not cause inflation in the UK, so instead we consider the growth in 'broad money' (technically M4, comprising all bank deposits, although the long-run series used here is spliced *ex post* from M2, M3 and M4 as the financial system and measurements evolved over time).

In a data-driven approach, observations on a larger set of $N > n$ variables (denoted $\{\mathbf{x}_t\}$) are collected to 'explain' y_t, which here could augment money with interest rates, growth in GDP and the National Debt, excess demand for goods and services, inflation in wages and other costs, changes in the exchange rate, changes in the unemployment rate, imported inflation, etc. To avoid simultaneous relations, where a variable is affected by inflation, all of these additional possible explanations will be entered lagged. The choice of additional candidate variables is based on looser theoretical guidelines, then some method of model selection is applied to pick the 'best' relation between y_t and a subset of the $\{\mathbf{x}_t\}$ within a class of functional connections (such as a linear relation with constant parameters and small, identically-distributed errors e_t independent of the $\{\mathbf{x}_t\}$). When N is very large ('big data', which could include micro-level data on household characteristics or internet search data), most current approaches have difficulties either in controlling the number of spurious relationships that might be found (because of an actual or implicit significance level for hypothesis tests that is too loose for the magnitude of N), or in retaining all of the relevant explanatory variables with a high probability (because the significance level is too stringent): see e.g., Doornik and Hendry (2015). Moreover, the selected model may be hard to interpret, and if many equations have been tried (but perhaps not reported), the statistical properties of the resulting selected model are unclear: see Leamer (1983).

6.2 The Drawbacks of Using Each Approach in Isolation

Many variants of theory-driven and data-driven approaches exist, often combined with testing the properties of the e_t, the assumptions about the regressors, and the constancy of the relationship $f(\cdot)$, but with different strategies for how to proceed if any of the conditions required for viable inference are rejected. The assumption made all too often is that a rejection occurs because that test has power under the specific alternative for which the test is derived, although a given test can reject for many other reasons. The classic example of such a 'recipe' is finding residual autocorrelation and assuming it arose from error autocorrelation, whereas the problem could be mis-specified dynamics, unmodelled location shifts as seen above, or omitted autocorrelated variables. In our inflation example, in order to eliminate autocorrelation, annual dynamics need to be modelled, along with shifts due to wars, crises and legislative changes. The approach proposed in the next section instead seeks to include all likely determinants from the outset, and would revise the initial general formulation if any of the mis-specification tests thereof rejected.

Most observational data are affected by many influences, often outside the relevant subject's purview—as the 2016 Brexit vote has emphasized for economics—and it would require a brilliant theoretical analysis to take all the substantively important forces into account. Thus, a purely theory-driven approach, such as a monetary theory of aggregate inflation, is unlikely to deliver a complete, correct and immutable model that forges a new 'law' once estimated. Rather, to capture the complexities of real world data, features outside the theory remit almost always need to be taken into account, especially changes resulting from unpredicted events. Moreover, few theories include all the variables that characterize a process, with correct dynamic reactions, and the actual non-linear connections. In addition, the data may be mis-measured for the theory variables (revealed by revising national accounts data as new information accrues), and may even be incorrectly recorded relative to its own definition, leading to outliers. Finally, shifts in relationships are all too common—there is a distinct lack of empirical models that have stood the test of time or have an unblemished forecasting track record: see Hendry and Pretis (2016).

Many of the same problems affect a purely data-driven approach unless the $\mathbf{x}_t$ provide a remarkably comprehensive specification, in which case there will often be more candidate variables N than observations T: see Castle and Hendry (2014) for a discussion of that setting. Because included regressors will 'pick up' influences from any correlated missing variables, omitting important factors usually entails biased parameter estimates, badly behaved residuals, and most importantly, often non-constant models. Failing to retain relevant theory-based variables can be pernicious and potentially distort which models are selected. Thus, an approach that retains, but does not impose, theory-driven variables without affecting the estimates of a correct, complete, and constant theory model, has much to offer, if it also allows selection over a much larger set of candidate variables, avoiding the substantial costs when relevant variables are omitted from the initial specification. We now describe how the benefits of the two approaches can be combined to achieve that outcome based on Hendry and Doornik (2014) and Hendry and Johansen (2015).

6.3 A Combined Approach

Let us assume that the theory correctly specifies the set of relevant variables. This could include lags of the variables to represent an equilibrium-correction mechanism. In the combined approach, the theory relation is retained while selecting over an additional set of potentially relevant candidate variables. These additional candidate variables could include disaggregates for household characteristics (in panel data), as well as the variables noted above. To ensure an encompassing explanation, the additional set of variables could also include additional lags and non-linear functions of the theory variables, other explanatory variables used by different investigators, and indicator variables to capture outliers and shifts.

The general unrestricted model (GUM) is formulated to nest both the theory model and the data-driven formulation. As the theory variables and additional variables are likely to be quite highly correlated, even if the theory model is exactly correct the model estimates are unlikely to be the same as those from estimating the theory model directly. However, the theory variables can be orthogonalized with respect to the additional variables, which means that they are uncorrelated with the other variables. Therefore, inclusion of additional regressors will not affect the estimates of the theory variables in the model, regardless of whether any, or all, of the additional variables are included. The theory variables are always included in the model, and any additional variables can be selected over to see if they are useful in explaining the phenomona of interest. Thus, data-based model selection can be applied to all the potentially relevant candidate explanatory variables while retaining the theory model without selection.

> **Summary of the Combined Approach**
> The theory variables are given by the set $\mathbf{z}_t$ of n relevant variables entering $f(\cdot)$. We use the explicit parametrization for $f(\cdot)$ of a linear, constant parameter vector $\boldsymbol{\beta}$, so the theory model is:
> $y_t = \boldsymbol{\beta}'\mathbf{z}_t + e_t,$
> where $e_t \sim \mathsf{IN}[0, \sigma_e^2]$ is independent of $\mathbf{z}_t$.
> Define the additional set of M candidate variables as $\{\mathbf{w}_t\}$.
>
> Formulate the GUM as:
> $y_t = \boldsymbol{\beta}'\mathbf{z}_t + \boldsymbol{\gamma}'\mathbf{w}_t + v_t,$
> which nests both the theory model and the data-driven formulation when $\mathbf{x}_t = (\mathbf{z}_t, \mathbf{w}_t)$, so v_t will inherit the properties of e_t when $\boldsymbol{\gamma} = \mathbf{0}$.
>
> Without loss of generality, $\mathbf{z}_t$ can be orthogonalized with respect to $\mathbf{w}_t$ by projecting the latter onto the former in:
> $\mathbf{w}_t = \boldsymbol{\Gamma}\mathbf{z}_t + \mathbf{u}_t$
> where $\mathsf{E}[\mathbf{z}_t\mathbf{u}_t'] = \mathbf{0}$ for estimated $\boldsymbol{\Gamma}$. Substitute the estimated components $\boldsymbol{\Gamma}\mathbf{z}_t$ and $\mathbf{u}_t$ for $\mathbf{w}_t$ in the GUM, leading to:
>
> $$y_t = \boldsymbol{\beta}'\mathbf{z}_t + \boldsymbol{\gamma}'(\boldsymbol{\Gamma}\mathbf{z}_t + \mathbf{u}_t) + v_t = (\boldsymbol{\beta}' + \boldsymbol{\gamma}'\boldsymbol{\Gamma})\mathbf{z}_t + \boldsymbol{\gamma}'\mathbf{u}_t + v_t.$$
>
> When $\boldsymbol{\gamma} = \mathbf{0}$, the coefficient of $\mathbf{z}_t$ remains $\boldsymbol{\beta}$, and because $\mathbf{z}_t$ and $\mathbf{u}_t$ are now orthogonal by construction, the estimate of $\boldsymbol{\beta}$ is unaffected by whether or not any or all $\mathbf{u}_t$ are included during selection.

To favour the incumbent theory, selection over additional variables can be undertaken at a stringent significance level to minimize the chances of spuriously selecting irrelevant variables. We suggest $\alpha = \min(0.001, 1/N)$. However, the approach protects against missing important explanatory variables, one such example of which is location shifts. The critical value for 0.1% in a Normal distribution is $c_{0.001} = 3.35$, so substantive regressors or shifts should still be easily retained. As noted in Castle et al. (2011), using IIS allows near Normality to be a reasonable approximation. However, a reduction from an integrated to a non-integrated representation requires non-Normal critical values, another reason for using tight significance levels during model selection. In practice, unless the parameters of the theory model have strong grounds for being of special interest, the orthogonalization step is unnecessary since the same outcome will be found just by retaining the theory variables when selecting over the additional candidates. An example of retaining a 'permanent income hypothesis' based consumption function relating the log of aggregate consumers' expenditure, c, to logs of income, i, and lagged c, orthogonalized with respect to the variables in Davidson et al. (1978), denoted DHSY, is provided in Hendry (2018).

When should an investigator reject the theory specification? As there are M additional variables included in the combined approach (in addition to the n theory variables which are not selected over), on average αM will be significant by chance, so if $M = 100$ and $\alpha = 1\%$ (so $c_{0.01} = 2.6$), on average there will be one adventitiously significant selection. Thus, finding that one of the additional variables was 'significant' would not be surprising even when the theory model was correct and complete. Indeed, the probabilities that none, one and two of the additional variables are significant by chance are 0.37, 0.37 and 0.18, leaving a probability of 0.08 of more than two being retained. However, using $\alpha = 0.5\%$ ($c_{0.005} = 2.85$), these probabilities become 0.61, 0.30 and 0.08 with almost no probability of 3 or more being significant; and 0.90, 0.09 and <0.01 for $\alpha = 0.1\%$, in which case retaining 2 or more of the additional variables almost always implies an incomplete or incorrect theory model.

When the total number of theory variables and additional variables exceeds the number of observations in the data sample (so $M + n = N > T$), our approach can still be implemented by splitting the variables into feasible sub-blocks, estimating separate projections for each sub-block, and replacing these subsets by their residuals. The n theory variables are retained without selection at every stage, only selecting over the (putatively irrelevant) variables at a stringent significance level using a multi-path block search of the form implemented in the model selection algorithm *Autometrics* (see Doornik 2009; Doornik and Hendry 2018). When the initial theory model is incomplete or incorrect—a likely possibility for the inflation illustration here—but some of the additional variables are relevant to explaining the phenomenon of interest, then an improved empirical model should result.

6.4 Applying the Combined Approach to UK Inflation Data

> **Interpreting regression equations**
> The simplest model considered below relates two variables, the dependent variable y_t and the explanatory variable x_t, $t = 1, \ldots, T$:
> $$y_t = \beta_0 + \beta_1 x_t + u_t.$$
> To conduct inference on this model, we assume that the innovations $u_1, \ldots u_T$ are independent and Normally distributed with a zero mean and constant variance, $u_t \sim \text{IN}\left[0, \sigma_u^2\right]$, and that the parameter space for the parameters of interest $(\beta_0, \beta_1, \sigma_u^2)$ is not restricted. These assumptions need to be checked for valid inference, which is done by tests for residual autocorrelation (F_{ar}), non-Normality (χ^2_{nd}), autoregressive conditional heteroskedasticity (ARCH: F_{arch}, see Engle 1982), heteroskedasticity (F_{Het}), and functional form (F_{RESET}). If the assumptions for valid inference are satisfied, then we can interpret β_1 as the effect of a one unit increase in x_t on y_t, or an elasticity if x and y are in logs.

We start from the simplest equation relating inflation (denoted $\Delta p_t = p_t - p_{t-1}$ so Δ signifies a difference) to broad money growth (i.e., Δm_t) where lower case letters denote logs, P is the UK price level and M is its broad money stock:

$$\Delta p_t = \beta_0 + \beta_1 \Delta m_t + e_t \tag{6.1}$$

The two time series for annual UK data over 1874–2012 are shown in Fig. 6.1(a) and their scatter plot with a fitted regression line and the deviations therefrom in Panel (b).

At first sight, the hypothesis seems to have support: the two series are positively related (from Panel (b)) and tend to move together over time (from Panel (a)), although much less so after 1980. However, that leaves open the question of why: is inflation responding to money growth, or is more (less) money needed because the price level has risen (fallen)?

6 The Polymath: Combining Theory and Data

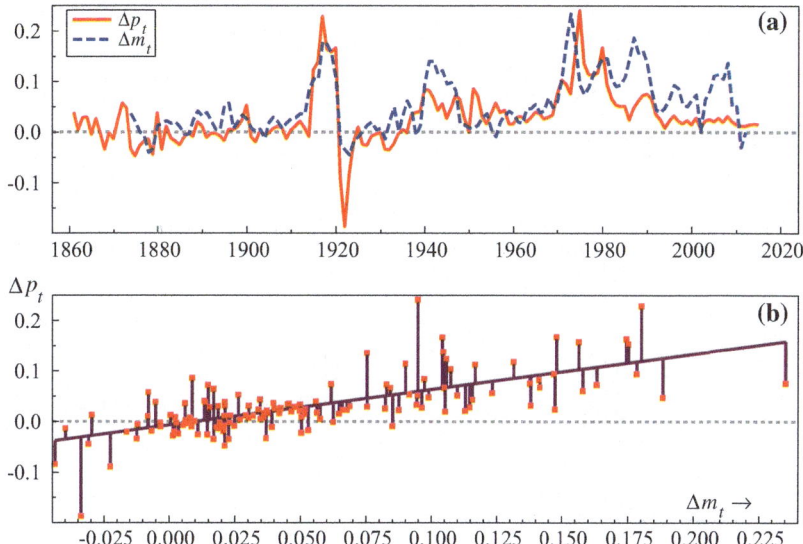

Fig. 6.1 (a) Time series of Δp_t and Δm_t; (b) scatter plot with the fitted regression of Δp_t on Δm_t and the deviations therefrom

The regression in (6.1) is estimated over 1877–2012 as:

$$\Delta p_t = \underset{(0.005)}{-0.005} + \underset{(0.063)}{0.69} \Delta m_t \tag{6.2}$$

$\widehat{\sigma} = 4.1\%$ $R^2 = 0.47$ $\mathsf{F}_{\mathsf{ar}}(2, 132) = 30.7^{**}$ $\mathsf{F}_{\mathsf{Het}}(2, 133) = 4.35^*$
$\chi^2_{\mathsf{nd}}(2) = 36.6^{**}$ $\mathsf{F}_{\mathsf{arch}}(1, 134) = 8.94^{**}$ $\mathsf{F}_{\mathsf{RESET}}(2, 132) = 1.27$

The residual standard deviation, $\widehat{\sigma}$, is very large at 4%, with a 95% uncertainty range of 16%, when for the last 20 years, inflation has only varied between 1.5% and 3.5%.

Moreover, tests for residual autocorrelation (F_{ar}), non-Normality (χ^2_{nd}), autoregressive conditional heteroskedasticity (ARCH: $\mathsf{F}_{\mathsf{arch}}$) and heteroskedasticity ($\mathsf{F}_{\mathsf{Het}}$) all reject. Figure 6.2(a) records the fitted and actual values of Δp_t; (b) shows the residuals $\widehat{e}_t/\widehat{\sigma}$, (c) their density with a standard Normal for comparison; and (d) their residual correlogram.

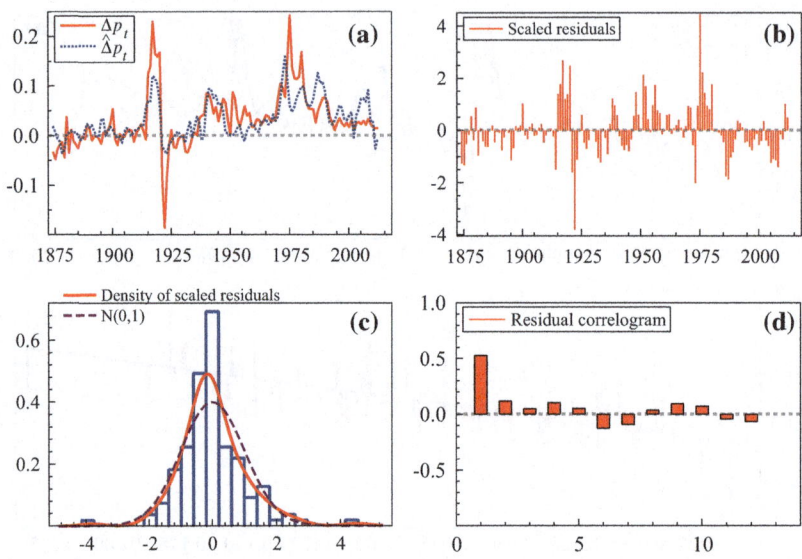

Fig. 6.2 (a) Fitted, $\widehat{\Delta p_t}$, and actual values, Δp_t, from (6.2); (b) scaled residuals $\widehat{e}_t/\widehat{\sigma}$; (c) their density with a standard Normal for comparison and (d) their residual correlogram

A glance at the test statistics in (6.2) and Fig. 6.2 shows that the equation is badly mis-specified, and indeed recursive estimation reveals considerable parameter non-constancy. The simplicity of the bivariate regression provides an opportunity to illustrate MIS, where both β_0 and β_1 are interacted with step indicators at every observation, so there are 271 candidate variables. Using $\alpha = 0.0001$ found 7 shifts in β_0 and 5 in β_1, halving $\widehat{\sigma}$ to 1.9%, and revealing a far from constant relationship between money growth and inflation.

Such a result should not come as a surprise given the large number of major regime changes impinging on the UK economy over the period as noted in Chapter 3, many relevant to the role of money. In particular, key financial innovations and changes in credit rationing included the introduction of personal cheques in the 1810s and the telegraph in the 1850s both reducing the need for multiple bank accounts just before our sample; credit cards in the 1950s; ATMs in the 1960s; deregulation of banks and building societies (the equivalent of US Savings and Loans) in the 1980s;

interest-bearing chequing accounts around 1984; and securitization of mortgages; etc.

First, to offer the incumbent theory a better chance, we added lagged values of Δp_{t-i} and Δm_{t-i} for $i = 1, 2$ to (6.2), but without indicators, which improves the fit to $\hat{\sigma} = 3.3\%$ although three significant misspecification tests remain as (6.3) shows.

$$\Delta p_t = \underset{(0.09)}{0.67} \Delta p_{t-1} - \underset{(0.08)}{0.19} \Delta p_{t-2} + \underset{(0.10)}{0.40} \Delta m_t$$
$$- \underset{(0.15)}{0.01} \Delta m_{t-1} - \underset{(0.11)}{0.02} \Delta m_{t-2} - \underset{(0.004)}{0.003} \quad (6.3)$$

$$\hat{\sigma} = 3.3\% \quad R^2 = 0.66 \quad F_{ar}(1, 128) = 0.20 \quad F_{Het}(10, 125) = 5.93^{**}$$
$$\chi^2_{nd}(2) = 76.9^{**} \quad F_{arch}(1, 134) = 7.73^{**} \quad F_{RESET}(2, 128) = 0.13$$

Neither lag of money growth is relevant given the contemporaneous value, but both lags of inflation matter, suggesting about half of past inflation is carried forward, so there is a moderate level of persistence. Now applying IIS+SIS at $\alpha = 0.0025$ to (6.3) yielded $\hat{\sigma} = 1.6\%$ with 4 impulse and 6 step indicators retained, but with all the coefficients of the economics variables being much closer to zero.

As the aim of this section is to illustrate our approach, and a substantive model of UK inflation over this period is available in Hendry (2015), we just consider four of the rival explanations that have been proposed. Thus to create a more general GUM for Δp_t, we also include the unemployment rate ($U_{r,t}$) relating to the original Phillips curve model of inflation (Phillips 1958); the potential output gap (measured by ($g_t - 0.019t$) and adjusted to give a zero mean) and growth in GDP (Δg_t) to represent excess demand for goods and services (an even older idea dating back to Hume); wage inflation (Δw_t) as a cost push measure (a 1970s theme); and changes in long-term interest rates ($\Delta R_{L,t}$) reflecting the cost of capital. To avoid simultaneity, all variables are entered lagged one and two periods (including money growth) and the 2-period lag of the potential output gap is excluded to avoid multicollinearity between growth in GDP and the potential output gap, making $N = 14$ including the intercept before any indicators. The five additional variables are then orthogonalized with respect to Δm_t and lags of it and lags of Δp_t. To fully implement the strategy, lags of regressors should also be orthogonalized, but the resulting coefficients of the variables in common are close to those in the simpler model. Estimation delivers $\widehat{\sigma} = 3.3\%$ with an F-test on the additional variables of $F(9, 121) = 2.66^{**}$, thereby rejecting the simple model, still with the three mis-specification tests significant.

Since the baseline theory model is untenable, its coefficients are not of interest, so we revert to the original measures of all the economic variables to facilitate interpretation of the final model. The economic variables are all retained while we select indicators by IIS and SIS at $\alpha = 0.0025$, choosing that significance level so that only a few highly significant indicators would be retained, with almost none likely to be significant by chance (with a theoretical retention rate of $271 \times 0.0025 = 0.68$ of an indicator). Nevertheless, five impulse and ten step indicators were selected, producing $\widehat{\sigma} = 1.2\%$ now with no mis-specification tests significant at 1%. Such a plethora of highly significant indicators implies that inflation is not being well explained even by the combination of all the theories. In fact the more general model in Hendry (2015) still needed 7 step indicators (though for somewhat different unexplained shifts) as well as dummies for the World Wars: sudden major shifts in UK inflation are not well explained by economic variables. We then selected over the 13 economic variables at the conventional significance level of 5%, forcing the intercept to be retained. Six were retained, with $\widehat{\sigma} = 1.2\%$ to deliver (only reporting the economic variables):

$$\Delta p_t = \underset{(0.04)}{0.17 \Delta m_{t-2}} - \underset{(0.10)}{0.46 U_{r,t-1}} + \underset{(0.09)}{0.43 U_{r,t-2}} - \underset{(0.03)}{0.10 gap_{t-1}}$$

$$+ \underset{(0.03)}{0.23 \Delta w_{t-1}} + \underset{(0.24)}{0.54 \Delta R_{L,t-1}} + \underset{(0.01)}{0.02} \qquad (6.4)$$

$$\widehat{\sigma} = 1.2\% \quad (R^*)^2 = 0.96 \quad F_{ar}(2, 112) = 0.14$$

$$F_{Het}(22, 108) = 1.97^*$$

$$\chi^2_{nd}(2) = 1.63 \quad F_{arch}(1, 134) = 0.15$$

$$F_{RESET}(2, 112) = 4.25^*$$

In contrast to the simple monetary theory of inflation, the model retains aspects of all the theories posited above. Now there is no direct persistence from past inflation, but remember that the step indicators represent persistent location shifts, so the mean inflation rate persists at different levels. Interesting aspects are how many shifts were found and that these location shifts seem to come from outside economics. The dates selected are consistent with that: 1914, 1920 and 1922, 1936 and 1948, 1950 and 1952, 1969, 1973 and 1980, all have plausible events, although they were not the only large unanticipated shocks over the last 150 years (e.g., the general strike). There is a much bigger impact from past wage growth than money growth as proximate determinants, but we have not modelled those to determine 'final' causes of what drives the shifts and evolution. Finally, the − then + coefficients on unemployment suggest it is changes therein rather than the levels that affect inflation.

The long-run relation after solving out the dynamics is:

$$\Delta p = \underset{(0.03)}{0.23\, \Delta w} + \underset{(0.04)}{0.17\, \Delta m} - \underset{(0.07)}{0.03\, U_r} - \underset{(0.03)}{0.10\, gap} + \underset{(0.24)}{0.54\, \Delta R_L}$$

(6.5)

The first two signs and magnitudes are easily interpreted as higher wage growth and faster money growth raise inflation. The negative unemployment coefficient is insignificant, consistent with its role probably being through changes. The hard to interpret output gap could be reflecting omitted variables and changes in the cost of capital raising inflation.

It is easy to think of other variables that could have an impact on the UK inflation rate, including the mark-up over costs used by companies to price their output; changes in commodity prices, especially oil; imported inflation from changes in world prices; changes in the nominal exchange rate; and changes in the National Debt among others, several of which are significant in the inflation model in Hendry (2015). Moreover, there is no strong reason to expect a constant relation between any of the putative explanatory variables and inflation given the numerous regime shifts that have occurred, the changing nature of money, and increasing globalization. In principle, MIS could be used where shifts are most likely, but in practice might be hard to implement at a reasonable significance level.

In our proposed combined theory-driven and data-driven approach, when the theory is complete it is almost costless in statistical terms to check the relevance of large numbers of other candidate variables, yet there is a good chance of discovering a better empirical model when the theory is incomplete or incorrect. Automatic model selection algorithms that allow retention of theory variables while selecting over many orthogonalized candidate variables can therefore deliver high power for the most likely explanatory variables while controlling spurious significance at a low level. Oh for having had the current technology in the 1970s! This is only partly anachronistic, as the theory in Hendry and Johansen (2015) could easily have been formulated 50 years ago. Combining the theory and data based approaches improves the chances of discovering an empirically well-specified, theory-interpretable model.

References

Castle, J. L., Doornik, J. A., and Hendry, D. F. (2011). Evaluating automatic model selection. *Journal of Time Series Econometrics*, **3(1)**. https://doi.org/10.2202/1941-1928.1097.

Castle, J. L., and Hendry, D. F. (2014). Semi-automatic non-linear model selection. In Haldrup, N., Meitz, M., and Saikkonen, P. (eds.), *Essays in Nonlinear Time Series Econometrics*, pp. 163–197. Oxford: Oxford University Press.

Davidson, J. E. H., Hendry, D. F., Srba, F., and Yeo, J. S. (1978). Econometric modelling of the aggregate time-series relationship between consumers' expenditure and income in the United Kingdom. *Economic Journal*, **88**, 661–692.

Doornik, J. A. (2009). Autometrics. In Castle, J. L., and Shephard, N. (eds.), *The Methodology and Practice of Econometrics*, pp. 88–121. Oxford: Oxford University Press.

Doornik, J. A., and Hendry, D. F. (2015). Statistical model selection with big data. *Cogent Economics and Finance*. http://www.tandfonline.com/doi/full/10.1080/23322039.2015.1045216#.VYE5bUYsAsQ.

Doornik, J. A., and Hendry, D. F. (2018). *Empirical Econometric Modelling Using PcGive: Volume I*, 8th Edition. London: Timberlake Consultants Press.

Engle, R. F. (1982). Autoregressive conditional heteroscedasticity, with estimates of the variance of United Kingdom inflation. *Econometrica*, **50**, 987–1007.

Hendry, D. F. (2015). *Introductory Macro-econometrics: A New Approach*. London: Timberlake Consultants. http://www.timberlake.co.uk/macroeconometrics.html.

Hendry, D. F. (2018). Deciding between alternative approaches in macroeconomics. *International Journal of Forecasting*, **34**, 119–135, with

'Response to the Discussants', 142–146. http://authors.elsevier.com/sd/article/S0169207017300997.

Hendry, D. F., and Doornik, J. A. (2014). *Empirical Model Discovery and Theory Evaluation*. Cambridge, MA: MIT Press.

Hendry, D. F., and Johansen, S. (2015). Model discovery and Trygve Haavelmo's legacy. *Econometric Theory*, **31**, 93–114.

Hendry, D. F., and Pretis, F. (2016). *All Change! The Implications of Non-stationarity for Empirical Modelling, Forecasting and Policy*. Oxford University: Oxford Martin School Policy Paper. http://www.oxfordmartin.ox.ac.uk/publications/view/2318.

Leamer, E. E. (1983). Let's take the con out of econometrics. *American Economic Review*, **73**, 31–43. Reprinted in Granger, C. W. J. (ed.) (1990), *Modelling Economic Series*. Oxford: Clarendon Press.

Phillips, A. W. H. (1958). The relation between unemployment and the rate of change of money wage rates in the United Kingdom, 1861–1957. *Economica*, **25**, 283–299. Reprinted as pp. 243–260 in R. Leeson (ed.) (2000) *A. W. H. Phillips: Collected Works in Contemporary Perspective*. Cambridge: Cambridge University Press.

Open Access This chapter is licensed under the terms of the Creative Commons Attribution 4.0 International License (http://creativecommons.org/licenses/by/4.0/), which permits use, sharing, adaptation, distribution and reproduction in any medium or format, as long as you give appropriate credit to the original author(s) and the source, provide a link to the Creative Commons license and indicate if changes were made.

The images or other third party material in this chapter are included in the chapter's Creative Commons license, unless indicated otherwise in a credit line to the material. If material is not included in the chapter's Creative Commons license and your intended use is not permitted by statutory regulation or exceeds the permitted use, you will need to obtain permission directly from the copyright holder.

7

Seeing into the Future

Abstract While empirical modelling is primarily concerned with understanding the interactions between variables to recover the underlying 'truth', the aim of forecasts is to generate useful predictions about the future regardless of the model. We explain why models must be different in non-stationary processes from those that are optimal' under stationarity, and develop forecasting devices that avoid systematic failure after location shifts.

Keywords Forecasting · Forecast failure · Forecast uncertainty · Hedgehog forecasts · Outliers · Location shifts · Differencing · Robust devices

In a stationary world, many famous theorems about how to forecast optimally can be rigorously proved (summarised in Clements and Hendry 1998):

1. causal models will outperform non-causal (i.e., models without any relevant variables);
2. the conditional expectation of the future value delivers the minimum mean-square forecast error (**MSFE**);

3. mis-specified models have higher forecast-error variances than correctly specified ones;
4. long-run interval forecasts are bounded above by the unconditional variance of the process;
5. neither parameter estimation uncertainty nor high correlations between variables greatly increase forecast-error variances.

Unfortunately, when the process to be forecast suffers from location shifts and stochastic trends, and the forecasting model is mis-specified, then:

1. non-causal models can outperform correct in-sample causal relationships;
2. conditional expectations of future values can be badly biased if later outcomes are drawn from different distributions (see Fig. 4.5);
3. the correct in-sample model need not outperform in forecasting, and can be worse than the average of several devices;
4. long-run interval forecasts are unbounded;
5. parameter estimation uncertainty can substantively increase interval forecasts; as can
6. changes in correlations between variables at or near the forecast origin.

The problem for empirical econometrics is not a plethora of excellent forecasting models from which to choose, but to find any relationships that survive long enough to be useful: as we have emphasized, the stationarity assumption must be jettisoned for observable variables in economics. Location shifts and stochastic trend non-stationarities can have pernicious impacts on forecast accuracy and its measurement: Castle et al. (2019) provide a general introduction.

7.1 Forecasting Ignoring Outliers and Location Shifts

To illustrate the issues, we return to the two data sets in Chapter 5 which were perturbed by an outlier and a location shift respectively, then modelled by IIS and SIS. The next two figures use the indicators found in those examples. In Fig. 7.1, the 1-step forecasts with and without the indicator show the former to be slightly closer to the outcome, and with a smaller interval forecast.

Both features seem sensible: an outlier is a transient perturbation, and providing it is not too large, its impact on forecasts should also be transient and not too great. The increase in the interval forecast is due to the rise in the estimated residual standard error from the outlier. Nevertheless, failing to model outliers can be very detrimental as Hendry and Mizon (2011) show when modelling an extension of the US food expenditure data noted above, which was of course, the origin of IIS finding the very large outliers in the 1930s, discussed in Sect. 5.1 as a robust estimation method.

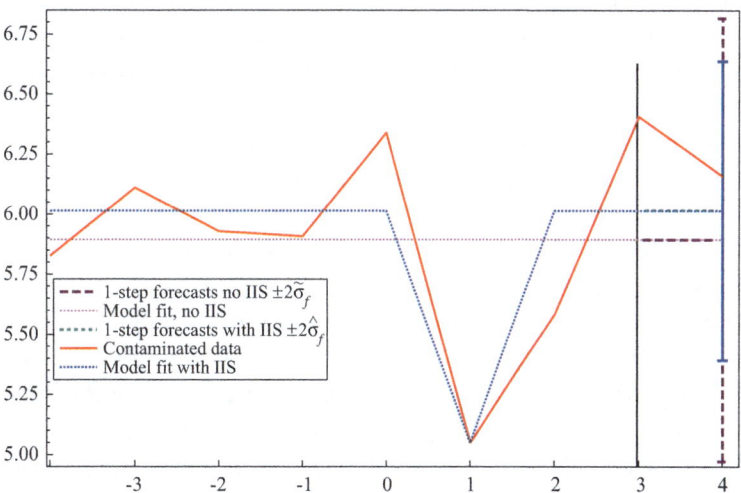

Fig. 7.1 1-step forecasts with and without the impulse indicator to model an outlier

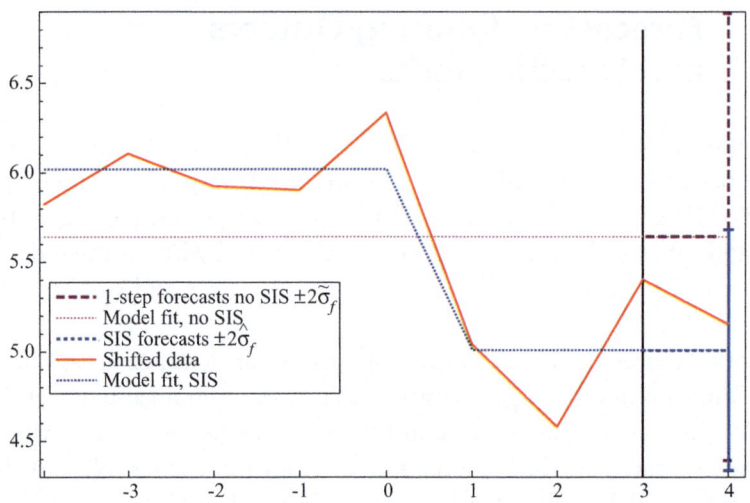

Fig. 7.2 1-step forecasts with and without the step indicator

However, the effect of omitting a step indicator that matches a location shift is far more serious as Fig. 7.2 shows. The 1-step forecast with the indicator is much closer to the outcome, with an even smaller interval forecast than that from the model without. Moreover, the forecast without the step indicator is close to the top of the interval forecast from the model with.

In Fig. 7.2, we (the writers of this book) know that the model with SIS matches the DGP (albeit with estimated rather than known parameters), whereas the model that ignores the location shift is mis-specified, and its interval forecast is hopelessly too wide—wider than the range of all previous observations. Castle et al. (2017) demonstrate the use of SIS in a forecasting context, where the step-indicator acts as a type of intercept correction when there has been a change in policy resulting in a location shift. An intercept correction changes the numerical value of the intercept in a forecasting model by adding a recent forecast error to put the forecast 'back on track'. SIS, along with other forms of robust device such as a conventional intercept correction, can greatly improve forecasts when they are subject to shifts at or near the forecast origin: see Clements and Hendry (1996).

7.2 Impacts of Stochastic Trends on Forecast Uncertainty

Because I(1) processes cumulate shocks, even using the correct in-sample model leads to much higher forecast uncertainty than would be anticipated on I(0) data. This is exemplified in Fig. 7.3 showing multi-period forecasts of log(GDP) starting in 1990 till 2030: the outcomes to 2016 are shown, but not used in the forecasts. Constant-change, or difference stationary, forecasts (dotted) and deterministic trend forecasts (dashed) usually make closely similar central forecasts as can be seen here. But deterministic linear trends do not cumulate shocks, so irrespective of the data properties, and hence even when the data are actually I(1), their uncertainty is measured as if the data were stationary around the trend.

Although the data properties are the same for the two models in Fig. 7.3, their estimated forecast uncertainties differ dramatically (bars and bands respectively), increasingly so as the horizon grows, due to the linear trend model assuming stable changes over time. Thus, model

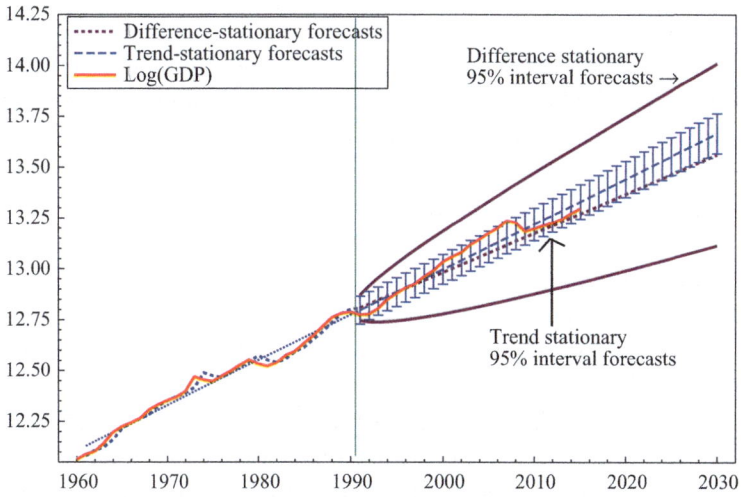

Fig. 7.3 Multi-period forecasts of log(GDP) using a non-stationary stochastic-trend model (dotted) and a trend-stationary model (dashed) with their associated 95% interval forecasts

choice has key implications for measuring forecast uncertainty, where misspecifications—such as incorrectly imposing linear trends—can lead to understating the actual uncertainty in forecasts. Although the assumption of a constant linear trend is rarely satisfactory, nevertheless, here almost all the outcomes between 1990 and 2016 lie within the bars. Conversely, the difference stationary interval forecasts are very wide. In fact, that model has considerable residual autocorrelation which the bands do not take into account, so over-estimate the uncertainty. However, caution is always advisable when forecasting integrated time series for long-periods into the future by either approach, especially from comparatively short samples.

7.3 Impacts of Location Shifts on Forecast Uncertainty

Almost irrespective of the forecasting device used, forecast failure would be rare in a stationary process, so episodes of forecast failure confirm that many time series are not stationary. Conversely, forecasting in the presence of location shifts can induce systematic forecast failure, unless the forecasting model accounts for the shifts.

Figure 7.4 shows some recent failures in 8-quarter ahead forecasts of US log real GDP. There are huge forecast errors (measured by the vertical distance between the forecast and the outcome), especially at the start of the 'Great Recession', which are not corrected till near the trough. We call these 'hedgehog' graphs since the successively over-optimistic forecasts lead to spikes like the spines of a hedgehog. It can be seen that the largest and most persistent forecast errors occur after the trend growth of GDP slows, or falls. This is symptomatic of a fundamental problem with many model formulations, which are equilibrium-correction mechanisms (EqCMs) discussed in Sect. 4.2: they are designed to converge back to the previous equilibrium or trajectory. Consequently, even when the equilibrium or trajectory shifts, EqCMs will persistently revert to the old equilibrium—as the forecasts in Fig. 7.4 reveal—until either the model is revised or the old equilibrium returns.

Figure 7.4 illustrates the difficulties facing forecasting deriving from wide-sense non-stationarity. However, the problem created by a location

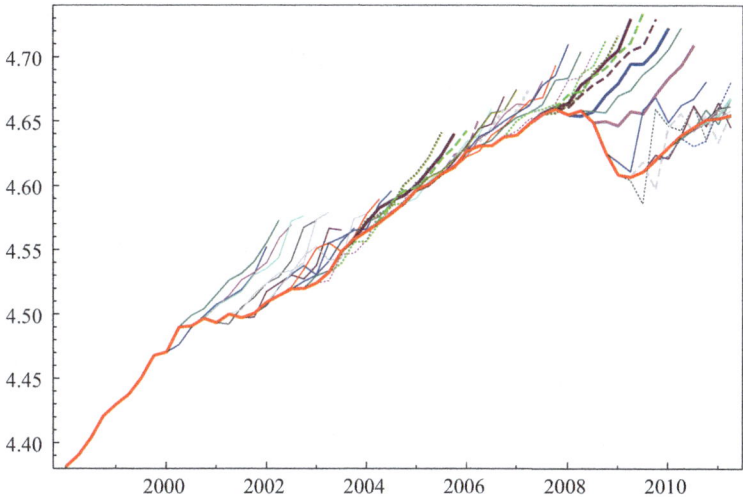

Fig. 7.4 US real GDP with many successive 8-quarter ahead forecasts

shift is not restricted to large forecast errors, but also affects the formation of expectations by economic actors: in theory models, today's expectation of tomorrow's outcome is often based on the 'most likely outcome', namely the conditional expectation of today's distribution of possible outcomes. In processes that are non-stationary from location shifts, previous expectations can be poor estimates of the next period's outcome. Figure 4.5 illustrated this problem, which has adverse implications for economic theories of expectations based on so-called 'rational' expectations. This issue also entails that many so-called structural econometric models constructed using mathematics based on inter-temporal maximization behavioural assumptions are bound to fail when the distributions involved shift as shown in Sect. 4.4.

7.4 Differencing Away Our Troubles

Differencing a break in a trend results in a location shift, as can be seen in Fig. 7.5, and in turn differencing a location shift produces an impulse, and a final differencing creates a 'blip'. All four types occur empirically.

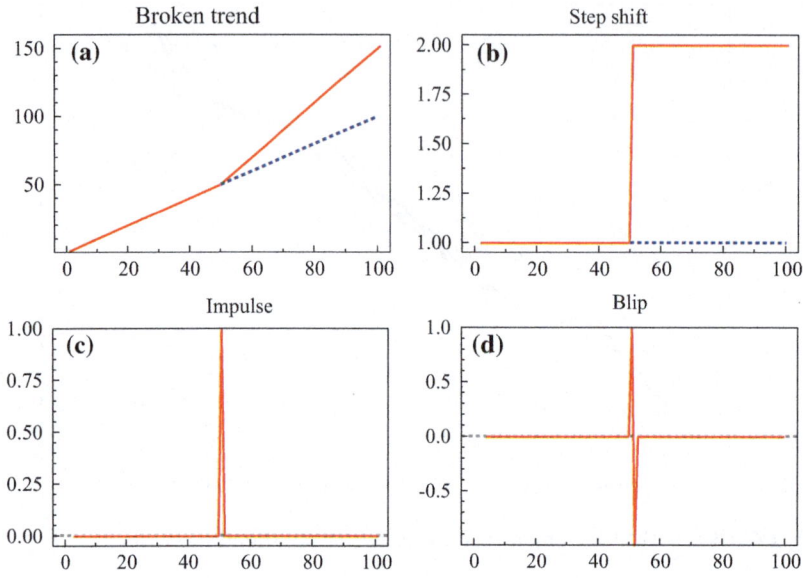

Fig. 7.5 Successively differencing a trend break in (a) creates a step shift in (b) an impulse in (c) and a 'blip' in (d)

Failing to allow for trend breaks or location shifts when forecasting entails extrapolating the wrong values and can lead to systematic forecast failure as shown by the dotted trajectories in Panels (a) and (b). However, failing to take account of an impulse or a blip just produces temporary errors, so forecasts revert back to an appropriate level rapidly. Consequently, many forecasts are reported for growth rates and often seem reasonably accurate: it is wise to cumulate such forecasts to see if the entailed levels are correctly predicted.

Figure 7.6 illustrates for artificial data: only a couple of the growth-rate outcomes lie above the 95% interval forecasts, but the levels forecasts are systematically downward biased from about observation 35. This is because the growth forecasts are on average slightly too low, which cumulates over time. The graphs show multi-step forecasts, but being simply a constant growth-rate forecast, the same interval forecasts apply at all steps ahead.

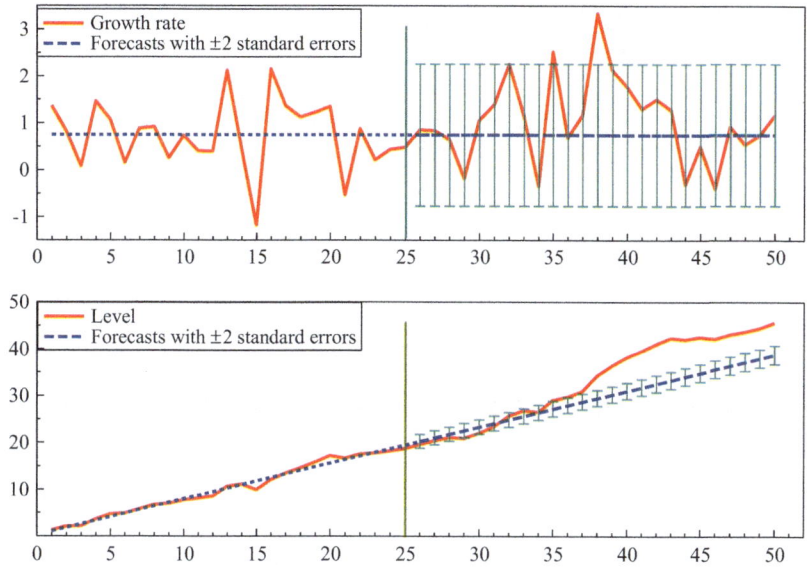

Fig. 7.6 Top panel: growth-rate forecasts; lower panel: implied forecasts of the levels

Constant growth-rate forecasts are of course excellent when growth rates stay at similar levels, but otherwise are too inflexible. An alternative is to forecast the next period's growth rate by the current value, which is highly flexible, but imposes a unit root even when the growth rate is I(0). Figure 7.3 contrasted deterministic trend forecasts with those from a stochastic trend, which had huge interval forecasts. Such intervals correctly reflect the ever increasing uncertainty arising from cumulating unrelated shocks when there is indeed a unit root in the DGP.

However, forecasting an I(0) process by a unit-root model also leads to calculating uncertainty estimates like those of a stochastic trend: the computer does not know the DGP, only the model it is fed. We must stress that interval forecasts are based on formulae that are calculated for the model used in forecasting. Most such formulae are derived under the assumption that the model is the DGP, so can be wildly wrong when that is not the case.

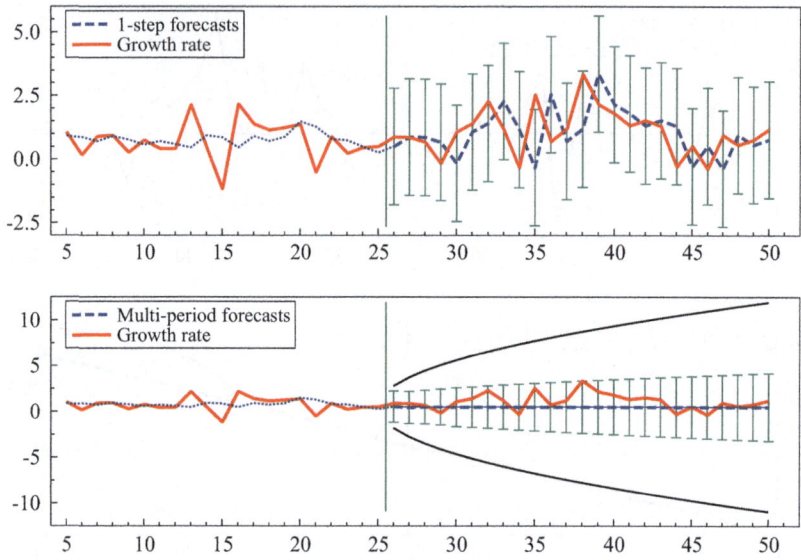

Fig. 7.7 Top panel: 1-step growth-rate forecasts from a 4-period moving average; lower panel: multi-period growth-rate forecasts with ±2 standard errors from a random walk (bands) and a 4-period moving average of past growth rates (bars)

The top panel in Fig. 7.7 shows that 1-step growth-rate forecasts from a 4-period moving average of past growth rates with an imposed unit coefficient are much more flexible than the assumed constant growth rate, and only one outcome lies outside the 95% error bars. The two sets of multi-period interval forecasts in the lower panel of Fig. 7.7 respectively compare the growth rate and the 4-period moving average of past growth rates as their sole explanatory variables, both with an imposed unit coefficient to implement a stochastic trend. The average of the four most recent growth rates at the forecast origin, as against just one, produces a marked reduction in the interval forecasts despite still cumulating shocks.

A potential cost is that it will take longer to adjust to a shift in the growth rate. Here the growth rate is an I(0) variable, and it is the imposition of the unit coefficient that creates the increasing interval forecasts, but even so, the averaging illustrates the effects of smoothing. This idea of smoothing applies to the robust forecasting methods noted in the next section. Care is required in reporting interval forecasts for several steps ahead as their

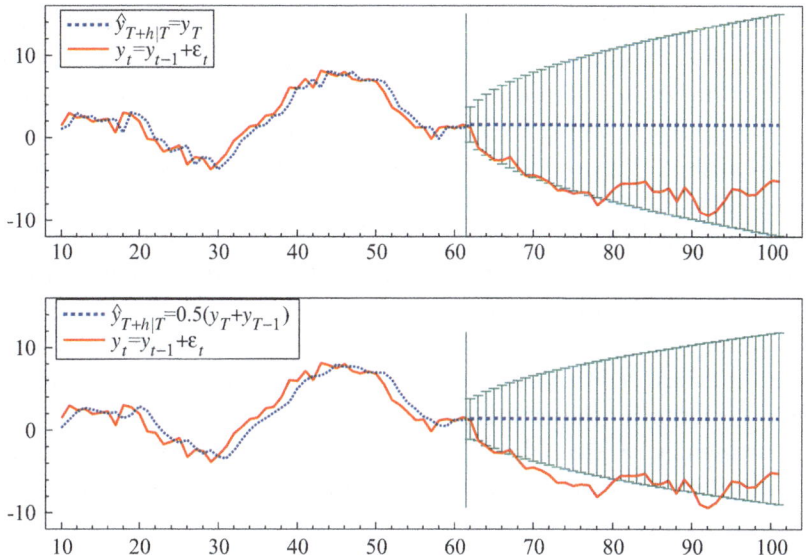

Fig. 7.8 Top panel: multi-period forecasts with ±2 standard errors from the DGP of a random walk; lower panel: multi-period forecasts from a 2-period moving average with ±2 calculated standard errors

calculation may reflect the properties of the model being used more than those of the DGP.

Conversely, trying to smooth a genuine random walk process by using a short moving average to forecast can lead to forecast failure as Fig. 7.8 illustrates. The DGP is the same in both panels, but the artificially smoothed forecasts in the lower panel have too small calculated interval forecasts.

7.5 Recommendations When Forecasting Facing Non-stationarity

Given the hazards of forecasting wide-sense non-stationary variables, what can be done? First, be wary of forecasting I(1) processes over long time horizons. Modellers and policy makers must establish when they are dealing with integrated series, and acknowledge that forecasts then entail increasing uncertainty. The danger is that uncertainty can be masked by using mis-specified models which can falsely reduce the reported uncertainty. An important case noted above is enforcing trend stationarity, as seen in Fig. 7.3, greatly reducing the measured uncertainty without reducing the actual, a recipe for poor policy and intermittent forecast failure. As Sir Alex Cairncross worried in the 1960s: 'A trend is a trend is a trend, but the question is, will it bend? Will it alter its course through some unforeseen force, and come to a premature end?' Alternatively, it is said that the trend is your friend till it doth bend.

Second, once forecast failure has been experienced, detection of location shifts (see Sect. 4.5) can be used to correct forecasts even with only a few observations, or alternatively it is possible to switch to more robust forecasting devices that adjust quickly to location shifts, removing much of any systematic forecast biases, but at the cost of wider interval forecasts (see e.g., Clements and Hendry 1999).

Nevertheless, we have also shown that one aspect of the explosion in interval forecasts from imposing an integrated model after a shift in an I(0) process (i.e., one that does not have a genuine unit root) is due to using just the forecast-origin value, and that can be reduced by using moving averages of recent values. In turbulent times, such devices are an example of a method with no necessary verisimilitude that can outperform the in-sample previously correct representation. Figure 7.9 illustrates the substantial improvement in the 1-step ahead forecasts of the log of UK GDP over 2008–2012 using a robust forecasting device compared to a 'conventional' method. The robust device has a much smaller bias and MSFE, but as it is knowingly mis-specified, clearly does not justify selecting it as an economic model—especially not for policy.

That last result implies that it is important to refrain from linking out-of-sample forecast performance of models to their 'quality' or verisimilitude. When unpredictable location shifts occur, there is no necessary link between forecast performance and how close the underlying model is to the truth. Both good and poor models can forecast well or badly depending on unanticipated shifts.

Third, the huge class of equilibrium-correction models includes almost all regression models for time series, autoregressive equations, vector autoregressive systems, cointegrated systems, dynamic-stochastic general

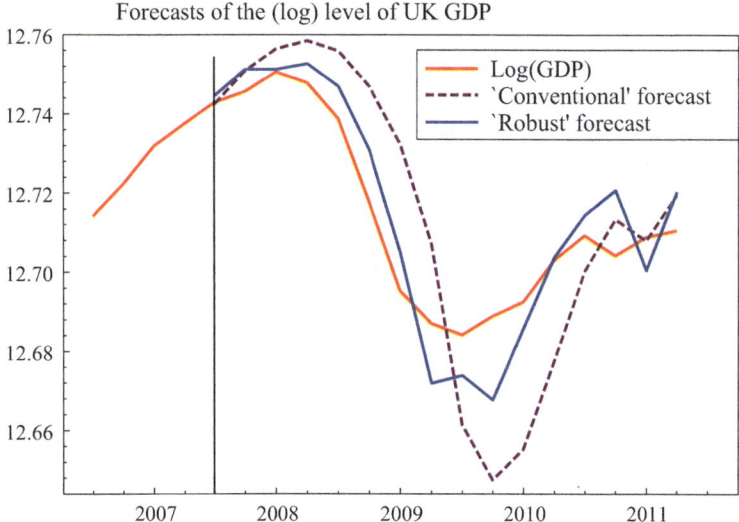

Fig. 7.9 1-step ahead forecasts of the log of UK GDP over 2008–2012 by 'conventional' and robust methods

equilibrium (DSGE) models, and many of the popular forms of model for autoregressive heteroskedasticity (see Engle 1982). Unfortunately, all of these formulations suffer from systematic forecast failure after shifts in their long-run, or equilibrium, means. Indeed, because they have in-built constant equilibria, their forecasts tend to go up (down) when outcomes go down (up), as they try to converge back to previous equilibria. Consequently, while cointegration captures equilibrium correction, care is required when using such models for genuine out-of-sample forecasts after any forecast failure has been experienced.

Fourth, Castle et al. (2018) have found that selecting a model for forecasting from a general specification that embeds the DGP does not usually entail notable costs compared to using the estimated DGP—an infeasible comparator with non-stationary observational data. Indeed when the exogenous variables need to be forecast, selection can even have smaller **MSFE**s than using a known DGP. That result matches an earlier finding in Castle et al. (2011) that a selected equation can have a smaller root mean square error (**RMSE**) for estimated parameters than those from estimating the DGP when the latter has several parameters that would not be significant on conventional criteria. Castle et al. (2018) suggest using looser than conventional nominal significance levels for in-sample selection, specifically 10% and 16% depending on the number of non-indicator candidate variables, and show that this choice is not greatly affected by whether or not location shifts occur either at, or just after, the forecast origin. The main difficulty is when an irrelevant variable that happens to be highly significant by chance has a location shift, which by definition will not affect the DGP but will shift the forecasts from the model, so forecast failure results. Here rapid updating after the failure will drive that errant coefficient towards zero in methods that minimize squared errors, so will be a transient problem.

Fifth, Castle et al. (2018) also conclude that some forecast combination can be a good strategy for reducing the riskiness of forecasts facing location shifts. Although no known method can protect against a shift after a forecast has been made, averaging forecasts from an econometric model, a robust device and a simple first-order autoregressive model frequently came near the minimum **MSFE** for a range of forecasting models on 1-step ahead forecasts in their simulation study. This result is consistent with many findings since the original analysis of pooling forecasts in Bates and Granger (1969), and probably reflects the benefits of 'portfolio diversification' known from finance theory. Clements (2017) provides a careful analysis of forecast combination. A caveat emphasized by Hendry and Doornik (2014) is that some pre-selection is useful before averaging to eliminate very bad forecasting devices. For example, the GUM is rarely a good device as it usually contains a number of what transpire to be irrelevant variables, and location shifts in these will lead to poor forecasts. Granger and Jeon (2004) proposed 'thick' modelling as a route to overcoming model uncertainty, where forecasts from all non-rejected specifications are combined. However, Castle (2017) showed that 'thick' modelling by itself neither avoids the problems of model mis-specification, nor handles forecast origin location shifts. Although 'thick' modelling is not formulated as a general-to-simple selection problem, it could be implemented by pooling across all congruent models selected by an approach like *Autometrics*.

References

Bates, J. M., and Granger, C. W. J. (1969). The combination of forecasts. *Operations Research Quarterly*, **20**, 451–468. Reprinted in T. C. Mills (ed.), *Economic Forecasting*. Edward Elgar, 1999.

Castle, J. L. (2017). Sir Clive W. J. Granger model selection. *European Journal of Pure and Applied Mathematics*, **10**, 133–156. https://ejpam.com/index.php/ejpam/article/view/2954.

Castle, J. L., Clements, M. P., and Hendry, D. F. (2019). *Forecasting: An Essential Introduction*. New Haven, CT: Yale University Press.

Castle, J. L., Doornik, J. A., and Hendry, D. F. (2011). Evaluating automatic model selection. *Journal of Time Series Econometrics*, **3(1)**. https://doi.org/10.2202/1941-1928.1097.

Castle, J. L., Doornik, J. A., and Hendry, D. F. (2018). Selecting a model for forecasting. Working paper, Economics Department, Oxford University.

Castle, J. L., Hendry, D. F., and Martinez, A. B. (2017). Evaluating forecasts, narratives and policy using a test of invariance *Econometrics*, **5(39)**. https://doi.org/10.3390/econometrics5030039.

Clements, M. P. (2017). Sir Clive W. J. Granger's Contributions to Forecasting. *European Journal of Pure and Applied Mathematics*, **10(1)**, 30–56. https://www.ejpam.com/index.php/ejpam/article/view/2949.

Clements, M. P., and Hendry, D. F. (1996). Intercept corrections and structural change. *Journal of Applied Econometrics*, **11**, 475–494.

Clements, M. P., and Hendry, D. F. (1998). *Forecasting Economic Time Series*. Cambridge: Cambridge University Press.

Clements, M. P., and Hendry, D. F. (1999). *Forecasting Non-stationary Economic Time Series*. Cambridge, MA: MIT Press.

Engle, R. F. (1982). Autoregressive conditional heteroscedasticity, with estimates of the variance of United Kingdom inflation. *Econometrica*, **50**, 987–1007.

Granger, C. W. J., and Jeon, Y. (2004). Thick modeling. *Economic Modelling*, **21**, 323–343.

Hendry, D. F., and Doornik, J. A. (2014). *Empirical Model Discovery and Theory Evaluation*. Cambridge, MA: MIT Press.

Hendry, D. F., and Mizon, G. E. (2011). Econometric modelling of time series with outlying observations. *Journal of Time Series Econometrics*, **3(1)**. https://doi.org/10.2202/1941-1928.1100.

Open Access This chapter is licensed under the terms of the Creative Commons Attribution 4.0 International License (http://creativecommons.org/licenses/by/4.0/), which permits use, sharing, adaptation, distribution and reproduction in any medium or format, as long as you give appropriate credit to the original author(s) and the source, provide a link to the Creative Commons license and indicate if changes were made.

The images or other third party material in this chapter are included in the chapter's Creative Commons license, unless indicated otherwise in a credit line to the material. If material is not included in the chapter's Creative Commons license and your intended use is not permitted by statutory regulation or exceeds the permitted use, you will need to obtain permission directly from the copyright holder.

8

Conclusions: The Ever-Changing Way Forward

Abstract In a world that is always changing, 'conclusion' seems an oxymoron. But we can summarize the story. First, that non-stationary data are pervasive in observational disciplines. Second, there are two main sources of non-stationarity deriving from evolutionary change leading to stochastic trends that cumulate past shocks and abrupt changes, especially location shifts, that lead to sudden shifts in distributions. Third, the resulting 'wide sense' non-stationarity not only radically alters empirical modelling approaches, it can have pernicious implications for inter-temporal theory, for forecasting and for policy. Fourth, methods for finding and neutralizing the impacts of distributional shifts from both sources are an essential part of the modeller's toolkit, and we proposed saturation estimation for modelling our changing world.

Keywords Theory formulations · Empirical modelling · Forecasting · Policy

Non-stationarity has important implications for inter-temporal theory, empirical modelling, forecasting and policy. Theory formulations need to account for humans inevitably facing disequilibria, so needing strategies for correcting errors after unanticipated location shifts. Empirical models must check for genuine long-run connections between variables using cointegration techniques, detect past location shifts, and incorporate feedbacks implementing how agents correct their previous mistakes. Forecasts must allow for the uncertainty arising from cumulating shocks, and could switch to robust devices after systematic failures. Tests have been formulated to check for models not being invariant to location shifts, and for policy changes even causing such shifts, potentially revealing that those models should not be used in future policy decisions.

Policy makers must recognise the challenges of implementing policy in non-stationary environments. Regulation of integrated processes, such as atmospheric CO_2 concentrations, is challenging due to their accumulation: for example, in climate policy, net-zero emissions are required to stabilise outcomes (see Allen 2015). Invariance of the parameters in policy models to a policy shift is a necessary condition for that policy to be effective and consistent with anticipated outcomes. The possibility of location shifts does not seem to have been included in risk models of financial institutions, even though such shifts will generate many apparently extremely unlikely successive bad draws relative to the prevailing distribution, as seen in Fig. 4.5.

Caution is advisable when acting on forecasts of integrated series or during turbulent times, potentially leading to high forecast uncertainty and systematic forecast failure, as seen in Figs. 7.8 and 7.9. Conversely, as noted in Sect. 3.2, the tools described above for handling shifts in time series enabled Statistics Norway to quickly revise their economic forecasts after Lehmann Brothers' bankruptcy. Demographic projections not only face evolving birth and death rates as in Fig. 2.3, but also sudden shifts, as happens with migration, so like economics, must tackle both forms of non-stationarity simultaneously.

Location shifts that affect the equilibrium means of cointegrating models initially cause systematic forecast failure, then often lead to incorrectly predicting rapid recovery following a fall, but later under-estimating a subsequent recovery. Using robust forecasting devices like those recorded in Fig. 7.9 after a shift or forecast failure can help alleviate both problems.

While this book has mainly considered time series data, similar principles apply to cross section and panel observational data. Panel data poses an additional problem of dependence. Time series data has the advantage of historical ordering, enabling sequential factorization to remove temporal dependence. Panel data requires a suitable exogenous ordering to apply sequential factorization which may not be obvious to the modeller. Methods to detect and model outliers and structural breaks may be particularly important in panel data, where individual heterogeneity accounts for much of the data variability. See Pretis et al. (2018) for an example of IIS applied to a fixed-effects panel model looking at the impacts of climate change on economic growth. IIS is equivalent to allowing for a 'fixed effect' for every observation in the panel, and accounting for these country-year individual effects proved invaluable in isolating the effects of climate variation on economic growth.

References

Allen, M. (2015). Short-lived promise? The science and policy of cumulative and short-lived climate pollutants. Oxford Martin policy paper, Oxford Martin School, Oxford, UK. https://www.oxfordmartin.ox.ac.uk/downloads/briefings/PolicyNote-SLCPs.pdf.

Pretis, F., Schwarz, M., Tang, K., Haustein, K., and Allen, M. R. (2018). Uncertain impacts on economic growth when stabilizing global temperatures at 1.5°C or 2°C warming. *Philosophical Transactions of the Royal Society*, **A376**, 20160460. https://doi.org/10.1098/rsta.2016.0460.

Open Access This chapter is licensed under the terms of the Creative Commons Attribution 4.0 International License (http://creativecommons.org/licenses/by/4.0/), which permits use, sharing, adaptation, distribution and reproduction in any medium or format, as long as you give appropriate credit to the original author(s) and the source, provide a link to the Creative Commons license and indicate if changes were made.

The images or other third party material in this chapter are included in the chapter's Creative Commons license, unless indicated otherwise in a credit line to the material. If material is not included in the chapter's Creative Commons license and your intended use is not permitted by statutory regulation or exceeds the permitted use, you will need to obtain permission directly from the copyright holder.

Author Index

A

Akaike, H., 27
Allen, M., 118, 119
Anderson, D.R., 28
Anderson, T.W., 27
Augustin, N.H., 28

B

Bachelier, L., 47, 48
Bates, J.M., 114
Bock, M.E., 29
Bontemps, C., 25
Box, G.E.P., 49
Brown, R.L., 21
Buckland, S.T., 28
Burnham, K.P., 28

C

Campos, J., 31
Carter, L.R., 47, 48
Castle, J.L., 2, 22, 57, 60, 75, 76, 78, 81, 82, 88, 90, 102, 104, 113, 114
Chow, G.C., 21
Claeskens, G., 27
Clements, M.P., 2, 22, 26, 101, 104, 112, 114
Corsi, P., 22

D

Davidson, J.E.H., 51, 91
Derksen, S., 28
Doornik, J.A., vi, 22, 25, 28, 29, 31, 57, 60, 75, 87, 89–91, 113, 114
Duffy, J.A., 60

Durbin, J., 21

E
Efron, B., 28
Engle, R.F., 17, 92, 113
Ericsson, N.R., 22, 23, 31, 80
Esper, J., 81
Evans, J.M., 21

F
Friedman, W.A., 17

G
Gilbert, C.L., 27
Govaerts, B., 25
Granger, C.W.J., 17, 52, 82, 114
Grinsted, A., 39

H
Hamilton, J.D., 23, 82
Hannan, E.J., 27
Hansen, B.E., 21
Hartl-Meier, C., 81
Hastie, T., 28
Haustein, K., 119
Hendry, D.F., vi, 2, 16, 17, 22, 25, 26, 28–31, 42, 51, 52, 54–57, 59–61, 70, 72, 75, 78, 82, 87–91, 95–97, 101–104, 112–114
Hjort, N.L., 27
Hoeting, J., 28
Hoover, K.D., 25, 28, 31

J
Jackson, L.P., 40
James, W., 28
Jansen, E.S., 21
Jenkins, G.M., 49
Jeon, Y., 114
Jevrejeva, S., 40
Johansen, S., 22, 29, 60, 70, 72, 89, 98
Johnstone, I., 28
Judge, G.G., 29
Juselius, K., 42

K
Kaufmann, R.K., 53
Kauppi, H., 53
Kennedy, P., 61
Keselman, H.J., 28
Kitov, O.I., 80
Krolzig, H.-M., 28, 30, 31

L
Leamer, E.E., 27, 87
Lee, R.D., 47, 48
Lehmann, E.L., 24
Lovell, M.C., 28

M
Madigan, D., 28
Mallows, C.L., 28
Mann, M.L., 53
Martinez, A.B., 60
Mills, T.C., 17
Mizon, G.E., 17, 53–56, 77, 103
Moore, J.C., 40
Morgan, M.S., 16

Muellbauer, J.N.J., 56

N
Newbold, P., 17
Nielsen, B., v, 22, 29, 60, 72
Nyblom, J., 21
Nymoen, R., 57

P
Perez, S.J., 25, 28, 31
Perron, P., 17, 21
Phillips, A.W.H., 95
Phillips, P.C.B., 17, 27, 28
Ploberger, W., 27
Pollock, R.E., 22
Prakken, J.C., 22
Pretis, F., 22, 53, 60, 81, 88, 119
Priestley, M.B., 82

Q
Qin, D., 16
Quinn, B.G., 27

R
Raftery, A., 28
Reade, J.J., 60
Richard, J.-F., 25
Riva, R.E.M., 40

S
Santos, C., 60, 61, 70, 75
Schneider, L., 22, 81
Schwarz, G., 27
Scott, S.L., 28
Smerdon, J.E., 22, 81
Smith, B.B., 17
Soros, G., 55
Spanos, A., 10
Srba, F., 51
Stein, C., 28
Stock, J.H., 53
Sucarrat, G., 60

T
Tabor, M.N., 80
Taleb, N.N., 54
Teräsvirta, T., 21, 82
Tibshirani, R., 28

V
Varian, H.R., 28
Volinsky, C., 28

W
White, H., 61

Y
Yeo, J.S., 51
Yule, G.U., 16, 50

Subject Index

A

Aggregation, 7
ARCH, 92, 93
Autocorrelation, 25, 70, 88
Automatic Model Selection, v, 31, 98
Autometrics, 31, 60, 69, 82, 91, 114
Autoregression, 27

B

Bayesian, 27, 29
Bias, 27, 30, 112
  —correction, 30

C

Causality, 61
Chow
  —test, 74
Cointegrating
  —relation, 51

Cointegration, 17, 45, 50, 52, 54, 58, 60, 113, 117, 118
  recursive estimation, 74
Collinearity, 61
Congruence, 24
consumption, 91
Correlation, 2, 8, 14, 16, 28, 45, 48, 61, 102
  —coefficient, 16
Correlogram, 48
Critical values, 90

D

Data, 88
  —mining, 27, 85
DGP, 69, 109, 113
DHSY (Davidson, Hendry, Srba and Yeo, 1978), 91
Difference, 17, 23, 48, 53, 54, 58, 107
  seasonal, 7

Dummy variable, 75

E
Econometric models, 57, 59, 107
Efficiency, 72
Empirical model, vi, 3, 5, 6, 21–23, 25, 26, 37, 44, 50, 57, 60, 88, 91, 98, 117, 118
Encompassing, 24, 89
 parsimonious—, 25
Equilibrium, 2, 50, 58, 106, 113, 118
 —correction, 51, 53, 89, 112
Exogenous variable, 113

F
Feedback, 45, 117, 118
Food expenditure, 12
Forecast
 —error, 18, 22, 44, 101, 106
 —origin, 102, 110, 112, 114
F-test, 75
Functional form, 24

G
Gauge, 29, 72
General model, v, 25
General-to-specific, 114
General-to-specific (Gets)
 History of, 3, 17
Goodness of fit, 27
Growth rate, 40, 53, 78, 108, 110
GUM, 89–90, 114

H
Histogram, 61

Hypothesis
 null—, 28
 test, 21, 24, 28, 75, 87

I
Inference, 3, 21, 24, 42, 54, 61, 67, 68, 87
Information
 —criteria, 27
Innovation, 11, 55
Instrument, 26, 75
Instrumental variables, 75
Integrated
 —data, 53
 —process, 47, 48
 —series, 111, 118
Integratedness, 47, 48
Invariance, 26, 60, 61, 75, 118

L
Lasso, 28
Law of Iterated Expectations, 57
Limiting distribution, 72
Location shift, 12, 18, 21, 22, 44, 45, 52, 53, 55, 57, 58, 60, 62, 67, 68, 70, 75, 76, 78, 82, 88, 90, 102, 103, 106, 107, 112, 114, 117, 118
Long run, 7, 45, 50, 60, 79, 102, 113, 117, 118

M
Measurement, 2, 26, 102
 —errors, 45, 60
Mis-specification, 69, 88, 114

Subject Index

Model, 101–105
—averaging, 28
—formulation, 23, 25, 106
—selection, v, 3, 22, 23, 28, 69, 87, 89
—specification, 73
Moments, 10
Monte Carlo, vi, 22
More Variables than Observations, 69

N

Nesting, 14
Non-constancy, 22
Non-linear, 23, 82, 85, 86, 88, 89
—ity, 69, 82
Non-normality, 75
Non-stationarity, 3, 5, 10–12, 14, 16, 31, 39, 42, 43, 45, 48, 53, 60, 106, 111, 117, 118
Nonsense
—correlation, 16
—regression, 17, 44, 50
Normal distribution, 25, 54, 72, 90
Normality, 90

O

Observational equivalence, 60
Omitted variables, 30
Orthogonal, 25, 30, 76, 90
Outlier, 12, 22, 24, 29, 54, 59, 67–70, 72, 73, 75, 85, 86, 88, 89, 103
OxMetrics, vi

P

Parameter constancy, 74, 87, 90
Parsimony, 27

PcGets, 31
PcGive, vi
Policy, 3, 12, 16, 18, 21, 24, 26, 37, 42, 44, 45, 56, 57, 61, 81, 111, 117, 118
Population, 2, 16, 47, 48, 72
Potency, 75, 76
Progress, 40

R

Random number, 7
Random walk, 47, 48, 111
Rational expectations, 107
Reduction, 90, 110
Regression
  Static—, 70
Residual(s), 17, 24, 68, 88, 91
—autocorrelation, 22, 88, 92, 93
Robust, 73, 112, 114, 117, 118
—forecasting, 110, 112, 119
—statistics, 72

S

Sample
—period, 22
—size, 26, 27, 72
Seasonal, 7
Serial correlation, 17
Shifts, vi, 3, 5, 6, 9, 11, 17, 19, 21–24, 26, 29, 40, 42, 44, 45, 51, 53, 55–58, 61, 67, 68, 75, 77, 81, 85, 86, 88, 89, 106, 112, 117, 118
Sign, 2, 54, 59, 72, 76
Significance level, 28, 70, 72, 75, 87, 90
Simulation, vi, 3, 16, 81, 114

Standard deviation, 55
Stationarity, 10, 42, 44, 48, 50, 53, 56, 102, 112
Statistical
—theory, 60
Step-wise regression, 28
Structural
—break, 3, 17, 18
—change, 67–69, 82

T
Taxonomy, 22
Test, 69, 75, 87, 98
   portmanteau statistic, 69
   significance, 26, 30, 70, 72, 74, 98

Theory, 3, 17, 24, 26, 29, 44, 86, 88, 89, 98, 107, 114, 117, 118
—information, 85, 86
Thick modelling, 114
Trend, vi, 7, 20, 22, 40, 42, 45, 48, 50, 56, 58, 60, 62, 67, 68, 72, 102, 105–107, 109, 112

U
Unbiased, 56, 70
Unconditional
—variance, 102

V
Volatility, 12

The manufacturer's authorised representative in the EU is Springer Nature Customer Service Centre GmbH, Europaplatz 3, 69115 Heidelberg, Germany. If you have any concerns regarding our products, please contact ProductSafety@springernature.com

Printed and bound by CPI Group (UK) Ltd, Croydon, CR0 4YY

25/03/2026

02077962-0002

Enabling Sustainable Energy Transitions

"If we are to close the gap between words and deeds on decarbonisation, emission reductions need to go much faster and further than at present. *Enabling Sustainable Energy Transitions* steps directly into this gap, arguing that inadequate action relative to the scale of the problem constitutes a crisis of accountability. This crisis is sustained, the authors propose, by four 'practices of legitimation' through which states, firms and other key actors are effectively insulated from the political and economic consequences of inaction. In tune with the recent pivot in energy research from innovation to incumbency, and the post-Paris challenge of rapidly dismantling fossil energy regimes, this compact book argues that ideas about accountability and legitimation—drawn from work on environmental governance—can open up new analytical perspectives on what is holding back effective energy system transformation. With bite-size chapters and illustrative cases that draw on the work of five expert witnesses, this is a novel intervention into debates over the politics of energy transition."
—Gavin Bridge, Professor, *Department of Geography, Durham University*

"In this comprehensive and much-needed book, Dr. Siddharth Sareen with colleagues provides a compelling analysis of the sustainable energy transition and the role of legitimation practices and accountability therein. The book theorizes and advances the research frontier on legitimation practices and accountability with a carefully crafted analysis bridging scholarly fields of environmental governance, political economy, energy research and democratic theory. *Enabling Sustainable Energy Transition* presents a novel empirical analysis of the politics of energy transition across the world through rich case studies of countries such as Portugal, Germany, Norway, USA as well as cities such as Berlin. This book is a must-read for all students and scholars interested in shaping more legitimate, democratic and accountable energy transition from the local to global context."
—Karin Bäckstrand, Professor, *Department of Political Science, Stockholm University*

Siddharth Sareen
Editor

Enabling Sustainable Energy Transitions

Practices of legitimation and accountable governance

Editor
Siddharth Sareen
Department of Geography
Centre for Climate and Energy Transformation
University of Bergen, Bergen, Norway

ISBN 978-3-030-26890-9   ISBN 978-3-030-26891-6 (eBook)
https://doi.org/10.1007/978-3-030-26891-6

© The Editor(s) (if applicable) and The Author(s) 2020 This book is an open access publication, corrected Publication 2020
Open Access This book is licensed under the terms of the Creative Commons Attribution 4.0 International License (http://creativecommons.org/licenses/by/4.0/), which permits use, sharing, adaptation, distribution and reproduction in any medium or format, as long as you give appropriate credit to the original author(s) and the source, provide a link to the Creative Commons licence and indicate if changes were made.
The images or other third party material in this book are included in the book's Creative Commons licence, unless indicated otherwise in a credit line to the material. If material is not included in the book's Creative Commons licence and your intended use is not permitted by statutory regulation or exceeds the permitted use, you will need to obtain permission directly from the copyright holder.
The use of general descriptive names, registered names, trademarks, service marks, etc. in this publication does not imply, even in the absence of a specific statement, that such names are exempt from the relevant protective laws and regulations and therefore free for general use.
The publisher, the authors and the editors are safe to assume that the advice and information in this book are believed to be true and accurate at the date of publication. Neither the publisher nor the authors or the editors give a warranty, express or implied, with respect to the material contained herein or for any errors or omissions that may have been made. The publisher remains neutral with regard to jurisdictional claims in published maps and institutional affiliations.

This Palgrave Pivot imprint is published by the registered company Springer Nature Switzerland AG.
The registered company address is: Gewerbestrasse 11, 6330 Cham, Switzerland

The original version of this book was revised. Copyright holder has been updated. Author has acknowledged their funder in the book. The correction to this book can be found at
https://doi.org/10.1007/978-3-030-26891-6_11

Prologue

When I was 11, I lived in the river plains of northern India, a region poorer than sub-Saharan Africa (Alkire and Santos 2014). It was before the turn of the millennium, and while the mercury routinely went past 45 °C, my household struggled to cope with frequent power cuts totalling a dozen hours a day. We had the relative luxury of a diesel generator and an inverter, cooked using gas cylinders and a parabolic solar cooker, used electric water heaters, and the nightwatchman burnt charcoal to stay warm on winter nights and cooked his morning meals on a woodstove.

When I was 21, I lived on an elite university campus where the government ensured round-the-clock power supply so the lights never went out. Months before Copenhagen hosted the United Nations Framework Convention on Climate Change (UNFCCC) Conference of Parties (CoP) 15, I was an invited student delegate at a global sustainable development summit. Midway through, during a plenary session with the then-head of the Intergovernmental Panel on Climate Change (IPCC) and a leading British Broadcasting Corporation news anchor, I posed a question in the limelight. In two days of discussions on how to address the climate change challenge, why had nobody discussed the role of the United States of America (Christoff 2010), since our prospects looked bleak without its geopolitical backing and political economic will?

Now 31 years old, I live in Norway, one of the richest countries in the world with a fortune built on oil, with hydropower its predominant domestic energy source. My home runs almost entirely on electricity, from heating to cooking to hot water. Our transport systems are increasingly electric, except air travel which continues to be carbon emissions intensive and popular. During the CoP 24 in Katowice, the centre of coal in Europe, someone half my age spoke truth to power. Greta Thunberg said that our political representatives have failed us and that we must act now to address the climate crisis for today's youth and the vulnerable to have livable futures.

Those three decadal conjunctures of material configuration, institutional context and relative privilege reveal a great deal about the spatiotemporally contingent nature of how we experience the deeply entangled climate and energy crises. My concern with these contemporary crises has continued and increased in my transition from childhood to mid-career researcher; and so has the associated urgency. We live in a time of many crises—local, national and global; short-, medium- and long-term; social, environmental and economic—and the heart of each one is political. This book concerns the greatest crisis of our times, which spans generations. It is about addressing the drivers and impacts of climate change, which means rapidly decarbonising our energy systems, and deeply changing whom they benefit (Bickerstaff et al. 2013). This is a mammoth task with competing stakes, too vital to be left to privileged sets of decision-makers who have already failed to safeguard and secure public interest for decades, and much too big for a modest book. Rather, its envisaged contribution is to show how to make this crisis visible for what it truly is—a crisis of accountability—opening up space to discuss and establish anew (Dowdle 2017) the terms for more accountable governance to enable sustainable energy transitions. For the purpose of this book, the term 'sustainable energy transitions' signifies changes to our energy systems that enhance both decarbonisation and social equity.

I undertake this ambitious task in good company. That of countless excellent scientists past and present who have furnished a rigorous basis in knowledge and whose work I draw on—we already know much of what we need to know for sustainable energy transitions. Your company as a reader, as someone interested in understanding and addressing this crisis—this book is accessible to laypersons and experts, and aspires to be an engaging, inspiring read. The company of environmental governance researchers who have spent a great deal of their eminent careers examining various aspects of energy transitions and kindred subjects, which span many sectors and domains. And finally of the many people these colleagues and I have interacted with in the field—for our research is empirically informed—who help keep our work grounded and relevant. This combination is key in making an argument that at its crux concerns practices of legitimation.

What is legitimation, why does it feature practices, and what does it have to do with a crisis of accountability? Notably, an accountability crisis is distinct from the Habermasian notion of a legitimation crisis, which refers to a confidence deficit in leadership, institutions or administrative functions among the subjects of the state in an era of late capitalism. To wit:

> The state can avoid legitimation problems to the extent that it can manage to make the administrative system independent of the formation of legitimating will. To that end, it can, say, separate expressive symbols (which create a universal willingness to follow) from the instrumental functions of administration.... The scope for manipulation, however, is narrowly delimited, for the cultural system remains peculiarly resistant to administrative control. There is no administrative creation of meaning, there is at best an ideological erosion of cultural values. The acquisition of legitimation is self-destructive as soon as the mode of acquisition is exposed. Thus, there is a systematic limit for attempts at making up for legitimation deficits by means of well aimed manipulation. This limit is the structural dissimilarity between areas of administrative action and cultural tradition. (Habermas 1973: 657)

This book adopts a similar premise but a different point of entry. Taking forward an approach developed by Kraft and Wolf (2018), legitimation is a relationally produced artefact that can be empirically scrutinised to characterise accountability. Where an accountability crisis occurs, it need not manifest as breakdown (a legitimation crisis) but can be upheld through practices of legitimation even as things run aground. In this sense, we have been in an accountability crisis for centuries, and in the case of many actors knowingly so for decades, extracting and consuming resources with deeply inequitable distributions and emitting carbon (and other greenhouse gases—this book uses 'decarbonisation' as shorthand) that far exceed sustainable limits. Legitimation refers to the process through which an act (by its doer) is recognised as valid (by its authoriser and its public) in relation to societal norms. This process involves a set of distinct practices. Practices of legitimation are social relations premised on accountability and constitutive of it. Sectoral changes manifest in and through them. Thus, practices of legitimation embody the very means by which an act becomes legitimate and normalised (Luckmann 1987). They are necessarily also the relational sites where such normalisation can be laid bare and challenged. Such informed exposure represents Habermas' systematic limit, beyond which manipulation cannot make up for legitimation deficit. In the contemporary context of increasing right-wing authoritarian tendencies and climate scepticism, informed exposure is not straight-forward but tautly contested and requires rigorous evidence.

Questioning a practice of legitimation is a way of bringing an act to account, by holding accountable its doer, its authoriser, or both, to the broader publics affected by their actions. There is no singular public or normative standard (West and Davis 2011), as scholarly theorisations of institutional orders and orders of worth remind us (Boltanski and Thévenot 2006; Patriotta et al. 2011). Yet environmental governance and political ecology research have made inroads into questions of power and representation, and a normative goal such as sustainability has secured broad, albeit not uncontested, social legitimacy in terms of the desirability of decarbonisation that also enhances social equity. Nation states—and, in a polycentric world, trans-local networks of multi-scalar actors—have made strong verbal, political, policy and in some cases even legal commitments to achieving substantive transitions to sustainability. Nonetheless, global carbon emissions continue to increase, and human-made disasters are becoming normed into the anthropocene, with exacerbated threats of wildfires and floods causing widespread loss of human life, infrastructure and biodiversity. With a crisis of accountability of this magnitude—where societal foundations such as the energy system must open up to questioning—being increasingly recognised with public demands to address it, practices of legitimation occur wherever action is observable, whether to resolve the crisis or to profit by prolonging it. These practices are our windows to institutional change in the making (Dansou and Langley 2012), and our points of entry to not only examine and understand but also to inform and intervene.

To me, this is both a professional and personal quest: 45 °C summer days with no electricity for half the day is not just a memory from my childhood; it embodies the reality of the current lives of mind-bogglingly many people. We continue to shy away from some of the most pressing and difficult questions when it comes to acting on climate change: how is it that the powerful continue to act in unacceptable, unabashedly consumerist ways without being held to account, while highly vulnerable groups bear the brunt of the impact with precious little say?

We cannot change everything at once; what is in place keeps the world as we know it in play and nourishes very powerful parts of it. But we must pick it apart (through informed analysis) to improve upon it (for constructive change); for if we let things continue as they are, we are condemning billions of people and many other organisms besides to the suffering entailed by runaway climate change (Wallace-Wells 2019).

The energy system is not only a huge contributor to climate change, it is also humankind's greatest accomplishment and most devastating horror all rolled into one. Nothing has enabled greater human achievement and progress; nothing has led to more pronounced inequity and irreversible destruction. Consider the sophisticated command over resources to supply the energy needs of billions on the one hand, and the ruination of entire ways of life in extracting resources and setting up supply chains to do so on the other hand. Or a transatlantic jetplane for a millionaire versus a habitation flooded by damming respectively; or a neon-lit city versus a fracking landscape—the list is endless.

This book, then, seeks to provide a pick-axe of sorts. It offers an analytical approach to cut into practices of legitimation and examine how things are propped up, what must yield, and who is pushing for the sorts of changes that will enable sustainable energy transitions. A scientific way to evidence common-sense (Jovchelovitch 2008), get an empirical handle on the opportunities to decarbonise and render equitable our changing energy systems, and provide a basis for the public to put its feet down against the acts and actors who would rather watch the world burn, literally, than lose the untenable privileges of a small but powerful group of elites.

Part I of the book frames what research has already conclusively shown about feasible and necessary energy transitions, and puts forward an analytical typology of practices of legitimation to make headway towards sustainability in any given instance of energy transition. Part II explains the invitation to five colleagues to reflect on their varied cases related to energy transitions in terms of accountability and legitimation, and comprises their responses to this invitation in the form of five case chapters. Part III synthesises our reflections on how to take forward energy transitions analysis along such lines. We thus aim to pave a pathway for enmeshed empirical and theoretical studies of practices of legitimation towards accountable governance that can enable sustainable energy transitions.

Bergen, Norway   Siddharth Sareen

References

Alkire, S., & Santos, M. E. (2014). Measuring acute poverty in the developing world: Robustness and scope of the multidimensional poverty index. *World Development, 59*, 251–274.

Bickerstaff, K., Walker, G., & Bulkeley, H. (Eds.). (2013). *Energy justice in a changing climate: Social equity and low-carbon energy*. Zed Books Ltd.

Boltanski, L., & Thévenot, L. (2006). *On justification: Economies of worth*. Princeton, NJ: Princeton University Press.

Christoff, P. (2010). Cold climate in Copenhagen: China and the United States at COP15. *Environmental Politics, 19*(4), 637–656.

Dansou, K., & Langley, A. (2012). Institutional work and the notion of test. *Management, 15*(5), 503–527.

Dowdle, M. W. (2017). Public accountability: Conceptual, historical and epistemic mappings. In P. Drahos (Ed.), *Regulatory theory: Foundations and applications* (pp. 197–215). Canberra: Australian University Press.

Habermas, J. (1973). What does a crisis mean today? Legitimation problems in late capitalism. *Social Research, 40*, 643–667.

Jovchelovitch, S. (2008). The rehabilitation of common sense: Social representations, science and cognitive polyphasia. *Journal for the Theory of Social Behaviour, 38*(4), 431–448.

Kraft, B., & Wolf, S. (2018). Through the lens of accountability: Analyzing legitimacy in environmental governance. *Organization & Environment, 31*(1), 70–92.

Luckmann, T. (1987). Comments on legitimation. *Current Sociology, 35*(2), 109–117.

Patriotta, G., Gond, J. P., & Schultz, F. (2011). Maintaining legitimacy: Controversies, orders of worth, and public justifications. *Journal of Management Studies, 48*(8), 1804–1836.

Wallace-Wells, D. (2019). *The uninhabitable earth: Life after Warming*. Tim Duggan Books.

West, K., & Davis, P. (2011). What is the public value of government action? Towards a (new) pragmatic approach to values questions in public endeavours. *Public Administration, 89*(2), 226–241.

Acknowledgments

Siddharth Sareen: "The author gratefully acknowledges funding from a University of Bergen postdoctoral research fellowship (financed by Bergen Research Foundation and University of Bergen-Equinor Akademia Agreement), the Open Access publication fund at the University of Bergen, the Strategic Programme for International Research Collaboration and the Faculty of Social Sciences at the University of Bergen."

Timothy Moss: "Gerda Henkel Foundation"

Christian Lund: "The research for this paper has benefitted from generous funding from the Danish Research Council and the European Research Council (ERC). ERC Grant: State Formation Through the Local Production of Property and Citizenship (Ares (2015)2785650—ERC-2014-AdG—662770-Local State)."

Contents

Part I Introduction   1

1 Reframing Energy Transitions as Resolving
   Accountability Crises   3
   Siddharth Sareen

2 A Typology of Practices of Legitimation to Categorise
   Accountability Relations   15
   Siddharth Sareen

Part II Cases   33

3 Five Easy Pieces: Legitimation at Work in Cases Related
   to Energy Transitions   35
   Siddharth Sareen

4 Historicising Accountability: Berlin's Energy Transitions   41
   Timothy Moss

5 A Few Reflections on Accountability   53
   Christian Lund

6 Do Climate Targets Matter? The Accountability of
   Target-setting in Urban Climate and Energy Policy   63
   Håvard Haarstad

7 Governance and Legitimation in the Transition to Nordic
   Electric Mobility   73
   Benjamin Sovacool

8 Accountability and the Regulation of Legitimacy:
   Biodiversity Conservation and Energy Extraction in the
   American West   89
   Steven Wolf

Part III   Conclusion   103

9 Practices of Legitimation and Accountability Crises in a
   Range of Energy Transitions   105
   Siddharth Sareen

10 Conclusion: Legitimation and Accountability in Energy
   Transitions Research   117
   Siddharth Sareen, Timothy Moss, Christian Lund, Håvard
   Haarstad, Benjamin Sovacool, and Steven Wolf

Correction to: Enabling Sustainable Energy Transitions   C1

Appendix A   137

Appendix B   141

Index   167

NOTES ON CONTRIBUTORS

Håvard Haarstad is Professor of Human Geography at the University of Bergen. He is interested in sustainability, climate change and energy in relation to cities. He focuses on how mobile ideas and policies shape the way cities become sustainable, and on social theory about climate and energy transformation.

Christian Lund is Professor of Development, Resource Management and Governance at the University of Copenhagen. He has a keen interest in discussions about the state and politico-legal institutions, and the ways in which social action produces public authority. His research focuses on property, local politics and state formation.

Timothy Moss is a senior researcher at the Integrative Research Institute on Transformations of Human-Environment Systems, Humboldt University of Berlin. With a history and political science background, his research revolves around the processes of institutional change relating to public goods and their spatiality in general, and urban infrastructure systems in particular.

Siddharth Sareen is a postdoctoral researcher at the Centre for Climate and Energy Transformation and the Department of Geography at the University of Bergen. He has an interdisciplinary background in the environmental social sciences, and works on the governance of energy transitions and questions of resource access and authority.

Benjamin Sovacool is Professor of Energy Policy at the University of Sussex. He works on energy policy, energy security, and climate change mitigation and adaptation. His research focuses on renewable energy and energy efficiency, large-scale energy infrastructure politics, improving public policy for energy access, and building adaptive capacity.

Steven Wolf is Associate Professor of Environmental Social Science at Cornell University. His research on environmental governance focuses on efforts to secure public goods from private landscapes. His training and approach engage sociology and economics, with an interest in socioecological dynamics in both industrialised and rapidly industrialising societies.

LIST OF FIGURES

Fig. 4.1	Map showing size of Berlin prior to 1920 (marked core area) and territory of municipalised power utilities by 1925 (vertically striped area). (Source: Bruno Thierbach, 1925, Die gegenwärtige Versorgung der Stadt Berlin und der Provinz Brandenburg mit elektrischer Arbeit. *Elektrotechnische Zeitschrift*, 46(39), 1465)	45
Fig. 4.2	Protest camp against the planned power plant in Spandau Forest, 1976. (Source: Landesarchiv Berlin, F Rep 290, No. 0194-662)	46
Fig. 4.3	Campaign poster of the Berlin Energy Roundtable for the 2013 referendum, reading 'Our municipal utility, our power grid, our Berlin'. (Source: http://www.berliner-energietisch.net/materialien)	47
Fig. 7.1	Diffusion of electric vehicles in the five Nordic countries, 2009 to 2017. (Source: Kester et al. 2018)	79
Fig. 8.1	Co-evolution of nature and society mediated by accountability mechanisms and legitimacy tests	93
Fig. B1.1	Setting up the exhibition at Bergen Public Library	142
Fig. B1.2	The 'Idea box for energy transitions' exhibition. (Photo credit: Hordaland Kunstsenter)	143
Fig. B1.3	The idea box as part of the exhibition at Bergen Public Library. (Photo credit: Hordaland Kunstsenter)	144
Fig. B1.4	Workshop participants browse the idea box for energy transitions exhibition	145

Fig. B1.5	Bridging the exhibitions at Bergen Public Library and Hordaland Kunstsenter	146
Fig. B1.6	'Rhythmic energy mixes: Days and years with Dr. Siddharth Sareen' by Margrethe Brekke	147
Fig. B1.7	Margrethe Brekke's 'Potential exceeds the demand' exhibition at Hordaland Kunstsenter	148
Fig. B1.8	Margrethe Brekke reflects on her art exhibition while giving a guided tour	149
Fig. B1.9	The forces behind the artistic events	150
Fig. B1.10	'Imaginaries of energy transition: Public, artistic and academic' with Margrethe Brekke and Benjamin Sovacool	151
Fig. B1.11	Exchanges between the arts, academia and the public	152
Fig. B1.12	Theatrical performances by International School of Bergen students directed by Annie Sareen	153
Fig. B1.13	The accountability analysis workshop at Bergen Public Library	154
Fig. B1.14	Timothy Moss gives a keynote talk at the workshop on accountability analysis	155
Fig. B1.15	Christian Lund and Håvard Haarstad during a workshop keynote session	156
Fig. B1.16	Discussions among the workshop participants continued over dinner	157
Fig. B1.17	Closing workshop dinner with keynote speakers	158
Fig. B1.18	Starting festivities on the national day of Norway	159
Fig. B1.19	A traditional torchlight procession through Bergen	160
Fig. B1.20	The annual fireworks on 17 May in Bergen	161

LIST OF TABLES

Table 7.1	An overview of the electricity and mobility regimes in the Nordic region	76
Table 7.2	Positive and negative synergies with electric mobility and sustainability	84
Table 7.3	Policy mechanisms for more sustainable and just Nordic electric mobility	85
Table 10.1	Practices of legitimation with indicative dimensions for five wide-ranging cases	119

PART I

Introduction

CHAPTER 1

Reframing Energy Transitions as Resolving Accountability Crises

Siddharth Sareen

Abstract Using the concrete case of solar energy uptake in Portugal, Chap. 1 illustrates how energy transitions can be regarded as attempts to resolve crises of accountability. While Portugal is among the countries that lead globally on energy transitions, close attention to its apparently promising solar energy prospects reveals a paradox: progress has been slow and modest. Yet, there seems to be a major change on the horizon, and a potentially powerful explanation for these dynamics is premised on relations of accountability amongst stakeholders in Portugal's energy sector. Having argued that such a reframing of energy transitions has explanatory power, the chapter deconstructs accountability as an underlying relationship which is produced by various practices that manifest as legitimation. It argues for an analytical typology of legitimation.

Keywords Accountability crisis • Legitimation • Energy transitions • Solar • Portugal

---

S. Sareen (✉)
Department of Geography, Centre for Climate and Energy Transformation, University of Bergen, Bergen, Norway
e-mail: Siddharth.Sareen@uib.no

© The Author(s) 2020
S. Sareen (ed.), *Enabling Sustainable Energy Transitions*,
https://doi.org/10.1007/978-3-030-26891-6_1

1.1 Sustainable Energy Transition as a Response to an Accountability Crisis

In terms of national performance on energy transitions, few countries are more remarkable than Portugal. Already among Europe's leaders on renewable energy, its carbon mitigation from 2017 to 2018 was 9 per cent, the highest rate on the continent and over thrice the European average.[1] This small and relatively isolated country bordering Spain in the western part of the Iberian Peninsula with ten million residents has, thus, exceeded expectations.

Solar energy uptake in Portugal poses a surprising paradox: despite Portugal's leadership on renewable energy in the progressive energy policy context of Europe, with strong wind and hydro power assets and some of the continent's best solar irradiation conditions for cost-competitive low-carbon generation (Krajačić et al. 2011), till 2019, it has only installed modest solar energy capacity. Combined with no fossil fuel assets to speak of as an importer of coal, oil and natural gas, it would seem a no-brainer for Portugal to capitalise on remarkable global decreases in the price of solar energy infrastructure and promote a rapid solar uptake to move towards a largely decarbonised energy sector (Fortes et al. 2019).

Empirical research and mainstream media reports have unearthed numerous barriers for solar energy uptake, such as the lack of policy visibility, a restrictive regulatory framework, limited licences, grid constraints and limited credit access. These explain the relatively modest increases in installed solar capacity and surface some narratives of frustration. Emerging studies and reports, most notably Portugal's National Energy and Climate Plan, convey a sense that eventually things will work themselves out and solar projects will increasingly go ahead (Coelho et al. 2017), especially at utility scale, meaning in the multi-million dollar range. There has been insufficient transmission grid capacity for the national energy regulator to allow very many new solar installation in the locations with highest irradiation down south; till 2019, guidelines on how existing grid capacity should be allocated were unclear; and when transparent guidelines did emerge it was into a context with a little informed public debate on such crucial priorities regarding the country's energy future and low-carbon transition

---

[1] Eurostat news release 81/2019, dated 08.05.2019. Accessed 24.05.2019 at https://ec.europa.eu/eurostat/documents/2995521/9779945/8-08052019-AP-EN.pdf/9594d125-9163-446c-b650-b2b00c531d2b.

(Sareen and Haarstad 2018; Vasconcelos 2018). Then, a scandal in another ministry ahead of a national election year led to a cabinet reshuffle. The emergence of a new ministry with a new minister of environment and energy transition, as well as European Commission mandates, prompted the launch of a national climate and energy policy and a national decarbonisation roadmap 2050 (Sareen in review). At the time of writing, Portugal had scheduled solar capacity auctions for over 2 Giga Watts during 2019, and adopted a newly ambitious target that includes a tenfold increase in solar energy capacity within a decade.

To those well versed with energy sector dynamics, 'incumbency' and 'path dependence' (Sovacool 2016; Lockwood et al. 2017) are terms that will suggest themselves easily given the particular trajectory up to 2019, and potentially also disruption to describe evolving circumstances (Winskel 2018). Portugal has a history of a veritable monopoly in its energy sector by Energias de Portugal (EDP). Like many other countries, it moved from electricity being a largely publicly held sector to increased privatisation during the past quarter century. EDP remains an outsize vertically integrated player in this sector but is multinational and privately held. A great deal of control over its own energy infrastructure has shifted out of Portuguese hands of late with sustained interest by Chinese investors (Pareja-Alcaraz 2017), not least during Portugal's battle with economic recession and European Union pressure during 2009–2015.

The sector has changed, but the memory of a particular mode of functioning maintains a stronghold in the mind of decision-makers (Delicado et al. 2016). EDP is a major player in renewables—hydro and wind power in Portugal—but its solar energy assets are held abroad rather than in Portugal. Here, it has leveraged its presence in fossil fuel generation and protected investments in thermal plants in the hope that these will turn over a tidy profit for years hence. Timing is thus crucial in terms of who stands to benefit from Portugal's solar energy transition (Sareen et al. 2018). It is perhaps not all that surprising that so far there has been no particular rush to implement a dramatic increase in solar uptake. After all, things are running smoothly, Portugal is meeting European targets on renewable energy, and a cash-strapped economy has competing priorities, so why mess with a good enough energy sector? And yet, with the announcement of solar auctions for summer 2019 by the government of Portugal signalling a clear pathway, EDP publicly stated its interest in participating and submitting bids.

It is crucial to unpack this tension between a 'good enough' status quo that has lingered for years and the promise of upcoming large-scale dynamism in order to understand the changing energy sector and the adaptive behaviour of various stakeholders. What is the underlying normative commitment—what suffices and why, and by contrast, what catalyses change and when? Does Portugal exemplify a sustainable energy transition underway? Or does it normalise something well short of reasonable action, simply because legal and discursive space permit it without sufficiently rigorous tests (Dansou and Langley 2012)? These questions approach the nub of the argument presented below: in the Portuguese case of gradual solar uptake as in most current energy transitions, we know what the problem is, we know a good deal about how to solve it and yet do little about it, and this disjuncture is a crisis of accountability (Mason 2008).

From the normative standpoint of decarbonisation, Portugal should be putting all the weight it can behind rapid, even exponential, solar uptake, dealing with its disruptive effects head-on in order to decarbonise quickly. Adding an equity dimension, it should be encouraging a vibrant public debate about how to ensure that such a sectoral transition enhances social equity or at least does not work against it. Till recently, these discussions barely existed, and as they emerge, they play out amongst 'experts' and those who often represent specific stakes in the sector (cf. West and Davis 2011). There has been at best a fringe discussion on various public stakes in energy transitions and the necessity for a solar energy transition to happen rapidly and to produce public benefits (Delicado et al. 2014; Sareen and Haarstad 2018)—both in terms of enhancing current social equity and by way of securing improved intergenerational equity through climate change mitigation.

What does solar energy have to do with social equity? Within Europe, Portugal has one of the highest national rates of energy poverty, a condition whereby people cannot secure adequate home energy services. Some 800,000 of the country's ten million residents avail subsidised electricity tariffs. Yet, the current energy sector regime does not incentivise 'prosuming', or selling solar energy back to the grid. It mainly promotes self-consumption (Camilo et al. 2017), which does not appeal much to small households considering installing rooftop solar panels when they are usually not at home during peak solar generation hours. Nor does the national framework support community energy, and Portugal's first solar energy cooperative in Lisbon has struggled to gain recognition as an electricity supplier in order to increase the benefits its members can access from the addition of solar energy to the electric grid supply mix. Only solar developers installing solar capacity in the Mega Watts (MW), with each MW corresponding to close to a million dollar investment, find themselves able to turn a tidy profit by trading on the wholesale market. This does help in terms of climate change mitigation, as it enlarges the percentage of low-carbon energy sources feeding the electric grid, and thereby lowers the carbon emissions associated with electricity generation. But, current figures constitute nominal progress, gradual increments, that benefit a few private developers; Portugal is not witnessing some disruptive revolution in the energy sector that benefits tens of thousands of small households and communities and moves rapidly towards a democratic, low-carbon energy future (Camilo et al. 2017; Jaegersberg and Ure 2017; Sareen and Haarstad 2018; see also Jacobson et al. 2017).

So, we find ourselves in a peculiar, but comprehensible, situation. Solar energy is cost-competitive with dirtier energy sources, can be installed in large parts of a country that does not have fossil fuels and, yet, continues to struggle to comprise a significant chunk of Portugal's energy mix. What makes it understandable is the acceptance of a simple, horrifying fact: this is a crisis of accountability, one that flies under the radar even as we animatedly debate sustainable energy transitions within a global system that legitimates pathways of carbon capitalism (Mitchell 2011). Lisbon has hosted some of the most prominent global meetings on such matters, such as Sustainable Energy for All in 2018, and has even been awarded the label of European Green Capital 2020. Do such overt public displays of commitment to the ideal of sustainable energy transition serve as a spectacle that disguises or substitutes for a lack of ambition, action and implementation (Sareen and Grandin in review)? What other horrors lie in store if we extend our gaze to various energy transitions elsewhere, and would it help to call them out? What if we reframe energy transitions as a response to accountability crises? In order to do so, we must articulate how such accountability crises are upheld. What magic is this that keeps them going? I argue next that this 'magic' manifests as discrete practices of legitimation.

1.2 Deconstructing Accountability into Practices of Legitimation

I claim above that we know what the problem is, that we know how to solve it and yet do little about it, and that this disjuncture constitutes a crisis of accountability. Commenting on our contemporary efforts to undertake energy transitions and meet the climate challenge at the United Nations High Level Political Forum 2018 in New York, Alex Steffen pointed out to the world that in this case, winning slowly is the same as losing (also see McKibben 2017), and underscored a predatory delay by powerful actors with entrenched interests, both commercial and political. Greta Thunberg addressed an audience of the rich in Davos stating that it is now time to panic. The IPCC released a special report on keeping global warming below 1.5 °C, showing that we have our work cut out and must make critical advances by 2030. The exponential climate action roadmap 2018 highlighted proven technological solutions that already exist and can cut our emissions by half every decade till 2050, pointing out policy, political will and other blocks as the chief barriers to overcome (Falk et al. 2018). But, how can dramatic action proportionate to current drastic circumstances be enabled, when those in corridors of power do not feel the same heat, when the privileged maintain the illusion of time while the poor burn in wildfires and suffer climate risk and uncertainty over already vulnerable livelihoods? The energy sector has long been regarded as technical, is often run bureaucratically and technocratically, and is financed in deeply entrenched ways that remain far from transparent (Szulecki 2018)—is the first step towards decarbonising this sector (for decarbonise it we must) to bring it into public discourse as something that concerns us all, as a sector that we all have a stake in steering together?

These questions have answers. They have long been discussed by environmental governance scholars as a matter of accountability in various cognate sectors and a range of academic disciplines. Who makes decisions about resource use and allocation, and how are they held to account (Kraft and Wolf 2018) and by whom? This is partly a question of formal institutional authority—in whom society has vested the power to decide. But the world is rarely limited to formal structures alone. Authority is often contested, raw power sometimes prevails and, sometimes, the powerful are simply too powerful to be held to account by the standards that might appease a moral philosopher (Sareen 2016). And yet, powerful actors and organisations always seek ways to legitimate their power to wider publics to create a new moral economy in which they can take on the roles of new institutional authorities (de Sardan 1999; Sareen 2017). This is not simply attributable to some assumed innate desire in these actors to be recognised as authoritative; the explanation is simpler. Authority makes it easier for power to endure without constantly battling resistance (Scott 1998; Sivaramakrishnan 2005).

Authority comes from legitimation; hence, it affords its bearer the practical privilege of being able to claim recognition as the one with the *right* to make important decisions. Ordinary actors have to organise themselves and contest against the odds to secure outcomes that go against a systematised norm—this is the stuff of public protest, legal appeals and riots on the streets. Institutional authority can claim to uphold the system in executing its decisions; it need only cloak them in the guise of what has *already* been deemed socially acceptable, what is already valid because it is an outcome of due process (Ferguson 1990). Power legitimated as authority freezes legitimacy as embodied in action by virtue of the doer, rather than as a property of the act itself. The onus is on ordinary actors to validate both their claims and an alternative morality in order to challenge particular acts, whereas authoritative institutions use a range of garbs to validate acts.

Such a *de facto* understanding of authority as not being limited to traditional formal structures complicates how one understands accountability. Emerging scholarship on polycentric climate governance has articulated some of the challenges—accountability cannot be construed as pertaining solely to the state along some vertical and horizontal relations within a centralised and delegated governance framework because this is not an accurate descriptor of how climate governance is, in fact, conducted (Jordan et al. 2018; Bäckstrand and Kuyper 2017). Rather, there are many actors in the folds, each hankering after their own version of what transitions to sustainability should look like. Intergovernmental bodies co-exist with city networks co-exist with aligned interests between business and politics co-exist with federated civil society organisations, each staking its claims (Coenen et al. 2012). Who is to be held accountable for what? Each would have its success measured along customised metrics that favour its ability to showcase progress on sustainability (Kramarz and Park 2016), which runs the risk of double counting many successes that actors see as low-hanging fruit while sidelining attention to intractable problems nobody wants to be held responsible to address (Osofsky 2013).

As with climate governance, so is the case with transitioning energy sectors, albeit these transitions more commonly concern national and regional scales rather than global ones. Fossil fuel actors have entrenched interests, usually complemented by deep political and financial reach, and many are transitioning into leveraged positions in the expanding renewable energy sector, which is also populated by new actors such as solar developers.

Traditional authorities like ministries are changing their names and structures, demonstrating a commitment to an energy transition or even an ecological transition, responding to and reshaping social imaginaries (Tidwell and Tidwell 2018). Regulatory bodies are grappling with more complex issues than ever before with the advent of the 'smart grid' and questions of big data, ownership and privacy alongside energy efficiency, dynamic tariffs and prosuming (Sareen and Rommetveit 2019). There is emerging excitement linked with energy storage and the prospects of a highly flexible grid where electricity can be stored at decentralised nodes, opening up options for massive shares of renewable energy sources to be integrated into the grid supply mix. This is as complicated and technical as it sounds, and traditional authorities do not readily have the expertise at hand to deal satisfactorily with these questions, let alone inform and consult the wider public affected by the outcomes of these complex decisions. This is the recipe for an accountability crisis if ever there was one—technology is changing fast, institutional authority is being reconfigured and the basis for public oversight is lacking across key aspects of sectoral evolution (Jasanoff 2018; Delina and Janetos 2018). Energy futures are being decided but by whom, and how do those who will be affected—namely, the public—hold someone accountable, when both decision-making processes and decisions themselves appear to be so fuzzy and fluid?

This book, like Kraft and Wolf (2018), suggests that a closer link between legitimacy and accountability will help. What the problem outlined above needs is a relational understanding of accountability that focuses on relations between entities rather than on essentialist, fixed definitions of entities themselves (Bouzarovski and Haarstad 2018). Such a relational ontology is suitable to the context of fluid authority over decision-making and the shifting population of actors described as characterising contemporary energy sectors. How, then, are these relations of accountability constituted? In the present definition, this production of accountability takes place through discrete acts of legitimation. Practices of legitimation thus become relational constituents of accountability. They are empirically observable and contestable, as signifiers and enablers of deeper changes in institutional authority. A repertoire of these practices legitimates new acts and inflects accountability relations. It thereby serves as an adjustment mechanism for more embedded institutional logics (e.g., modest solar uptake to claim a commitment to sustainability while continuing reliance on fossil fuels), or as a transformational moment that alters these logics (e.g., exponential solar uptake as a response to the emerging new economics of the energy sector). To understand, and eventually influence, accountability in transitioning energy sectors, we must, therefore, attend to practices of legitimation that embody changing relations between entities. We can thus examine and reveal in what instances and to what extent they signify accountable modes of governance to enable sustainable energy transitions or not.

References

Bäckstrand, K., & Kuyper, J. W. (2017). The democratic legitimacy of orchestration: The UNFCCC, non-state actors, and transnational climate governance. *Environmental Politics, 26*(4), 764–788.

Bouzarovski, S., & Haarstad, H. (2018). Rescaling low-carbon transformations: Towards a relational ontology. *Transactions of the Institute of British Geographers*. In press, https://doi.org/10.1111/tran.1227514

Camilo, F. M., Castro, R., Almeida, M. E., & Pires, V. F. (2017). Economic assessment of residential PV systems with self-consumption and storage in Portugal. *Solar Energy, 150*, 353–362.

Coelho, M. B., Cabral, P., & Rodrigues, S. (2017). Solar photovoltaic farms suitability analysis: A Portuguese case-study. *International Journal of Renewable Energy Research (IJRER), 7*(1), 243–254.

Coenen, L., Benneworth, P., & Truffer, B. (2012). Toward a spatial perspective on sustainability transitions. *Research Policy, 41*(6), 968–979.

Dansou, K., & Langley, A. (2012). Institutional work and the notion of test. *Management, 15*(5), 503–527.

de Sardan, J. O. (1999). A moral economy of corruption in Africa? *The Journal of Modern African Studies, 37*(1), 25–52.

Delicado, A., Figueiredo, E., & Silva, L. (2016). Community perceptions of renewable energies in Portugal: Impacts on environment, landscape and local development. *Energy Research & Social Science, 13*, 84–93.

Delicado, A., Junqueira, L., Fonseca, S., Truninger, M., & Silva, L. (2014). Not in anyone's backyard? Civil society attitudes towards wind power at the national and local levels in Portugal. *Science & Technology Studies, 27*(2), 49–71.

Delina, L., & Janetos, A. (2018). Cosmopolitan, dynamic, and contested energy futures: Navigating the pluralities and polarities in the energy systems of tomorrow. *Energy Research & Social Science, 35*, 1–10.

Falk, J., Gaffney, O., Bhowmik, A. K., Borgström-Hansson, C., Pountney, C., Lundén, D., ... Shalit, T. (2018). *Exponential climate action roadmap*. Stockholm: Future Earth Sweden. Retrieved from http://exponentialroadmap.futureearth.org

Ferguson, J. (1990). *The anti-politics machine: 'Development', depoliticization and bureaucratic power in Lesotho.* Cambridge: Cambridge University Press.
Fortes, P., Simoes, S. G., Gouveia, J. P., & Seixas, J. (2019). Electricity, the silver bullet for the deep decarbonisation of the energy system? Cost-effectiveness analysis for Portugal. *Applied Energy, 237,* 292–303.
Jacobson, M. Z., Delucchi, M. A., Bauer, Z. A., Goodman, S. C., Chapman, W. E., Cameron, M. A., ... Erwin, J. R. (2017). 100% clean and renewable wind, water, and sunlight all-sector energy roadmaps for 139 countries of the world. *Joule, 1*(1), 108–121.
Jaegersberg, G., & Ure, J. (2017). The Portuguese case: The cost of inequality. In *Renewable energy clusters* (pp. 63–83). Cham: Springer.
Jasanoff, S. (2018). Just transitions: A humble approach to global energy futures. *Energy Research & Social Science, 35,* 11–14.
Jordan, A., Huitema, D., Van Asselt, H., & Forster, J. (Eds.). (2018). *Governing climate change: Polycentricity in action?* Cambridge: Cambridge University Press.
Kraft, B., & Wolf, S. (2018). Through the lens of accountability: Analyzing legitimacy in environmental governance. *Organization & Environment, 31*(1), 70–92.
Krajačić, G., Duić, N, & da Graça Carvalho, M. (2011). How to achieve a 100% RES electricity supply for Portugal? *Applied Energy, 88*(2), 508–517.
Kramarz, T., & Park, S. (2016). Accountability in global environmental governance: A meaningful tool for action? *Global Environmental Politics, 16*(2), 1–21.
Lockwood, M., Kuzemko, C., Mitchell, C., & Hoggett, R. (2017). Historical institutionalism and the politics of sustainable energy transitions: A research agenda. *Environment and Planning C: Politics and Space, 35*(2), 312–333.
Mason, M. (2008). The governance of transnational environmental harm: Addressing new modes of accountability/responsibility. *Global Environmental Politics, 8*(3), 8–24.
McKibben, B. (2017, December 4). Winning slowly is the same as losing. *Rolling Stone.*
Mitchell, T. (2011). *Carbon democracy: Political power in the age of oil.* London and New York: Verso Books.
Osofsky, H. M. (2013). The geography of solving global environmental problems: Reflections on polycentric efforts to address climate change. *New York Law School Law Review, 58,* 777–827.
Pareja-Alcaraz, P. (2017). Chinese investments in Southern Europe's energy sectors: Similarities and divergences in China's strategies in Greece, Italy, Portugal and Spain. *Energy Policy, 101,* 700–710.
Sareen, S. (2016). Seeing development as security: Constructing top-down authority and inequitable access in Jharkhand. *South Asia Multidisciplinary Academic Journal, 13.* https://doi.org/10.4000/samaj.4146

Sareen, S. (2017). Discourses around logging: The moral economy of wood extraction from West Singhbhum's conflicted forests. *South Asia: Journal of South Asian Studies, 40*(4), 862–877.

Sareen, S. (in review). Metrics for an accountable energy transition? Legitimating the governance of solar uptake. Manuscript under review.

Sareen, S., Baillie, D., & Kleinwächter, J. (2018). Transitions to future energy systems: Learning from a community test field. *Sustainability, 10*(12), 4513.

Sareen, S., & Grandin, J. (in review). European green capitals: Branding, spatial dislocation or catalysts for change? Revised and resubmitted manuscript.

Sareen, S., & Haarstad, H. (2018). Bridging socio-technical and justice aspects of sustainable energy transitions. *Applied Energy, 228*, 624–632.

Sareen, S., & Rommetveit, K. (2019). Smart gridlock? Challenging hegemonic framings of mitigation solutions and scalability. *Environmental Research Letters*. In press, https://doi.org/10.1088/1748-9326/ab21e6

Scott, J. C. (1998). *Seeing like a state: How certain schemes to improve the human condition have failed.* Yale University Press.

Sivaramakrishnan, K. (2005). Introduction to "moral economies, state spaces, and categorical violence". *American Anthropologist, 107*(3), 321–330.

Sovacool, B. K. (2016). How long will it take? Conceptualizing the temporal dynamics of energy transitions. *Energy Research & Social Science, 13*, 202–215.

Szulecki, K. (2018). Conceptualizing energy democracy. *Environmental Politics, 27*(1), 21–41.

Tidwell, J. H., & Tidwell, A. S. (2018). Energy ideals, visions, narratives, and rhetoric: Examining sociotechnical imaginaries theory and methodology in energy research. *Energy Research & Social Science, 39*, 103–107.

Vasconcelos, J.. (2018). Testimony before the Portuguese Parliament on July 11, 2018.

West, K., & Davis, P. (2011). What is the public value of government action? Towards a (new) pragmatic approach to values questions in public endeavours. *Public Administration, 89*(2), 226–241.

Winskel, M. (2018). Beyond the disruption narrative: Varieties and ambiguities of energy system change. *Energy Research & Social Science, 37*, 232–237.

Open Access This chapter is licensed under the terms of the Creative Commons Attribution 4.0 International License (http://creativecommons.org/licenses/by/4.0/), which permits use, sharing, adaptation, distribution and reproduction in any medium or format, as long as you give appropriate credit to the original author(s) and the source, provide a link to the Creative Commons licence and indicate if changes were made.

The images or other third party material in this chapter are included in the chapter's Creative Commons licence, unless indicated otherwise in a credit line to the material. If material is not included in the chapter's Creative Commons licence and your intended use is not permitted by statutory regulation or exceeds the permitted use, you will need to obtain permission directly from the copyright holder.

CHAPTER 2

A Typology of Practices of Legitimation to Categorise Accountability Relations

Siddharth Sareen

Abstract This chapter presents the central element of an accountability analysis approach—a typology of four practices of legitimation: discursive, bureaucratic, technocratic and financial. These are empirically derived and defined in generic terms as social relations premised on accountability. Their study can characterise accountability under energy transitions. Discursive legitimation practices normalise certain perspectives over others through textual and spoken interventions across a variety of forums. Bureaucratic legitimation practices, often codified and sequential, validate some actions and actors and constrain others. Technocratic legitimation practices perform systematic checks and approval of actions that entail technical expertise. Financial legitimation practices, often spatially remote and materially elusive, enable actors to block action or to fulfil financial requirements and proceed with material actions, shaping sectoral change.

Keywords Practices of legitimation • Discursive • Bureaucratic • Technocratic • Financial

---

S. Sareen (✉)
Department of Geography, Centre for Climate and Energy Transformation, University of Bergen, Bergen, Norway
e-mail: Siddharth.Sareen@uib.no

There is an endless variety of practices of legitimation. But they draw on a number of common registers. Four such registers surfaced clearly from empirical research on solar energy uptake in Portugal during 2017–2019. These empirically derived registers are put forward as a typology of practices of legitimation. They are:

- Discursive legitimation
- Bureaucratic legitimation
- Technocratic legitimation
- Financial legitimation

Without elaborating the empirical basis for this typology, detailed elsewhere (Sareen in review), and without extending the initial foray into the Portuguese case, this chapter unpacks each of these four types of practices: what do they mean? Furthermore, it puts forward a few preliminary suggestions for how this typology is supported by extant research on accountability and legitimacy within environmental governance. Environmental governance research has on the whole been rather laggardly in taking up the important question of sustainable energy transitions at disaggregated scales (Falkner 2014; Smith and Stirling 2010), so this connection between its treatment of accountability and legitimacy and their application to the energy sector is overdue (Szulecki 2018). It is a task that requires multiple perspectives and many person-years of research. This book enlists the support of select colleagues who have an appreciation of both environmental governance and energy transitions scholarship. This chapter kickstarts the conversation by laying out the types of practices of legitimation. Then, Part II opens with an explanation of the invitation (Chap. 3) issued to the authors of five subsequent case chapters, each of which presents a perspective on accountable governance under energy transitions, drawing on the case author's own empirical research (Chaps. 4, 5, 6, 7 and 8). The concluding Part III synthesises learning about the analytical usefulness of practices of legitimation across the five cases (Chap. 9), then features collective reflection on how future environmental governance scholarship can generate analytical insights on accountability (Chap. 10). The book seeks both to guide the uptake of accountability within theoretical and applied energy transitions research in a broad range of fields and disciplines, and to inform strategic action, thereby contributing to both analysing energy sector transitions and enabling accountable governance towards sustainability.

With each type of practice of legitimation below, the intent is to fashion tools that can deconstruct what acts are being justified and validated (i.e., legitimated) by whom, to whom and in what manner. Each type of practice surfaces a specific register along which it evinces accountability relations that display commitment to sustainable outcomes. Within any given energy sector context, each type of practice is empirically observable to a sufficient degree to identify specific problem areas, accountability lacunae, scope for further gains and to challenge claims, and to pose normative questions of who gets to decide, and who should be consulted or otherwise involved.

2.1 Discursive Legitimation

Discursive legitimation refers to a set of practices that normalise certain perspectives over others through textual and spoken interventions across a variety of forums. These forums range from highly technical discussions among a narrow group of actors to mainstream debates for audiences as wide as the general public in the pages of national newspapers. Practices of legitimation manifest in many ways on these platforms: speaking in favour of one choice over another, thus advocating for something; referring to some things as commonplace and thereby stabilising them as a public imaginary; talking down some possibilities as being a threat to other desirable outcomes, thus creating or strengthening cognitive links; repeating the need for something as a matter of social necessity and thereby building public support for it; and dismissing some options as wishful thinking uninformed by reality, thus tightening the discursive space that might allow their propagation. These practices are all relational in the sense that they are enacted by actors in relation to audiences, and also because they position ideas in specific relation to other ideas.

A politician backing continued reliance on fossil fuels may, for instance, decry renewable energy sources as posing a debt burden on the public. A federation of solar energy developers may issue a statement against this, pointing out that they are able to compete with coal thermal plants without any public subsidies. Coal thermal plant owners may lobby national regulators to maintain the status quo in the energy sector, which has historically rewarded their power source as relatively 'reliable'. Energy market analysts may point out that this logic has changed, as greater interconnections between electric grids allow for more flexibility in energy sources. Those concerned with energy security might contend that more interconnections pose a threat to sovereignty due to increased reliance on neighbouring countries. Geopolitical experts might counter this argument by pointing out that greater interdependency can in fact foster regional cooperation. Each of these actors would be articulating their particular interests in relation to other competing or complementary perspectives, picking platforms and orders of worth that favour their message or ones that are crucial for securing particular desirable outcomes (von Benda-Beckmann 1981; Boltanski and Thévenot 2006; Patriotta et al. 2011), be it parliamentary hearings, newspaper columns, online blogs, public consultations on new sectoral policies, electoral rallies, thematic conferences, annual expos or even urban festivals.

What makes these practices relevant for the examination of accountability in energy transition is that they lend themselves to empirical study (Moezzi et al. 2017). They allow a contextualised appreciation of different actors' interests and how they articulate them in a disaggregated manner. This extends to actors within organisations as well, as a given organisation rarely consistently represents a single perspective on a complex issue such as energy transition. If one understands energy sector governance as comprising an assemblage of actors (cf. Rose 1999)—governmental institutions, emerging authorities such as ad hoc commissions for specialised decisions, private companies, citizen associations, administrative bodies—then practices of discursive legitimation offer insight into the numerous and shifting relations between this diverse mix of actors. Tweets by a key decision-maker, for instance, have lately emerged as a new way to keep up with the latest developments in a fast-changing sector, and offer new opportunities for public responsiveness—key figures can note and respond directly to comments by ordinary individuals—while also providing insight into the views of individuals within formal organisations (Morgan et al. 2018). Discursive legitimation is also susceptible to hegemonic tendencies—particular accounts can 'go viral' and spread rapidly, often exercising significant influence by shaping readers' or listeners' perceptions. Meanwhile, more detailed and often better substantiated claims such as those in academic articles can remain largely disregarded even by key decision-makers who usually have busy schedules and little time to access paywalled manuscripts that use heavy language.

Practices of discursive legitimation thus play a key role in energy transition: validating particular acts and shoring up the credibility of institutional authorities and their decisions against critique; issuing challenges to specific decisions and even decision-making processes and suggesting alternatives, thus opening up space for debate and the emergence of competing actors; and closing down particular claims by pointing to countervailing accounts, often more established ones with some formal backing. Observation and analysis of which actors legitimate what sort of action and on what basis, which actors level competing claims, and the platforms they pick to address specific target audiences, can furnish a telling picture of a given energy transition. Is it driven by a culture of informed public engagement, healthy debate, friendly critique and an effort at reflexive learning by authoritative institutions in the sector? Or are there several opposing camps, with those currently in a position of authority trying to maintain the status quo and others challenging their authority, vying to constitute their own authority, or to simply improve their position within structural limits they dare not challenge?

Discursive legitimation provides insight into this power interplay precisely because it serves as a means by which actors legitimate their own positions and decisions (Haarstad et al. 2018). In an ideal world, it enables deliberation along democratic lines to institute accountability in the manner in which energy transitions are discussed and implemented (Späth and Rohracher 2010). Deliberative democracy remains hard to obtain in most political contexts, and a technical sector like energy hardly lends itself easily to informed public debate and engagement. Given its bureaucratic, often top-down history, a transition in this sector faces a real challenge to engender energy democracy, with the norm having long been to leave decision-making in the hands of narrow groups of experts (Sareen 2018). Examining discursive legitimation, then, is a sound approach to also identify specific opportunities to build public accountability into energy transitions.

2.2 Bureaucratic Legitimation

Bureaucratic legitimation pertains to practices, often codified and sequential, that validate some actions and actors and limit the range of possibilities for other actors. Readers will be familiar with bureaucracy as a particular method of ensuring conformity with existing laws and regulations (Ferguson and Gupta 2002). For instance, actors might have to furnish proof of a certain competence or qualification in order to secure approval necessary to take on a formal role, operate a private enterprise or maintain access to public services. Bureaucracy is ubiquitous; it is part of the paraphernalia of daily life whereby we conduct our everyday affairs. It also serves essential functions within society and is inevitable. But the flip side is that it accretes redundant requirements, conditions that are an artefact of old ways but remain embedded in current protocols due to inadequate adaptiveness by an organisation during sectoral change. Actors who have to meet such bureaucratic residue might protest and push for a change in formal requirements, an update, or they might find themselves in a position where they are unable to appeal due to limited time, financial wherewithal or a legal framework that, in turn, poses its own bureaucratic challenges. Authorities imposing bureaucratic requirements are often painfully well aware of the privilege their position accords them; depending on internal mechanisms to ensure checks and balances, particular individuals might even seek to abuse this privilege for personal gain, which is usually referred to as petty corruption.

There are several other aspects to bureaucratic legitimation (cf. Suchman 1995), such as a likely bias in favour of incumbent actors, and against emergent actors, on whom falls the onus to validate themselves and fulfil numerous existing requirements—to learn the rules of the game (Geels and Schot 2007). This is a potentially desirable trait in a well-functioning system to ensure system reliability and security, but poses challenges when change is imperative as in the case of energy transitions to address the urgent climate challenge. Several other relational tendencies also surface: there are likely to be information flow asymmetries, as practices in most sectors and contexts tend to feature a partially informal component. There is a risk that bureaucratic processes will extend processing time for critical decisions (Crawford 2015), lowering policy visibility during sectoral change and disadvantaging actors who are worst affected by ensuing uncertainty. And there is a further question concerning time and positionality: those who are well placed to devise bureaucratic requirements have often been closely acquainted with a sector for a long period, and hence, their embodied memory is of a certain mode of conducting affairs that is liable to often resemble business as usual (Sareen 2018; Szeman 2013). The bureaucratic mechanisms they proffer might thus favour the status quo and incumbent actors, allowing tacit bias to creep in. This risk is exacerbated by the fact that entrenched actors often occupy key positions from which to lobby and influence decision-makers in their sector; they can challenge and effectively quash protests from emergent actors by pointing to their superior experience and historically stellar credentials. When changes do come about, such actors can again leverage their positions to modulate what new bureaucratic frameworks are put in play

(Grandin and Sareen in review). This not only equips them with a potential information advantage, it also suggests that key actors can orchestrate sectoral change to unfold in a manner that works to their advantage over others without being held to account for their self-serving exercise of undue influence.

For instance, during energy sector transitions, solar developers might find themselves faced with the need to secure a number of different licences: to lease land for up to three decades, to conduct basic environmental impact assessments, to access grid infrastructure, to import solar modules and to gain the right to provide a certain quantum of stable supply to the electric grid over a stated period or to enter into bilateral contracts with users, to mention a few examples. These constitute practices of bureaucratic legitimation, and actors who are unable to navigate such demands might find themselves shut out from being able to participate as solar developers. An appropriate amount of bureaucratic process is important to secure requisite oversight over a number of interlocked functions in a technical sector like energy (Sareen and Kale 2018); a well-conceived bureaucratic system can feature in-built corrective measures that function as accountability mechanisms, internalised checks and balances. But what complicates matters is when bureaucratic requirements display overly zealous reach or are simply biased towards or against a particular technology or set of actors—especially emerging ones who tend to have less social capital—to an extent that interferes with the efficient functioning of the sector.

Sometimes such bureaucratic interference is expressly permitted and justified on normative grounds—renewable energy may be permitted to go ahead up to a certain component of the total energy supply, so as to meet clean energy targets as a percentage of the grid mix, consequently loosening up bureaucratic requirements for renewable producers up to this target. Yet, normative commitments are not always clearly articulated—fossil fuels are accorded numerous subsidies, both historically in terms of existing energy infrastructure and directly at present, to an extent that other sources would find it impossible to secure through any number of bureaucratic processes (Asmelash 2015). Bureaucratic preferences are not always easy to discern. Wholesale energy trading markets, for instance, follow bureaucratic sets of rules that have evolved historically in energy sectors with relatively small components of renewable energy, and as this proportion changes, the rules do not necessarily change in ways that are optimal for the grid or fair in terms of their effects on various actors, not least on the citizens and users whom the energy sector should serve in a manner responsive to their evolving needs. As part of energy transitions, these could include regulatory frameworks for individuals and communities to prosume and receive appropriate compensation for power sold to the grid from rooftop solar panels.

Studying such practices of bureaucratic legitimation can be challenging, but is an essential component of identifying whether and how energy transitions can proceed with public accountability (Kalkuhl et al. 2013; Saltzstein 1979). Such examination must often be undertaken in several locations across multiple scales (Krause and Meier 2005)—down the corridors of power where bureaucracy is executed; in policy documents, where its formal contours are delineated; by listening to the accounts of actors who claim they are marginalised; through attention to emergent material changes that open new possibilities and how these possibilities are bureaucratised; and by triangulating between the various concurrent changes in bureaucratic requirements during sectoral evolution (Sareen and Kale 2018). Where such examination uncovers bureaucratic mediation that forecloses opportunities for energy transition to aid decarbonisation and social equity, these practices can be specifically challenged to build accountability gains within specific contexts of energy transition.

2.3 Technocratic Legitimation

Technocratic legitimation refers to a set of practices that perform systematic checks and approval of actions that entail technical expertise. This is distinct from bureaucratic legitimation in that it extends beyond filling forms or ticking boxes to secure validation from a designated authority, to a practice that is itself substantive along the same register as the action that it evaluates for approval. This requires some clarification: practices of technocratic legitimation devise a method to assess whether specific actions by specific actors should be permitted or not, and this method itself exhibits a certain element of sophistication in order to lend credibility to the approval as something that takes place after due consideration of the technicalities involved.

Energy transitions raise many highly technical questions that require expert knowledge and do not always have existing scientific consensus around one answer. There may be several possibilities and a basis is needed to determine which ones to permit and prioritise, and which actors should be in charge of executing them and on what basis (Chilvers and Longhurst

2016). An important but relatively easy to resolve example is that of the debate between 80 and 100 per cent renewable energy-based systems. While there is still some disagreement on the possibility of complete decarbonisation despite highly detailed analyses of an impressive number of actual contexts in which this should work, it does not complicate too many current decisions, as most energy systems are well short of even 80 per cent renewable energy sources; hence, decisions can be made to decarbonise rapidly, and the question of the final 20 per cent can be resolved later in the energy transition (Jacobson and Delucchi 2009). A more complicated question and one that does require technocratic legitimation is whether a given quantum of new renewable energy capacity can be installed in a decentralised manner and added to an existing electric grid infrastructure. It is important not to overload transmission capacity beyond what the grid can withstand to ensure reliable energy supply and to consider the basis for 'curtailment', which refers to letting surplus power generation simply go unused, or to shutting it down when it runs into grid capacity constraints. Before giving the go-ahead to a number of solar projects, an energy regulator or national ministry would be keen to ensure that the terms on which this new capacity is installed are clear to everyone concerned, marking a clear instance of a case for technocratic legitimation. This is crucial not only to enable energy transitions, but to safeguard citizens against unreliable energy services and debt burdens in case support schemes are not designed to have equitable effects, as well as to prevent losses to the public exchequer, utilities and developers due to inadequate attention to aspects like grid stability and coordination.

This presents an interesting challenge for accountability in energy transitions. When matters are technical, they can hardly be left up to some sort of popular vote, as the public is rarely sufficiently knowledgeable to weigh in usefully on matters of such sophistication. But simply entrusting them to experts risks eventual public backlash, especially in contemporary contexts of rising distrust against authority and the rule of experts; history also bears evidence to the risk of elite capture and large-scale corruption under such conditions (cf. Lennon 2017). Practices of technocratic legitimation present a reasonable compromise—devising a relatively sophisticated system to secure technically appropriate decisions, but with an element of checks and balances and the participation of multiple types of actors who can hold each other accountable. Examples include standing committees, special taskforces and other such ad hoc measures; also more institutionalised mechanisms such as stringent public procurement rules, well-defined guidelines for public tenders to ensure competitive bidding on various contracts, and algorithms that automate the allocation of particular opportunities to actors who best fulfil pre-specified and publicised criteria to secure optimal performance.

Yet, both ad hoc and more embedded mechanisms, when situated within a temporal perspective, can be appreciated as facing risks of co-optation and being reduced to an empty shell without securing the very accountable outcomes that their technocratic components are ostensibly put in place to ensure (Hendriks 2009). Actors often move between key organisations in the same sector over time, and collegial and personal networks overlap in complex ways that render secrecy almost impossible, so upcoming changes in assessment or selection routines often set off pre-emptive adjustments within organisations that are in the loop, even before they are formally announced (Hargreaves et al. 2013). Moreover, sectoral contexts often feature limited expertise within a region or country; hence, expertise is subcontracted in to furnish inputs for terms of reference. This again courts the risk that some well-networked actors may be tipped off in advance of any technocratic legitimation procedures and maximise their chances over competitors.

Probing these relational practices of technocratic legitimation in concrete instances can generate and advance a technically robust and politically informed understanding of energy transitions. Technocratic legitimation is perhaps most visible at times when a sector undergoes rapid change, as effort-intensive mechanisms are put in place to enable change while simultaneously maintaining stability (Pellizzoni 2011). Over time, these practices tend to be absorbed into reconfigured systemic practices and become part of bureaucratic legitimation, which is more routinised and embedded within existing organisational functions. In this sense, practices of technocratic legitimation offer a raw, direct opportunity to shape energy futures towards decarbonisation and enhancement of social equity—by examining, critiquing and adjusting specific practices, it is possible to impact how the energy sector reorientates itself in relation to current changes. This translation function, between experts who are entrusted with framing and conducting technocratic legitimation and the public whose interests they should in principle safeguard, is one that researchers and analysts are well equipped to weigh in on (Fischer 1993). Those who inform themselves of the empirics of technocratic legitimation in a sectoral context can credibly provide policymakers with inputs on specific measures they should establish in order to move energy transitions towards sustainability, with a clear basis in evidence.

2.4 Financial Legitimation

Financial legitimation pertains to practices, often spatially remote and materially elusive, that enable actors to either block out scope for action, or to fulfil financial requirements and proceed with material actions in order to retain relevance within a sectoral context. They are perhaps the most crucial and telltale signifier of the characteristics of an energy transition—which actors are able to secure financial legitimation, through which practices, for what activities? By structuring the fields of action, capital and access to credit quite directly shape energy transitions (Hess 2014); thus, the practices that make up financial legitimation indirectly capture the core of any sectoral change. One of the refrains iterated by international agencies trying to steer towards rapid global decarbonisation and equitable access to energy has been the need to make much more capital available for universal access to clean energy (also see Polzin et al. 2017); the global divestment movement is trying to push money out of fossil fuel energy to secure contractions of carbon-intensive sources and accelerate investment in renewable energy (Healy and Barry 2017).

Practices of financial legitimation thus render explicit the relevance of spatial and scalar connections. But what practices are observable and how can their study contribute towards more accountable energy transitions? At the household or individual scale, germane issues include determining the appropriate levels of compensation for flexibility added to the grid based on distributed storage, as batteries become affordable and electric vehicles proliferate, as well as disincentives to prevent users from loading the grid during peak demand periods (Sareen and Rommetveit 2019). Several aspects of financial legitimation can in fact be studied in great empirical detail: what are the challenges actors have to face in securing financial backing to install and operate different energy sources; how do these requirements vary across sources; how are these financial parameters set and by which authority? For instance, renewable energy projects face a rather different challenge than fossil fuel projects. Most of their lifetime project costs are concentrated up front: procurement of licences, land and infrastructure. Once equipment is set up and grid connected, operating costs are negligible compared to coal or gas thermal plants which consume a great deal of fuel throughout their lifespan, fuel that additionally often has to be brought in from afar. Yet renewable energy projects are often characterised as variable sources and have up to recently faced considerable scepticism from financial institutions regarding their future revenue flows, making it relatively expensive to secure investment capital (Kim and Park 2016).

With the rapid decrease in costs of both wind and, especially, solar energy technologies, these dynamics have begun to shift, and even large fossil fuel majors are beginning to leverage their portfolios with some investments in clean energy. But the challenges are significantly different for relatively small entrants to the energy sector who do not have as much financial weight. By contrast, shell companies have also begun to emerge rapidly as vehicles for speculative financial investments in renewable energy projects. How to maintain an energy sector that remains open to smaller actors while also safeguarding against potentially risky short-term players is a challenge that can only be resolved through a keen appreciation of various practices of financial legitimation (Mazzucato and Semieniuk 2018).

Even tracking these observable practices, however, uncovers only the tip of the proverbial iceberg. When it comes to energy finance, there is little transparency, with large sums and many international organisations involved, leveraging their presence across several different legal regimes including global tax havens. There are thus intrinsic problems to contend with to usher accountability into financial legitimation, and part of the task is to better visualise these global metabolisms at lower scales like the urban and national (Goodman and Marshall 2018). Many cities, regions and countries have begun to track their territorial emissions and set targets at lower scales, including sector specific ones. It is possible that such attempts will be accompanied by fees on high carbon emitters and mass mobilisation of greater investment in renewable energy. Many such initiatives have already been promoted in recent years, but these attempts at alternative financial legitimation have faced stiff resistance in most parts of the world, most notably from the powerful and well-funded fossil fuel lobby that such practices, if successful, directly threaten.

Financial legitimation extends beyond project finance. These practices are also embedded within other processes intrinsic to the everyday operation of the energy sector, such as wholesale and retail market trade. On the wholesale market, fossil fuels such as gas secure high returns due to their flexibility, being available 'on demand', whereas market designs do not always favour renewable energy sources as their percentage of the total supply mix increases rapidly (Ueckerdt et al. 2015). This again is a question of what characteristics are seen as worth rewarding financially, and whether the decision is made by default or based on exhaustive public discussion. Likewise on the retail market, rules vary vastly across countries in terms of how much actors such as households and communities can benefit from installing small-scale solar capacity. Another practice of financial legitimation embedded both deeply and historically in the energy sector pertains to investments in energy infrastructure, often made from the public purse, with major consequences for which actors and what energy sources gain support (Jerneck 2017). This support includes both being able to sell electricity to the grid and lowering costs for the energy producer, for instance by co-financing thermal power plant infrastructure by the sea to enable easy access to international coal shipments, a common practice that supports one of the highest carbon emitting sources. Studying the manner in which these issues of financial legitimation are discussed and settled, as well as whom they favour and penalise, can generate key insights into the nature of energy transitions.

Overall, then, practices of financial legitimation are possibly the trickiest to interrogate empirically; doing so is, nonetheless, vital in order to identify the points that warrant the most critical attention for moving towards accountable energy transitions. These practices take place across the spatial scale, but their effects are materialised in the sector, and various reporting mechanisms and mandates as well as investigations by civil society watchdogs render overall trends visible. When it comes to specific actors in a given context, the contrasting demands that financial legitimation places on them can often be clearly explicated, and serve as a basis to challenge and contest practices that maintain power differentials in favour of business as usual. Unpacking this can ease the way for financially competitive renewable energy sources to expand rapidly in a market made more even by bringing accountability into energy sector transitions.

2.5 LINKING HOLLOW AND SUBSTANTIVE ACCOUNTABILITY WITH SUSTAINABILITY OUTCOMES

The articulation of the four types of practices of legitimation that relationally constitute accountability, or the lack of it, in energy sector transitions, paves the way for the final step of the argument in Part I. Overall, any given transition comprises these practices, which can be disaggregated into performances of substantive or hollow accountability. At a disaggregated level, most acts can be empirically and relationally categorised as aiding or opposing interlinked shifts towards decarbonisation and social equity under energy transition.

Acts that aid such shifts, and are held to account by practices of legitimation in order to secure a durable outcome of this nature, can be characterised as contributing to a sustainable energy transition. This is a case where practices of legitimation constitute substantive accountability relations. Conversely, acts that oppose such shifts are not substantively held to account by practices of legitimation in the service of sustainable outcomes (Blühdorn 2013). Rather, they are supported by practices of legitimation that constitute a performance of hollow accountability; they support the persistence or even expansion of unsustainable outcomes in the energy sector.

It follows that practices of legitimation provide the basis for a relational toolkit to identify substantive and hollow accountability through empirical study of energy sector transitions. This fine-grained evidencing and analysis of the practices that constitute energy transitions can inform academics, and in turn policymakers, practitioners and the public, about acts that support sustainability and those that hold us back from it. Wielded well, this pickaxe can equip citizens with evidence for their own urgent axes to grind and create a strong push for public accountability to be instituted into energy transitions towards sustainability.

This intent—to contribute to rapid decarbonisation of our energy systems and deeply change whom they benefit, thus addressing climate change drivers and safeguarding public interest—is a guiding beacon. The logical next step after propounding a typology of practices of legitimation is to understand how to situate such an approach within scholarship on energy transitions, so that it can render accountability crises visible in contextualised ways that inform and enable action. To open up space for sustainable outcomes through more accountable governance of energy transitions, it is relevant to take point of departure in the variety of ways in which scholarship on environmental governance approaches accountability in energy transitions. The five case chapters in Part II capture a wide range of cases and different disciplinary perspectives.

References

Asmelash, H. B. (2015). Energy subsidies and WTO dispute settlement: Why only renewable energy subsidies are challenged. *Journal of International Economic Law, 18*(2), 261–285.
Blühdorn, I. (2013). The governance of unsustainability: Ecology and democracy after the post-democratic turn. *Environmental Politics, 22*(1), 16–36.
Boltanski, L., & Thévenot, L. (2006). *On justification: Economies of worth.* Princeton, NJ: Princeton University Press.
Chilvers, J., & Longhurst, N. (2016). Participation in transition(s): Reconceiving public engagements in energy transitions as co-produced, emergent and diverse. *Journal of Environmental Policy & Planning, 18*(5), 585–607.
Crawford, A. (2015). Temporality in restorative justice: On time, timing and time-consciousness. *Theoretical Criminology, 19*(4), 470–490.
Falkner, R. (2014). Global environmental politics and energy: Mapping the research agenda. *Energy Research & Social Science, 1,* 188–197.
Ferguson, J., & Gupta, A. (2002). Spatializing states: Toward an ethnography of neoliberal governmentality. *American Ethnologist, 29*(4), 981–1002.
Fischer, F. (1993). Citizen participation and the democratization of policy expertise: From theoretical inquiry to practical cases. *Policy Sciences, 26*(3), 165–187.
Geels, F. W., & Schot, J. (2007). Typology of sociotechnical transition pathways. *Research Policy, 36*(3), 399–417.
Goodman, J., & Marshall, J. P. (2018). Problems of methodology and method in climate and energy research: Socialising climate change? *Energy Research & Social Science, 45,* 1–11.
Grandin, J., & Sareen, S. (in review). What sticks? Ephemerality, permanence and urban transformation pathways. Revised and resubmitted manuscript.
Haarstad, H., Sareen, S., Wanvik, T. I., Grandin, J., Kjærås, K., Oseland, S. E., ... Wathne, M. (2018). Transformative social science? Modes of engagement in climate and energy solutions. *Energy Research & Social Science, 42,* 193–197.
Hargreaves, T., Hielscher, S., Seyfang, G., & Smith, A. (2013). Grassroots innovations in community energy: The role of intermediaries in niche development. *Global Environmental Change, 23*(5), 868–880.
Healy, N., & Barry, J. (2017). Politicizing energy justice and energy system transitions: Fossil fuel divestment and a "just transition". *Energy Policy, 108,* 451–459.
Hendriks, C. M. (2009). Policy design without democracy? Making democratic sense of transition management. *Policy Sciences, 42*(4), 341.
Hess, D. J. (2014). Sustainability transitions: A political coalition perspective. *Research Policy, 43*(2), 278–283.
Jacobson, M. Z., & Delucchi, M. A. (2009). A path to sustainable energy by 2030. *Scientific American, 301*(5), 58–65.

Jerneck, M. (2017). Financialization impedes climate change mitigation: Evidence from the early American solar industry. *Science Advances, 3*(3), e1601861.
Kalkuhl, M., Edenhofer, O., & Lessmann, K. (2013). Renewable energy subsidies: Second-best policy or fatal aberration for mitigation? *Resource and Energy Economics, 35*(3), 217–234.
Kim, J., & Park, K. (2016). Financial development and deployment of renewable energy technologies. *Energy Economics, 59,* 238–250.
Krause, G. A., & Meier, K. J. (Eds.). (2005). *Politics, policy, and organizations: Frontiers in the scientific study of bureaucracy.* University of Michigan Press.
Lennon, M. (2017). Decolonizing energy: Black Lives Matter and technoscientific expertise amid solar transitions. *Energy Research & Social Science, 30,* 18–27.
Mazzucato, M., & Semieniuk, G. (2018). Financing renewable energy: Who is financing what and why it matters. *Technological Forecasting and Social Change, 127,* 8–22.
Moezzi, M., Janda, K. B., & Rotmann, S. (2017). Using stories, narratives, and storytelling in energy and climate change research. *Energy Research & Social Science, 31,* 1–10.
Morgan, K., Cheong, M., & Bedingfield, S. (2018). "Power to the people!": Social media discourse on regional energy issues in Australia. *Australasian Journal of Information Systems, 22.* In press, https://doi.org/10.3127/ajis.v22i0.1678
Patriotta, G., Gond, J. P., & Schultz, F. (2011). Maintaining legitimacy: Controversies, orders of worth, and public justifications. *Journal of Management Studies, 48*(8), 1804–1836.
Pellizzoni, L. (2011). The politics of facts: Local environmental conflicts and expertise. *Environmental Politics, 20*(6), 765–785.
Polzin, F., Sanders, M., & Täube, F. (2017). A diverse and resilient financial system for investments in the energy transition. *Current Opinion in Environmental Sustainability, 28,* 24–32.
Rose, N. (1999). *Powers of freedom: Reframing political thought.* Cambridge: Cambridge University Press.
Saltzstein, G. (1979). Representative bureaucracy and bureaucratic responsibility: Problems and prospects. *Administration & Society, 10*(4), 465–475.
Sareen, S. (2018). Energy distribution trajectories in two Western Indian states: Comparative politics and sectoral dynamics. *Energy Research & Social Science, 35,* 17–27.
Sareen, S. (in review). Metrics for an accountable energy transition? Legitimating the governance of solar uptake. Manuscript under review.
Sareen, S., & Kale, S. S. (2018). Solar 'power': Socio-political dynamics of infrastructural development in two Western Indian states. *Energy Research & Social Science, 41,* 270–278.

Sareen, S., & Rommetveit, K. (2019). Smart gridlock? Challenging hegemonic framings of mitigation solutions and scalability. *Environmental Research Letters*. In press, https://doi.org/10.1088/1748-9326/ab21e6

Smith, A., & Stirling, A. (2010). The politics of social-ecological resilience and sustainable socio-technical transitions. *Ecology and Society, 15*(1). Retrieved from http://www.ecologyandsociety.org/vol15/iss1/art11/

Späth, P., & Rohracher, H. (2010). 'Energy regions': The transformative power of regional discourses on socio-technical futures. *Research Policy, 39*(4), 449–458.

Suchman, M. C. (1995). Managing legitimacy: Strategic and institutional approaches. *Academy of Management Review, 20*(3), 571–610.

Szeman, I. (2013). How to know about oil: Energy epistemologies and political futures. *Journal of Canadian Studies/Revue d'études canadiennes, 47*(3), 145–168.

Szulecki, K. (2018). Conceptualizing energy democracy. *Environmental Politics, 27*(1), 21–41.

Ueckerdt, F., Brecha, R., & Luderer, G. (2015). Analyzing major challenges of wind and solar variability in power systems. *Renewable Energy, 81*, 1–10.

von Benda-Beckmann, K. (1981). Forum shopping and shopping forums: Dispute processing in a Minangkabau village in West Sumatra. *The Journal of Legal Pluralism and Unofficial Law, 13*(19), 117–159.

Open Access This chapter is licensed under the terms of the Creative Commons Attribution 4.0 International License (http://creativecommons.org/licenses/by/4.0/), which permits use, sharing, adaptation, distribution and reproduction in any medium or format, as long as you give appropriate credit to the original author(s) and the source, provide a link to the Creative Commons licence and indicate if changes were made.

The images or other third party material in this chapter are included in the chapter's Creative Commons licence, unless indicated otherwise in a credit line to the material. If material is not included in the chapter's Creative Commons licence and your intended use is not permitted by statutory regulation or exceeds the permitted use, you will need to obtain permission directly from the copyright holder.

PART II

Cases

CHAPTER 3

Five Easy Pieces: Legitimation at Work in Cases Related to Energy Transitions

Siddharth Sareen

Abstract This chapter provides an overview of five energy transition cases by describing the questions posed to five authors to guide the flow of argument in their chapters and summarising case treatments with respect to accountability and legitimation. It links four proposed practices of legitimation with analytical takes on wide-ranging cases. The cases span urban energy transitions over time and space in Germany, forest and land conflicts over authority in Indonesia, urban climate targets based on carbon metrics in Norway, the modalities of Nordic electric mobility transitions, and biodiversity conservation and energy extraction in the USA. Pinpointing the relevance of each case to legitimation, this chapter explicates how questions of accountability are germane to how the energy transitions associated with these cases impact sustainability.

Keywords Accountability • Crisis • Energy transitions • Legitimacy • Sustainability

S. Sareen (✉)
Department of Geography, Centre for Climate and Energy Transformation, University of Bergen, Bergen, Norway
e-mail: Siddharth.Sareen@uib.no

It is imperative that we bear in mind the deep variation in how energy transitions are experienced by different actors, and that their ability to exercise their stakes in the outcomes differs by orders of magnitude. Part I reframed energy transitions as a response to accountability crises, deconstructed accountability into practices of legitimation and presented a typology of those practices. The cases in Part II surface a number of complex spatiotemporal conjunctures and deconstruct the climate and energy crises entangled therein.

If even privileged academics at Global North institutions, well-resourced and relatively free to choose our own research themes, were to shy away from attempts to mobilise knowledge to inform and steer action and hold power accountable, it would spell little hope for sustainable futures. These cases, and the collaborative project ensconcing them, constitute an argument that we can in fact make a meaningful difference, that we have a crucial role to play in making energy transitions accountable and directed towards sustainable outcomes. This is our contribution to make in addressing the climate crisis for those at risk today to have livable futures.

Accordingly, this middle section of the book provides short overviews of cases relevant to energy transitions in a variety of sectors and regions, with a focus on legitimation and accountability in the governance of environmental change. Each of the five chapters is authored by an accomplished environmental governance scholar working on energy transition cases and kindred subjects. Each has reframed their work on a particular case in terms of crises of accountability and practices of legitimation. The following questions guide their independently composed individual responses and constitute a general flow of argument:

- What is the case and why is it an energy transitions case?
- What crises of accountability are being maintained or challenged?
- How do environmental governance scholars characterise the case?
- What practices of legitimation appear to be at play in empirical work?
- What interventions could enable sustainable outcomes under transition?

Timothy Moss draws on the governance of urban energy infrastructure across time and space to unpack the changing relationship between energy transitions, accountability and practices of legitimation across the formidable range of contextual variation in Berlin over the past century. His historical analysis of accountability in the changing contexts that drove energy transitions in this city over the course of a century of political flux surfaces many potent concerns. Among these is the difficulty of evaluating past transitions in relation to sustainability, which only appeared in its familiar current form from the 1970s onwards and has gained notable attention beyond academia even more recently, mainly in the twenty-first century. He also foregrounds that accountability crises are not a new concern but rather have deep roots. What is new, in this sense, is the relevance of sustainability as a concern linked with energy transitions, which directs our attention in this book to accountability crises that are only beginning to be sufficiently recognised. Moss' historical analysis of Berlin's energy transitions, moreover, emphasises the context specificity of accountability as relationally negotiated within a spatiotemporally shifting and historically contingent political economy.

Christian Lund probes a case of forest and land conflict that is, at base, about struggles over authority and accountability. He considers the generative potential of an accountability lens when applied to questions of land governance that remain under-addressed in energy transitions scholarship. In his handling, authority is relationally and reflexively construed, through active and tacit contestations between competing actors. Rather than a state and non-state binary, governance here revolves around questions of claims to statehood and their recognition at multiple scales. Citizens seek to have their claims met by recognising the state at the more local village scale rather than a distant central government and, in doing so, try to reconfigure relations of power and authority. Power is unequally distributed, but its legitimation is necessarily contingent, and is what bestows an organisation with institutional authority to control resources in more persistent ways that can subdue resistance. In Lund's telling, this contingency is revealed as an opportunity for hitherto marginalised actors to not only vye over resources but to orchestrate a redefinition of where authority resides, and thereby of the state itself.

Håvard Haarstad examines the problematic of setting targets for carbon emission reduction at the urban scale both in general and specifically in Norway in terms of its pitfalls as well as potential. He first sets up a case for debunking urban climate and energy targets as the vanity projects of street-smart local politicians—the targets do not seem to be achievable and policies to realise them are not systematically deployed. Then he takes a step back to point out that the very act of target-setting has performative and discursive power, it imbues actors with the ability to point at a goal and orchestrate ambitious actions around it that might otherwise have failed to get off the ground. This normalising of mitigation targets in various forms at the urban scale, in Haarstad's rendering, enables energy transitions. It does so by establishing new accountability relations in a graduated manner that imbricates them within existing routines of decision-making and configurations of power. For strategies to legitimate carbon reduction, discretion may well be the better part of confrontation in shifting policy-making over vital domains to the urban scale for implementation in line with climate target creep.

Benjamin Sovacool bases his reflections on engagement with electric vehicle roll-out in the five Nordic countries, a region that is in the global lead on this energy infrastructure and mobility decarbonisation transition. Drawing on an impressive range of empirical material, this case highlights the many urgent reasons for a shift to electric mobility. It engages closely with the materiality and political economic dynamics of how this transition actually pans out in order to throw into relief how electric mobility alone can hardly address the problems it is commonly portrayed as resolving; these problems are deeply embedded within systems of mobility themselves. Sovacool flags unfolding accountability crises linked with inequitable access to electric vehicles, exclusionary and elitist planning, global externalities, and exacerbated social vulnerabilities. The chapter problematises the perpetuation of car-centric mobility alongside planning centred on public transport electrification and points to the perils and promises of how roll-out interfaces with electric grid flexibility and the integration of renewable energy sources. His treatment spans sectoral actors from national authorities to vehicle dealerships and from those affected by extraction to those buying Teslas, in keeping with an appreciation of accountability relations as multi-scalar, multi-sited, polycentric and amorphous in a sectoral layering of regimes.

Steven Wolf thinks through a case of dysfunctional habitat exchange markets around the sage-grouse in Colorado to interrogate the construction of hollow accountability. On the one hand, science-based assessment presents energy extractive industries with clear costs associated with oil and gas extraction activities so as to compensate for the displacement of this endangered species by provisioning for habitat replacement. Institutional orchestration creates the requisite paraphernalia around this, including actors to execute compensatory habitat exchange, a quantification tool and a market to facilitate these transactions. On the other hand, power trumps substantive assessment, as the extractive majors refuse to entertain the estimated costs and the habitat exchange fails to record a single transaction. Wolf argues that these developments are rightly understood as situated within accompanying changes at the federal and state levels pertaining to regulation and political dynamics. Rather than a case of abject failure, he reads it as the construction of requisite institutions to exercise accountability mechanisms that render energy extraction and biodiversity conservation not necessarily mutually exclusive, given political will and future enabling policy. This cross-sectoral analysis raises questions of legitimacy for the evolution of the energy sector in the American West, evidencing a lack of credibility to claims of energy transition.

After the five case chapters comes Part III, which comprises editorial reflections and a co-authored concluding synthesis. It takes a step back to revisit the cases at a higher level of abstraction. Chapter 9 draws out the various registers where practices of legitimation are at work in each case. Chapter 10 demonstrates application of the practices of legitimation within dimensions that are present in the five cases and highlights opportunities to cross-fertilise scholarship on energy transitions and environmental governance. Part III thus brings together openings in the fields that are broached by the case chapters and by the framing of the book. With this in mind, the reader is invited into the wide-ranging world of energy transitions over the course of Chaps. 4, 5, 6, 7 and 8.

Open Access This chapter is licensed under the terms of the Creative Commons Attribution 4.0 International License (http://creativecommons.org/licenses/by/4.0/), which permits use, sharing, adaptation, distribution and reproduction in any medium or format, as long as you give appropriate credit to the original author(s) and the source, provide a link to the Creative Commons licence and indicate if changes were made.

The images or other third party material in this chapter are included in the chapter's Creative Commons licence, unless indicated otherwise in a credit line to the material. If material is not included in the chapter's Creative Commons licence and your intended use is not permitted by statutory regulation or exceeds the permitted use, you will need to obtain permission directly from the copyright holder.

CHAPTER 4

Historicising Accountability: Berlin's Energy Transitions

Timothy Moss

Abstract This chapter explores accountability and energy transitions through the lens of historical analysis. It reinterprets empirical research on the history of Berlin's energy systems to illustrate how accountability and legitimacy are political constructs of a particular time and place. Three periods of reconfiguration to urban electricity and gas networks, chosen from across Berlin's turbulent past century, illustrate this diversity. The chapter outlines each selected case and its pertinence to energy accountability. It then describes what crisis of accountability was prevalent in each instance and its treatment in the literature. The practices of legitimation enrolled to justify energy strategies are subsequently highlighted, as are forms of resistance and attempts to delegitimise the dominant discourse. The conclusion summarises the implications of historicising accountability for energy transitions research.

Keywords Accountability • Legitimacy • Berlin • Energy • History

T. Moss (✉)
Integrative Research Institute on Transformations of Human-Environment Systems (IRI THESys), Humboldt University of Berlin, Berlin, Germany
e-mail: timothy.moss@hu-berlin.de

© The Author(s) 2020
S. Sareen (ed.), *Enabling Sustainable Energy Transitions*,
https://doi.org/10.1007/978-3-030-26891-6_4

4.1 What Is the Case and Why Is It an Energy Transitions Case?

This chapter explores ways of contextualising accountability and accountability crises, both temporally and spatially. Using the case of Berlin over the past 100 years, it aspires to enrich debate on accountability in energy transitions—the focus of this book—by reflecting on historical precedents that can challenge some 'presentist' assumptions underpinning much of this work. Following the editor's invitation (Sareen 2019), I reframe ongoing and published research on Berlin's multiple energy transitions (Moss 2014, 2016; Becker et al. 2017) in terms of crises of accountability and practices of legitimation. In doing so, I hope to sensitise future research on this topic to the importance of time and space. The underlying question guiding the chapter is: how can historicising accountability contribute to our understanding of energy transitions and ways of researching them?

Berlin lends itself to such an analysis in part because accountability has, today, become a key issue of contention over the future of the city's energy infrastructures (Becker et al. 2015, 2017; Blanchet 2015). Over the past decade, criticism of the city's electricity and gas utilities, which were both fully privatised during the 1990s, has targeted not only their reluctance to embrace the low carbon agenda but also—significantly—their resistance to public scrutiny and the democratisation of decision-making processes. A local referendum to remunicipalise Berlin's electricity grid narrowly failed in November 2013, but the campaign generated two social movements. These have since managed to reframe energy policy debates in the city around issues of accountability, participation and transparency. The first is the Berlin Energy Roundtable (Berliner Energietisch), a coalition of approximately 50 environmental, leftist and anti-gentrification organisations that calls for a democratic, ecologically oriented and socially just 'citizens' utility'. The second is an energy cooperative, Citizen Energy Berlin (BürgerEnergie Berlin), that is at least partly owned by a collective of consumers. Pressure from both organisations has succeeded in changing the city government's policy, which in its current red–red–green complexion has established a small publicly owned energy utility in direct competition with the incumbent Vattenfall. This utility—Berlin Energie—is designed to be more accountable not only to local politicians but also to local energy consumers.

While restricting attention to this ongoing experiment in urban energy democracy would be revealing enough about how accountability is being framed and institutionalised today, it would say nothing about the historical context of energy accountability in the city. What makes Berlin interesting in this context are the different kinds of energy transition it has witnessed during its turbulent recent history. In the course of the past 100 years, Berlin has experienced political regimes of unparalleled range—from democratic to fascist to state-socialist—that each tried to mould urban energy policy in their own image. It is these multiple energy transitions, rather than the one, low carbon energy transition of today, which are the empirical focus of this chapter. The task is to compare the current with earlier phases of energy transition (*in senso lato*) in order to reveal how accountability has been variously invoked and what practices of legitimation have been enrolled to justify action.

The challenges of this venture are considerable. Apart from investigating energy transitions very different to the one pursued today, the societal norms framing both form and content of legitimacy (cf. Bäckstrand et al. 2018) underwent massive shifts during the course of the twentieth century. Accountability under National Socialism was not about the government serving the people, but the people serving *Führer* and *Volk*. In East Germany, the Socialist Unity Party established itself as the steward of the working class to which all citizens should pay obeisance. These extreme examples illustrate how much accountability and legitimacy are political constructs of their time, and indeed, of specific places. Although focusing on such undemocratic regimes could be instructive, this chapter instead selects examples of urban energy transitions drawn from Berlin's more democratically constituted governance systems, in order to generate findings of greater relevance to most contexts today. Three periods of transition have been chosen: (1) creating model municipal energy utilities for the new Greater Berlin in the 1920s, (2) sustaining energy autarky in an isolated West Berlin during the Cold War and (3) democratising urban energy governance in the city today. As argued later, they constitute cases of the politics of distribution, protection and representation, respectively.

4.2 What Crises of Accountability Are Being Maintained or Challenged?

The crisis of accountability in 1920s Berlin revolved around who should be responsible for supplying the burgeoning metropolitan area with public services, including electricity and gas. Prior to 1920, Berlin was geographically minute, surrounded by powerful bourgeois-led municipalities that had successfully resisted amalgamation, thanks to the restrictive suffrage in Prussia. The large cities around Berlin each had their own energy utilities, which they zealously protected. The German revolution of 1918–1919 and the introduction of universal suffrage opened the floodgates for socialist schemes that were geared to substantiate the promise of democracy with more equitable and affordable public services for all. The creation of Greater Berlin in 1920 marked a milestone of this kind. Amalgamating seven cities, 59 smaller municipalities and 27 landed estates, the new Berlin grew 12-fold in size. It incorporated all existing municipal energy companies into its own electricity and gas utilities (Bewag and Gasag), which were, henceforth, entrusted with implementing territorial unification by means of uniform service standards, tariffs and working conditions. To the new government of Greater Berlin, it was of critical importance to have a single utility accountable to a single city authority in the provision of power or gas services. Equally important was the provision of electricity and gas produced by the city's own utilities. This involved resisting persistent approaches by the major national energy providers of the day, Reichselektrowerke A.G. and Ruhrgas A.G., to supply the capital as part of their own programmes of territorial expansion and system centralisation (Fig. 4.1).

In West Berlin of the 1970s, a very different crisis of accountability emerged around the city's energy provision. Ever since the Berlin blockade of 1948/1949 and the subsequent political division of the city, West Berlin had sought to minimise dependence on East Germany and East Berlin by generating its own electricity and producing its own (town) gas. This strategy of urban energy autarky required a huge number of power and gas plants to be built within the city limits, but this was tolerated—indeed, celebrated—by West Berlin residents throughout the 1950s and 1960s as a symbol of defiance of the 'insular city'. Decisions by the city's power utility to build ever more generating capacity were not questioned for fear of appearing to undermine West Berlin's very existence. By the 1970s, however, popular resistance to the serious environmental and public health hazards posed by continuous infrastructure expansion—especially to the city's air quality and ecosystems—was posing a massive threat to the compact of non-accountability between utility and citizen. The more the energy utilities insisted on the need for additional plants to keep West Berlin functioning, the more the protestors questioned the fun-

4 HISTORICISING ACCOUNTABILITY: BERLIN'S ENERGY TRANSITIONS   45

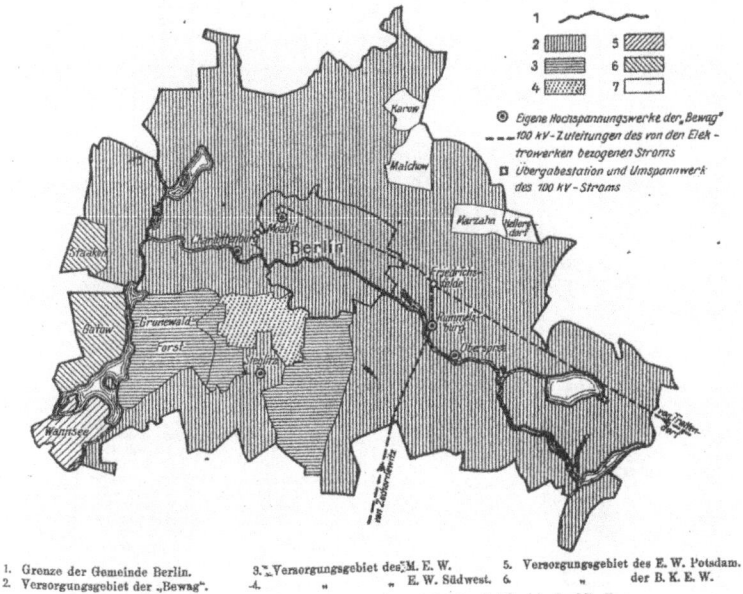

1. Grenze der Gemeinde Berlin.   3. Versorgungsgebiet des M. E. W.   5. Versorgungsgebiet des E. W. Potsdam.
2. Versorgungsgebiet der „Bewag".   4. "   "   E. W. Südwest.   6.   "   "   der B. K. E. W.

Fig. 4.1 Map showing size of Berlin prior to 1920 (marked core area) and territory of municipalised power utilities by 1925 (vertically striped area). (Source: Bruno Thierbach, 1925, Die gegenwärtige Versorgung der Stadt Berlin und der Provinz Brandenburg mit elektrischer Arbeit. *Elektrotechnische Zeitschrift, 46*(39), 1465)

damental assumptions on which the call for increased capacity was based. The issue came to a head in 1976–1977 over a decision by the city government and its power utility to build a new 600-Mega Watt power plant in the middle of one of the city's remaining forests. Massive protests and prolonged court cases resulted in the planned power plant being stopped, but not before it had been revealed to the public how both Bewag and the city government were prepared to ride roughshod over legal constraints and societal norms in order to achieve their common goal. Bewag's public image never really recovered from the damage this affront to public accountability caused amongst the population (Mielke and Weiß 1977). The case of the rejected power plant became a milestone of energy governance in Germany (Fig. 4.2).

Fig. 4.2 Protest camp against the planned power plant in Spandau Forest, 1976. (Source: Landesarchiv Berlin, F Rep 290, No. 0194-662)

Today's accountability crisis revolves around the ownership and control of the city's energy systems. The renewal of the concession agreements for the electricity grid and gas network in 2014 provided a window of opportunity for the two grassroots initiatives—the Berlin Energy Roundtable and Citizen Energy Berlin—to challenge the position of the incumbent utilities: Vattenfall and Gasag. Whilst the Roundtable has campaigned for the city to take over the electricity concession in one form or another, the cooperative has sought to take it on itself in partnership with others. A very public contestation has emerged between Vattenfall and its opponents over the future of Berlin's power grid. Vattenfall has argued that only it possesses the experience and expertise necessary to run a complex electricity system. The civil society organisations have countered that only an accountable municipal utility can deliver on policy targets for renewable energy and decarbonisation. The dispute landed in the courts and was only resolved—in favour of the new municipal utility Berlin Energie—in March 2019 (Fig. 4.3).

Fig. 4.3 Campaign poster of the Berlin Energy Roundtable for the 2013 referendum, reading 'Our municipal utility, our power grid, our Berlin'. (Source: http://www.berliner-energietisch.net/materialien)

4.3 How Do Environmental Governance Scholars Characterise the Case?

The story of Berlin's energy policy in the 1920s has been told only by the author, and to date only from selective perspectives. These perspectives have highlighted interest in balancing electricity load curves with demand management measures (Moss 2014) and the rise and fall of alternative energy technologies in the interwar years (Moss 2016).

The impact of political division on West Berlin's energy infrastructures and utilities was analysed initially by the political scientist Richard Merritt in the 1960s, but not with respect to environmental issues (Merritt 1968). The author of this chapter has explored how division nurtured a strategy of spatial reorientation and self-dependence of energy provision around the insular city (Moss 2009) that largely failed to entertain options for saving energy or using it more efficiently (Moss 2014).

By contrast, in Berlin today, there is considerable academic interest in initiatives to reform energy governance and reconfigure energy infrastructures (Becker et al. 2015, 2017; Blanchet 2015). What captivates these environmental governance scholars is the novel kind of collective control and accountability being advanced by the two social movements. Remunicipalisation, to these initiatives, means much more than returning a privatised utility to municipal ownership. It is about creating a wholly new kind of utility that is transparent to public scrutiny, open to joint decision-making by consumers and obliged by protocol to serve the public interest in keeping energy affordable and protecting the climate. This agenda is, as recent research reveals (Becker et al. 2015), broadening the scope of debate on energy governance in the city and undermining the previously unchallenged hegemony of the incumbent providers, notably Vattenfall.

4.4 What Practices of Legitimation Appear to Be at Play in Empirical Work?

In the 1920s, the core issue of legitimacy was creating uniform and affordable public services for the enlarged municipal entity of Greater Berlin. This had been the principal rationale for expanding the city's boundaries; after 1920, it needed to be put into practice. Municipal politicians never tired of emphasising the importance of the city's own energy (and water) utilities as instruments to this end. Practices enrolled to deliver the promise came in three forms: first, unitary tariffs across the territories of the newly united utilities (if not the whole city); second, uniform service standards for access, supply and maintenance; and third, fair and equal wages for employees across the city. These improvements to public services provided the justification for massive investments in urban infrastructure. The argument of uniform and fair services for Greater Berlin was mobilised repeatedly to rally local support for building state-of-the-art power stations (e.g., the Klingenberg plant) and experimenting with innovative technologies (e.g., heat storage for rapid power generation). The revenues generated from growing electricity sales, in particular, were used not only to fund these capital investments but also to support the beleaguered city budget, especially during the hyperinflation of 1922–1923 and depression during 1929–1933. The legitimacy of this policy of welfare expansionism did not go unchallenged. During the 1920s, the local Communist Party (KPD) criticised rising tariffs for hitting the poor hardest. Far more serious was the campaign launched by the Reichsbank President Hjalmar Schacht against the foreign loans used to fund much of Berlin's new energy infrastructure. By 1931, this culminated in the forced sale of most of the city's shares in Bewag to national and international energy conglomerates as a stop-gap measure to reduce the city's burgeoning debt.

In West Berlin during the Cold War, security was the overriding argument used to legitimise urban energy policy. Successive city governments and utility directors proclaimed, when any network expansion was planned, that failing to act would jeopardise the local economy and undermine West Berlin's capacity to provide its own electricity and gas. With the backing of the three Western Allied powers, high security standards were built into West Berlin's energy systems. These were epitomised by two core practices: first, storing sufficient reserves of primary energy (coal and oil) to power the city for at least three months and, second, creating a cascade of generating capacity capable of avoiding power outages even in the event that the largest generating block failed. The massive capital investments required for this security-oriented strategy did not need legitimising locally as they were heavily subsidised by the West German government. It was only in the 1970s, when fresh expansionist plans confronted an emergent environmentalist movement, that these practices of legitimation for West Berlin as an 'electricity island' were challenged seriously. For the first time, alternative models for energy provision in West Berlin were advanced by academics, activists and consultants. These revolved around reducing the need for new generating plant by promoting energy saving, using energy more efficiently (e.g., with small-scale co-generation), and, latterly, importing electricity from East German power plants upgraded with West German technology. These measures were deliberately framed to delegitimise the dominant narrative of build-and-supply.

The current conflict over Berlin's energy future is characterised by competing claims to legitimacy. On the one hand, the incumbent energy utilities (primarily Vattenfall, but also Gasag) present themselves to the public as the experts who, by virtue of their long-standing experience in running Berlin's energy systems, are the sole actors capable of managing the power grid and gas network. Technical expertise, track record and financial viability are the arguments they mobilise to justify their claims and belittle their competitors. On the other hand, the social movements campaigning for their kind of accountable remunicipalisation argue that it is precisely this reliance on traditional management criteria that is blocking attempts in the city to reduce energy use, cut carbon emissions and promote renewable sources of energy. They are advancing a very different logic of legitimacy which targets global sustainability and local accountability. Significantly, they have managed to induce a shift in city government policy, from supporting the incumbent utilities to embracing a new municipal utility and a strategy of decarbonising the city's energy systems.

4.5 What Interventions Could Enable Sustainable Outcomes Under Transition?

Assessing historical examples in terms of sustainability norms is highly problematic, since sustainability—as currently understood—was not then an issue. Past interventions to reconfigure urban energy systems were made in the name of other overarching principles prevalent at the time, such as social equality or political security. What this brief foray into the past has revealed is, first, that crises of accountability over energy are not new. They have accompanied the emergence, consolidation and adaptation of energy systems since their early beginnings. Second, we have illustrated that what accountability can mean, how it is invoked, to what ends and through what mechanisms varies hugely according to particular contexts of time and space. What passes without arousing public disapproval in one context can be highly controversial in another. This prompts us to pause and reflect, when recommending practices of legitimation or modes of accountability governance, on what temporality might mean for their shelf-life and future-proofing. Today's accountability fix should not become tomorrow's accountability trap (Kramarz and Park 2017). Finally, the examples drawn from Berlin's history have shown how processes of legitimising energy transitions are inextricably bound up in much wider societal concerns, such as—in our three cases—the politics of distribution, protection and representation. Efforts to institutionalise sustainable energy transitions would, it follows, be well advised to heed, enrol or resist concurrent movements that are likely to influence—one way or another—the viability of a particular preferred pathway (Bouzarovski and Haarstad 2018).

References

Bäckstrand, K., Zelli, F., & Schleifer, P. (2018). The legitimacy and accountability in polycentric climate governance. In A. Jordan, D. Huitema, H. van Asselt, & K. J. Forster (Eds.), *Governing climate change: Polycentricity in action* (pp. 338–356). Cambridge: Cambridge University Press.

Becker, S., Beveridge, R., & Naumann, M. (2015). Reconfiguring energy provision in Berlin. Commoning between compromise and contestation. In M. Dellenbaugh, M. Kip, M. Bieniok, A. K. Müller, & M. Schwegmann (Eds.), *Urban commons. Moving beyond state and market* (pp. 196–213). Basel: Birkhäuser.

Becker, S., Naumann, M., & Moss, T. (2017). Between coproduction and commons: Understanding initiatives to reclaim urban energy provision in Berlin and Hamburg. *Urban Research and Practice, 10*(1), 63–85.

Blanchet, T. (2015). Struggle over energy transition in Berlin: How do grassroots initiatives affect local energy policy-making? *Energy Policy, 78*, 246–254.

Bouzarovski, S., & Haarstad, H. (2018). Rescaling low-carbon transformations: Towards a relational ontology. *Transactions of the Institute of British Geographers*. https://doi.org/10.1111/tran.12275

Kramarz, T., & Park, S. (2017). Introduction: The politics of environmental accountability. *Review of Policy Research, 34*(1), 1–4.

Merritt, R. L. (1968). Political division and municipal services in postwar Berlin. In J. D. Montgomery & A. O. Hirschman (Eds.), *Public policy* (pp. 165–198). Cambridge, MA: Harvard University Press.

Mielke, H.-J., & Weiß, H. (1977). Kraftwerksbau im Landschaftsschutzgebiet Spandauer Forst. *Berliner Naturschutzblätter, 21*(60/61), 251–255, 286–288.

Moss, T. (2009). Divided city, divided infrastructures: Securing energy and water services in postwar Berlin. *Journal of Urban History, 35*(7), 923–942.

Moss, T. (2014). Socio-technical change and the politics of urban infrastructure: Managing energy in Berlin between dictatorship and democracy. *Urban Studies, 51*(7), 1432–1448.

Moss, T. (2016). Discarded surrogates, modified traditions, welcome complements: The chequered careers of alternative technologies in Berlin's infrastructure systems. *Social Studies of Science, 46*(4), 559–582.

Sareen, S. (2019). Five easy pieces: Legitimation at work in cases related to energy transitions. In *Enabling sustainable energy transitions: Practices of legitimation and accountable governance*. London: Palgrave Macmillan.

Open Access This chapter is licensed under the terms of the Creative Commons Attribution 4.0 International License (http://creativecommons.org/licenses/by/4.0/), which permits use, sharing, adaptation, distribution and reproduction in any medium or format, as long as you give appropriate credit to the original author(s) and the source, provide a link to the Creative Commons licence and indicate if changes were made.

The images or other third party material in this chapter are included in the chapter's Creative Commons licence, unless indicated otherwise in a credit line to the material. If material is not included in the chapter's Creative Commons licence and your intended use is not permitted by statutory regulation or exceeds the permitted use, you will need to obtain permission directly from the copyright holder.

CHAPTER 5

A Few Reflections on Accountability

Christian Lund

Abstract Accountability is a form of communication between people and institutions where one is held to account by the other. Parts of the scholarship distinguish between upward and downward accountability. Upward accountability would involve acknowledgement of an authority to sanction or validate operations or claims, whereas downward accountability refers to the institution of authority being responsible to the general public for their actions. While the directionality of accountability is important, a case from Indonesia suggests that they may indeed be co-constitutive. By deliberately and publicly complying with the idea of state land ownership, and by being selective about what institutions represent 'the state', the farmers used their upward accountability to produce downward accountability in terms of recognition of their rights. The farmers exploited the separation of powers in their attempt to gain a new visibility.

Keywords Accountability • Recognition • Social contract • Indonesia

---

C. Lund (✉)
Department of Food and Resource Economics, University of Copenhagen, Copenhagen, Denmark
e-mail: clund@ifro.ku.dk

> *Akk ja, retten, retten; hva hjelper det at du har retten når du ikke har noen makt?*
> *[Ah yes, rights, rights; what does it help that you have rights when you do not have any power?]*
> —Fru Stockmann in "En Folkefiende" (Henrik Ibsen *1882*)

5.1 Accountability and Social Contract

'Everyone realizes how praiseworthy it is for a prince to honour his word and to be straightforward rather than crafty in his dealings; nonetheless contemporary experience shows that princes who have achieved great things have been those who have given their words lightly, who have known how to trick men with their cunning, and who, in the end, have overcome those abiding by honest principles. ... There are two ways of fighting: by law or by force. The first way is natural to men, and the second to beasts. ... a prince must know how to act according to the nature of both, ... he cannot survive otherwise' (Machiavelli 1961: 99). The candour of this sixteenth-century Secretary and Second Chancellor to the Florentine Republic is refreshing. Moreover, his book is probably among the most concise of the 30,000+ offerings from Amazon.com when you punch in 'accountability'. Google.com suggests a menu of 128,000,000 items in less than 0.3 seconds. Power's interest in power is obvious and unabashedly stated as a fact by Machiavelli. It is not cloaked in bureaucratic niceties and unrealistic assumptions about the common good, and as a self-help book for politicians, *The Prince* remains unsurpassed.

The principle of power stands in tension with the principles of its division. Montesquieu's idea about the separation of powers (1977), Locke's suggestion to rein in tyranny (1980) and Rousseau's doctrine that government must rest on a social contract (1977) all recognise the truths of the drive for power described by Machiavelli, and they all share a concern for the danger of power's concentration. Each, in their own way, suggests checks and balances in the system of government, and within the European history of enlightenment, they may be the first to articulate concern with power's accountability. While Montesquieu focuses on the mutual accountability among institutions of power, Locke and Rousseau direct their attention to the relationship between the governors and the governed. In a nutshell, Rousseau argues that government (or the sovereign) derives its legitimacy to govern from the power freely surrendered by the governed in a social contract where the government is elected by the people as a representation of the general will and is therefore accountable to it. The social contract rests on an understanding of mutual recognition between state and citizenry when the population is subject to the laws of the state, and the state is subject to popular political franchise. This figure, however, is as abstract as it is beautiful.

In actual societies, and maybe especially in post-colonial societies, the number of institutions that operate in the name of the state approaches the infinite, and citizenship itself is fraught with intersecting qualifications derived from gender, race and caste, as well as class, creed and conviction (Lund 2016). In terms of social contract, this raises the question: as what are the contractual partners recognised? Who is visible to what institution, and what institution commands authority in what domain? A way to access the empirical complexity may be on offer from a broad philosophical tradition that takes recognition as a fundamental human expression of acknowledgement of the 'other' (Arendt 1973; Fraser 2001; Honneth 1996; Taylor 1989, 1994). Honneth, in particular, talks about visibility among and between actors, and I believe it can be extended to institutions. Social contracts of recognition require mutual visibility between actors and institutions. Actors must have a social, legal, fiscal or cultural presence visible and acknowledged by an institution, and the institution must legitimately appear capable of providing the desired recognition of a claim (Weber 1958). What actors *are* therefore comprises not individual features but relational, politically visible attributes. So, who is the actor? A tax payer, a peasant, or a red troublemaker, an indigene, a businessman, or a person without paper? And who defines the categories? And, similarly, we must ask what is the specific institution? Executive, legislative or judiciary, or can it be re-purposed to fit the task at hand?

This may seem a somewhat grandiose introduction to what is often seen as a governance routine question. I, however, suggest that any granular analysis of relations of accountability (Latour 2009; Strathern 2000) could do worse than to focus on power, its separation, the mutual recognition of claims and authority, and the representation of rights subjects (or citizens) and government. In the following, I present a summary case from my work in Indonesia to illustrate relations of mutual recognition (Lund 2020). While the case itself relates only indirectly to energy transitions, it surfaces concerns of conflict over land and forest that are germane to any discussion of energy transitions, not least given Indonesia's participation in a global carbon forestry programme (cf. Hein 2018).

5.2 Visibility and Recognition in Indonesia

Harumandala is a village in West Java in Indonesia. The village consists of several sub-villages or *kampungs* and is located within a steeply sloped landscape. After independence in 1945, the area saw many confrontations over land control between the Indonesian army and Communist groupings. The confrontations died down around 1961. The area was formally under the territorial authority of the Provincial Forestry Service of West Java, and the entire area was classified as 'forest'. However, most of the area was, in fact, populated with villages and *kampungs*. Generally, people were farming paddy rice on terraces, as well as different crops on forest plots. In practice, people could clear land for paddy rice farming and other activities without much interference from the authorities. No legal rights ensured people's access to land, but the Provincial Forestry Service tolerated farming and people regarded the land as their own.

In 1978, all the forestland controlled by the Provincial Forestry Service in West Java—close to a million hectares—was transferred to the State Forestry Corporation which had previously operated only in Central and East Java (Peluso 1992; Rachman 2011). As a parastatal institution with its own uniformed 'forest police', and as a part of an authoritarian regime, the State Forest Corporation was inaccessible to ordinary people seeking to argue or negotiate their case. The Corporation established boundaries to create teak and mahogany plantations, clearing the area of any farmed fields that might be in the way. Moreover, it started to act as a landlord charging rent for the fields people cultivated within the area. These farmers thus became tenants of the Corporation, and in the process consolidated its land control. The rent consisted of 33 per cent of the villagers' rice production: There was no legal basis for this rent, and it was never registered as official income of the company.

During the late 1990s, agrarian protest became ever more frequent as the Suharto regime spiralled into decline and crisis. Different social organisations, groups and movements were formed in a period of political transformation in Indonesia. Democratisation and decentralisation appeared to offer opportunities to transform society, and not least the agrarian structures. The protests were accompanied by land occupations, where farmers seized land from state forests or private and government plantations. The occupations were controversial. On the one hand, they were condoned and even hailed by popular movements as the realisation of the long-awaited land reform. On the other hand, government condemned occupations as theft (Lucas and Warren 2013).

In 2006, farmers and their organisation, Sundanese Peasant's Movement (*Serikat Petani Pasundan* [SPP]) realised that the Forest Corporation's collection of rent was illegal, and actions towards land reform could be launched. The first move was to refuse to pay rent to the State Forest Corporation. Instead, people paid 10,000 Rupiah (equivalent to a couple of US dollars) per month to SPP and turned their presence into a land occupation.

The West Java police commander and the Corporation director in Jakarta decided to re-establish the Corporation's control over the occupied forestlands by launching a so-called forest security operation funded by the Ministry of Forestry. The operation was preceded by a joint reconnaissance for forest security control conducted in March 2008. The State Forest Corporation provided the reconnaissance team with a detailed map that indicated 'forest security disturbances'. The team reported that approximately 290 hectares of forestland were occupied by nearly 1600 villagers from four villages within the district.

Three months after this reconnaissance report was issued, the West Java Police, the Ministry of Forestry and the State Forest Corporation launched a forest security operation. The main objectives of the operation were to re-establish control of the state forestland and to evict the people occupying it. The operation invoked the military terms, Security Operation and Dangerous Area, echoing the Suharto era. Similarly, the use of terms like 'illegal loggers', 'illegal occupiers', 'subversive' and 'anti-state' established an association between land occupation and organised crime. For a country the size of Indonesia, 290 hectares may seem trivial, but the significance of a successful occupation could be earth-shattering, literally breaking new ground for further challenges to state authority.

Officers from the State Forest Corporation and the Provincial Police came to Harumandala and its six *kampungs*, and more than 300 police officers set up camp and began to prepare the evictions. The operation was initiated by a ceremony, in which the police commander, the head of the Corporation's forest police and representatives from the local government Forestry and Plantation Unit went through the objectives of the operation—namely, to find evidence of illegal logging, to evict illegal occupants and destroy their farms and to remove any illegal construction from the area. First, the police and the Corporation officers made house-to-house searches for timber. Then, fields were ravaged and houses were burnt to the ground. Some houses were left standing, but the police marked them with chalk 'This house must be destroyed by yourself', or 'This house and land is not yours but the property of the state'. Finally, the police forced the villagers to sign a statement in which they renounced their membership of SPP and declared they would never join again. It is well worth recalling that this took place almost a decade into the post-New Order democratic era, and that SPP was a legal organisation.

After the police operation, people resumed the cultivation of their plots within the area but moved to *kampungs* outside of the State Forest Corporation area for a couple of years. By 2010, people had begun to move back to the abandoned *kampung* of Pasir Pilar within the Corporation-controlled area. People reconstructed their houses; and within six months, some 34 families had re-established themselves in the *kampung*. The local SPP chapter drew up a map of the area, registering each plot and its owner.

The State Forest Corporation contacted the settlement, but now with a new approach. They announced a planting ceremony of mahogany trees and invited villagers to witness. An area was cleared and 1000 seedlings were planted in rows. Each row was publicly named after a government institution. Thus, the first row was named, 'the row of the provincial governor', the next, 'the row of the police commander', 'the row of the Indonesian army' and so on. The intention, no doubt, was to impress upon the people of the area that these resources belonged to and were under the protection of the entire government structure of Indonesia. The State Forest Corporation had the whole episode filmed. The following night, however, all 1000 mahogany seedlings were uprooted. People remained in their *kampungs* on the disputed land; they resumed farming their plots and rice fields, and they continued *not* to pay rent to the State Forest Corporation. They were not beholden to the Corporation or the Indonesian government for their land rights. Instead, they held land thanks to 'the republic' of SPP, with the opportunities and dangers this implied.

As people moved back into their settlement, they asked the official local territorial administration—the village office—for new ID cards that would reflect this change. This was done. By that token, the settlement became an official *kampung*, situated within the area that the State Forest Corporation claimed to control as forest. Moreover, as people registered to vote for the 2014 elections, officials from the sub-district would visit all houses and place an official government sticker on the door with the name of the voter, and place of residence—their new official *kampung*.

The system of payment to SPP remained provisory, but with the smallholders' return to the contested lands in 2010, all *kampungs* of Harumandala also began to contribute to the Village Office to the tune of 1,000,000 Rupiah annually. At first, the Village Office, its mayor and its elected parliamentarians were reluctant to receive the funds. They were unsure whether they were entitled to recover tax, and what it would mean to accept it, but after some negotiation the Village Government of Harumandala accepted the money at a public ceremony. While still perceived as illegal occupants by the State Forest Corporation, smallholders were also beginning to be seen as taxpaying, voting, registered, Indonesian citizens. Their 'contribution', or tax, established a new substantive relationship between them as landholders and the formal structures of the Indonesian government at its lowest level, the Village Office. It remains to be seen what this new relationship represents. One might argue that this relationship not only established the SPP landholders as owners of property in the eyes of the Village Office; it also established the Village Office as a public authority on questions of property in land that was classified as forest. As the smallholders made claims to resources, they also invoked public authority in the Village Office. Tax collection attributed to it governing capacity and the authority to validate land claims. This may, eventually, put the Village Office in competition with other statutory institutions.

5.3 Reflections

Accountability is a form of communication between people and institutions where one is held to account by the other. Parts of the scholarship distinguish between upward and downward accountability (Fox 2018). Upward accountability would involve acknowledgement of an authority to sanction or validate operations or claims, whereas downward accountability refers to the institution of authority being responsible to the general public for their actions. While the directionality of accountability is important, the case from Indonesia suggests that they may indeed be co-constitutive. When the villagers shifted from payment of rent as tenants to one part of government (the Corporation), to payment of a community tax to another part of government (the lowest level assembly and government), they not only morphed from undercover tenants to enfranchised citizens, but also invoked capacities in the village government that it had not had before. By deliberately and publicly complying with the idea of state land ownership, and by being selective about what institutions represent 'the state', the farmers used their upward accountability to produce downward accountability in terms of recognition of their rights. The farmers exploited the separation (or multi-location) of powers in their attempt to gain a new visibility.

The power to define subjectivity—to define it for oneself or to impose it on others—is essential in any relation of accountability, because it defines actors' visibility and, consequently, the possible fields of engagement and contracts of recognition. The Ministry of Forestry and the State Forest Corporation had been long established as the consequential authorities holding the power to define who is entitled and who is a thief. Yet, the active re-orientation by the farmers re-drew the map of mutual recognition. To be sure, this relied on people's capacity and political space to recast themselves as responsible citizens and rights subjects rather than passively being defined as subversive squatters and enemies of the state.

Actors have different capacities to engage in the field of politics. However, the field itself is a result of engagement, not only by the powerful but also by those who resist and want change. This desire for change—expressed through local politics of land—may, in E.P. Thompson's words (1963: 12), be foolhardy. But the desire for change defines agency and is hardly inconsequential for the relations between people and institutions.

References

Arendt, H. (1973 [1951]). *The origins of totalitarianism*. New York: Harcourt Brace Janovich.
Fox, J. (2018). The political construction of accountability keywords. *IDS Bulletin*, 49(2), 65–80.
Fraser, N. (2001). Recognition without ethics? *Theory, Culture and Society*, 18(2–3), 21–42.
Hein, J. I. (2018). *Political ecology of REDD+ in Indonesia: Agrarian conflicts and forest carbon*. Abingdon and New York: Routledge.
Honneth, A. (1996). *The struggle for recognition. The moral grammar of social conflict*. Cambridge: Polity Press.
Ibsen, H. (1882). *En Folkefiende* [An Enemy of the People]. Oslo: Gyldendal.
Latour, B. (2009). *The making of law: An ethnography of the Conseil d'Etat*. Cambridge: Polity.
Locke, J. (1980 [1689]). *Two treatises of government*. Cambridge: Cambridge University Press.

Lucas, A., & Warren, C. (Eds.). (2013). *Land for the people: The state and Agrarian conflict in Indonesia.* Columbus, OH: Ohio University Press.
Lund, C. (2016). Rule and rupture. State formation through the production of property and citizenship. *Development and Change, 47*(6), 1199–1228.
Lund, C. (2020). *Nine-tenths of the law. Enduring dispossession in Indonesia.* New Haven, Yale University Press.
Machiavelli, N. (1961 [ca. 1532]). *The Prince.* London: Penguin.
Montesquieu, C.-L. (1977 [1748]). *The spirit of the laws.* Berkeley: University of California Press.
Peluso, N. L. (1992). *Rich forests, poor people. Resource control and resistance in Java.* Berkeley: University of California Press.
Rachman, N. F. (2011). *The resurgence of land reform policy and Agrarian movements in Indonesia.* PhD thesis, University of California, Berkeley.
Rousseau, J.-J. (1977 [1762]). *Du contrat social.* Paris: Éditions du Seuil.
Strathern, M. (2000). *Audit cultures. Anthropological studies in accountability, ethics and the academy.* London: Routledge.
Taylor, C. (1989). *Sources of the self. The making of modern identity.* Cambridge: Cambridge University Press.
Taylor, C. (1994). The politics of recognition. In A. Gutmann (Ed.), *Multiculturalism* (pp. 107–148). Princeton, NJ: Princeton University Press.
Thompson, E. P. (1963). *The making of the English working class.* London: Penguin.
Weber, M. (1958). *From Max Weber. Essays in sociology* (H. Gerth & C. W. Mills, Eds.). New York: Oxford University Press.

Open Access This chapter is licensed under the terms of the Creative Commons Attribution 4.0 International License (http://creativecommons.org/licenses/by/4.0/), which permits use, sharing, adaptation, distribution and reproduction in any medium or format, as long as you give appropriate credit to the original author(s) and the source, provide a link to the Creative Commons licence and indicate if changes were made.

The images or other third party material in this chapter are included in the chapter's Creative Commons licence, unless indicated otherwise in a credit line to the material. If material is not included in the chapter's Creative Commons licence and your intended use is not permitted by statutory regulation or exceeds the permitted use, you will need to obtain permission directly from the copyright holder.

CHAPTER 6

Do Climate Targets Matter? The Accountability of Target-setting in Urban Climate and Energy Policy

Håvard Haarstad

Abstract Climate-related targets abound, but are they important drivers of policy action? Given the apparent gap between ambitious targets and concrete actions to reach them, climate-related targets can easily be seen as representative of a crisis of accountability. At the same time, this chapter argues, there are practices of legitimation at work that can help overcome this crisis, and translate abstract and arbitrary targets into concrete policy implementation. Norway's Zero Growth Objective in transport policy represents a case of this. From its first formulation as a target around 2006 and until 2019, it has materialised as a "hard" target shaping funding streams and concrete policy interventions, and most likely, emission levels. Under certain conditions, abstract targets play important roles in legitimating transition policy.

Keywords Climate targets • Metrics • Implementation • Transport • Accountability

---

H. Haarstad (✉)
Department of Geography, Centre for Climate and Energy Transformation, University of Bergen, Bergen, Norway
e-mail: Havard.Haarstad@uib.no

6.1 Introduction

A casual observer of the official fight against climate change may get the impression that it is primarily about setting quantitative *targets* for emissions reduction. Who has committed to the 2 °C target? How did the world's leaders discuss the 1.5 °C target at the latest high-level meeting? Who has the most ambitious target for cuts in CO_2-emissions, or for growth of renewables? It may seem that setting targets is what climate policy *consists of*.

Cities have certainly entered this game. Since the city council of Freiburg in 1996 decided to cut 25% of its CO_2-emissions by 2010 (Leal and Azevedo 2016), cities all over the world have set ambitious and celebrated targets for a range of climate-related challenges such as emission cuts, renewable energy use, energy efficiency, electric vehicle uptake and growth of bicycle use and infrastructure. More than 7700 local and regional authorities have signed up to the Covenant of Mayors and thereby committed themselves to achieving and exceeding the EU climate and energy targets. The Covenant of Mayors initiative is one of many examples of how governance entities are organising themselves in networks rallying around particular targets.

The key question is, of course, what all this targeting and goal-setting means for actual climate policy. From a bird's-eye view of urban climate policy, it is tempting to conclude that these targets are not followed by policies that may realistically ensure that they are met.

It is not that cities are ignoring the climate challenge—on the contrary, many commentators view cities as leading the fight against climate change (Rosenzweig et al. 2010). Yet, considering the drastic transformations that many of these targets involve—for example, 72 cities have committed to the C40 network's Deadline 2020 programme of cutting CO_2 emissions in line with the Paris Agreement—one might suspect that the current practices of target-setting are unconnected to any realistic programme of delivering on what they promise. It would follow that the ambitious target-setting are exercises of vanity, wherein cities compete for the most ambitious targets but not the most transformative policies. And thereby that targets help politicians appear to be doing something when they are actually not. In this sense, we are faced with a *crisis of accountability* in which politicians can capitalise on climate-sensitive rhetoric but escape being held to account for that same rhetoric.

At the same time, the question of what all this targeting and goal-setting means for actual climate policy may also generate a different set of answers. What if target-setting is more important and substantive than it looks? Even if not all the rhetoric is translated into substantive policy, could there be ways in which target-setting actually percolates into substantive policy-making practices?

This chapter reflects on the nature of target-setting, focusing in particular on climate and energy policy in cities. I recognise that target-setting is a political-rhetorical practice, and therefore not necessarily representative of actual processes of transformation—we should expect a lot of hot air. But I aim to go beyond the readily-at-hand analysis that suggests targets are simply vanity exercises without practical implications, and to look deeper at the ways in which target-setting may in fact "trickle" up and down in governance systems and—in a gradual way—facilitate transitions.

6.2 Climate Governance as Political-rhetorical Practice

Scholars have often taken a sceptical view of official climate discourses, including their ambitious targets. It is common to see this discourse as evading or purposely obfuscating the conflicts of interest and difficult choices involved in meeting the climate challenge. Swyngedouw (2010), for example, holds that the policy discourse on climate change is characteristic of the "post-political condition." He has argued that reduction of CO_2 emissions is inserted into a vast techno-managerial apparatus, "ranging from new eco-technologies of a variety of kinds to unruly complex managerial and institutional configurations, with a view to producing a socio-ecological fix *to make sure nothing really changes*" (p. 220, italics mine).

In other words, instead of addressing the underlying substantive political challenges, conflicts of interests and difficult trade-offs of climate-friendly transformation, official climate discourse manages to produce a set of interventions that harmonise with economic growth, the fossil economy, and so on, thus perpetuating business-as-usual practices. This is why climate governance is, in the words of Methmann, an "empty signifier"—it serves to integrate climate protection into the global hegemonic order "without changing the basic social structures of the world economy" (Methmann 2010: 348). Hegemonic governmental agents have been able to remake almost any policy—free trade, continued oil exploration, economic growth—into being part of the solution.

A similar critique has been levelled against the entire sustainable development discourse, in a debate too vast to enter into here (but see While et al. 2010).

At the urban scale, these trade-offs and conflicts of interests may be harder to conceal. Yet even here, scholars have pointed to the contrast between rhetorical aspects of governance and substantive transformative interventions. In terms of rhetoric, cities generate and circulate high-profile stories and "best practice" narratives that highlight claims about achievements and successes (Bulkeley 2006; McCann 2011). In terms of substantive change, however, real effects may be more elusive. Grandin and Sareen (forthcoming) describe urban governance arrangements as "often characterised by voluntary action, weak institutions, non-binding commitments and uncoordinated efforts," and argue that it can be difficult to determine the substantive and enduring transformative impact of their interventions.

More concretely, researchers have also criticised the targets that cities are operating with. Leal and Azevedo (2016) reviewed the targets for local energy planning for a number of case cities, and found them to show a lack of standardisation of methodologies, "leading to a diversity that may not only hamper the comparison between different municipalities' action but also prevent a consistent assessment of their global impact." In similar vein, Kramers et al. (2013) found a wide variety of accounting methodologies, system boundaries, time frames and source of emissions included behind relatively similar targets. There is moreover limited awareness of these methodological limitations among city administrators.

In short, one can find grounds for deep scepticism against the practice of target-setting in the climate governance literature. In an abstract sense, these targets are often part of a post-political and techno-managerial climate governance discourse that simultaneously appears climate-friendly *without* addressing the underlying contradictions that produce the climate problem in the first place. At the urban level, target-setting can be seen as a part of the circulation of "best practice" and rhetorical competition to be *the most sustainable city*, while the actual commitments remain largely non-binding and voluntary.

In this sense, target-setting registers on several of the types of legitimation Sareen outlines in Chap. 2 of this book, but perhaps particularly *discursive* legitimation. These are legitimation practices that normalise particular ways of seeing, stabilising them in the public imaginary. In the worst-case scenario, targets are stabilising the idea that our decision-makers are tackling the climate challenge in an ambitious way, while actually, very little gets done.

However, what if we put aside the worst-case scenario for a moment, and consider the flip side of the coin? Is it possible that targets, even seemingly overly ambitious ones, may have real and substantive effects that contribute to a sustainable transition? Could there be mechanisms through which targets—even unrealistic ones—influence, push or nudge urban politics and processes of change? This is not to cast aside the critical perspectives outlined above, but to suggest that analogous mechanisms of legitimation may also work in the opposite direction.

6.3 METRICS THAT CAN LEGITIMATE THE SUSTAINABILITY TRANSITION

My starting point for thinking about ways targets may legitimate transitions is to consider the carrying power of numbers (or "metrics"). It is widely recognised that quantifying a phenomenon impregnates it with a particular type of force, transforming it from the particular and provincial into the language of the universal. Foucault, for instance, showed how scientific knowledge—where metrics play a central role—is the foundation for the birth of the modern state (Foucault 1991). Metrics is what we use to make the unknown *knowable*, and thereby, *governable*. Foucault's work showed how scientific knowledge advanced our ability to govern society and its individuals. Now, we are progressively using scientific knowledge to govern *nature* as well. As Jasanoff (2010) puts it, "Increasingly, however, the politics of nature occurs under the rubric of 'environment'—a domain of ideas and entities accessible only with the aid of science and technology."

In this sense, it is quite conceivable that climate targets take on a similar type of carrying power as other metrics have done in our governance of nature. Climate change is knowable and measurable in precise ways, through global aggregate temperatures traced far back in time, parts per million of CO_2 in the atmosphere, and carbon budgets, among many others. Measures to deal with climate change are also knowable and measurable in detailed ways, through percentage of rise in renewable energy uptake, energy efficiency measures, numbers of electric vehicles sold and so on. This means that policies can be assessed, scenarios can be crafted, decision-makers can—in principle—be held to account. And in the seductive ways that metrics work in governance, targets may work themselves into mind sets and documents even after they have been shed of their methodological and substantive attire.

It has been argued that due to this metrical legibility of carbon, climate change is actually more open to politicisation than the sustainable development discourse was. Sustainable development has of course also been subject to quantification (Miller 2005), but has lent itself too easily to being incorporated in the growth paradigm and neoliberal modes of governance. By contrast, argue While and co-authors (2010), the discourse of carbon control represents "a harder edge to state environmental regulation via non-negotiable target setting...". Shifting focus from the ambiguous and co-optable idea of sustainability towards the more measurable problem of carbon control, they argue, opens up for a harder type of regulation.

Carbon control may introduce a new set of values into state regulation, which could open possibilities for challenging mainstream modes of urban development in ways not possible under the sustainable development discourse (While et al. 2010). Jonas et al. (2011) suggest that the ranking of cities on the basis of carbon emissions is becoming part of the competition between cities for investment capital, headquarter locations and attraction of educated workers. In other words, carbon control and its target are becoming part of the calculus behind "rational" urban governance.

We are probably not quite there yet. But at least target-setting is becoming normalised, which in turn legitimates a whole set of practices that may advance sustainable energy transitions. The next section examines a concrete chain of events to illustrate how this may occur. Given the scope of a short chapter, this case study is cursory. Yet it seeks to identify certain *mechanisms* for how climate targets are legitimated.

The concrete case I look at traces the 2 °C target through the Norwegian Zero Growth Objective for urban transport. Within this, I am interested in how the climate problem, which has been distilled into a universal object of knowledge (as in the 2 °C target), cascades downwards in scale from the national to the local level.

6.4 Following the Target—Norway's Zero Growth Objective

Norway's *Zero Growth Objective* for transport in urban areas is a useful illustration of how climate-related targets work their way into concrete policy-making. The goal itself states that *all growth in personal traffic in the largest cities will be covered by public transport, walking and cycling*. The "zero growth" aspect implied in this is of course that there will be no growth in private car traffic.

The legitimation of the target has been incremental, and involves multiple actors with divergent interests. Still, the progression from abstract target formulation towards a tangible foundation for concrete policy implementation is traceable by examining a series of key documents over time.

The contours of the Zero Growth Objective can be traced back at least to the 2006 White Paper on Norwegian Climate Policy [Meld. St. 34, 2006–2007]. There the government put forward some initial goals for climate-related policy in the transport sector, writing that there is a "need to shift the use of transport modes towards public transport, walking and cycling." The overarching reference for this White Paper was the international 2 °C target, adopted by the Norwegian government a year prior. While the 2 °C target is somewhat arbitrary and has been a source of controversy (Randalls 2010), it is referred to here and in most climate-related Norwegian national policy documents in a way that sets the level of ambition and points to the global urgency. The 2 °C target, notwithstanding the controversy over its origins and usefulness, is providing the framing for Norwegian policy, including the Zero Growth Objective back in 2006.

That formulation—"shift the use of transport modes towards public transport, walking and cycling"—can be found in all the key national climate policy documents from then on. The 2008 Climate Accord between all parties in Parliament minus one, the 2012 White Paper on Norwegian Climate Policy, and the 2012 Climate Accord, all use that same formulation with miniscule variations. Notably, however, the context in which that formulation is placed gets increasingly concrete and binding. In the 2012 White Paper, it is actually formulated as a target ("The Government has the goal that..."). Around the same time, the National Transport Plan Working Group put forward a proposition as an official goal of Norwegian transport policy, that the large cities should have zero growth except in "public transport, walking and cycling," and simultaneously coined the

"Nullvekstmålet"—Zero Growth Objective. The leader of the Working Group has been quoted as saying "*We wanted to find a target that was easy to measure, that would be ambitious and not least reachable*" (quoted in Strand 2016).

Since then, the Zero Growth Objective has been mentioned, integrated and discussed in innumerable briefs, policy documents, talks and newspaper articles on transport policy in Norway. The way the target is formulated—with its simple quantification: "zero"—may account for some of its carrying power. And as a climate-related target, it has attained enormous success. It is an important element of the structural conditions for transport and mobility planning (Tennøy and Øksenholt 2018). We can quite concretely follow the process through which this occurs, through budget documents and funding agreements between the government and cities.

From 2014 onwards, the National Transport Plan adopted the Zero Growth Objective as the key target for transport policy in cities. The government, in launching the Urban Environment Agreements, also it was translated to a concrete agreement framework tied to a funding scheme for cities. It then transpired that the Government would negotiate with the largest cities in Norway and other regional authorities with responsibility for transport, to create "greater coherence in urban policy" by having these authorities collectively "commit to common goals written into the Urban Environment Agreements." Now, all relevant authorities are to sign a binding agreement on how to meet the Zero Growth Objective, and this agreement will be the basis for government funding for local transport.

From this point onwards, the amount of funding cities received for local transport infrastructure became tied to how well they worked towards meeting the Zero Growth Objective. This includes specific indicators that measure whether or not car traffic decreases. In 2016 and 2017, such Agreements were signed with Oslo, Trondheim, Bergen and Stavanger (Jæren); in short, the largest Norwegian cities.

Subsequently, the Zero Growth Objective has been mainstreamed and absorbed into the planning and land use regulation of the cities themselves. It is a ubiquitous condition for decision-making within the wide range of issues that affect the abilities of cities to reach the goal, such as location of housing, retail, transport infrastructure, congestion charging and much more. It introduces a simple calculus for decision-makers in cities: failure to meet the target will affect the amount of government money available in the next round of negotiations. Even beyond this, the effectiveness of the target transcends this simple calculus. It has become a standard reference point for ambitions in the climate field, and percolated into the urban policy discourse at many levels. Trends in actual traffic patterns are following suit—all cities mentioned above underwent a reduction in private car traffic in 2018 (Miljødirektoratet). Arguably, the target has contributed to normalising and routinising a way of thinking about transitions in cities that was considered highly ambitious only a few years ago.

6.5 Legitimating Sustainable Transitions

Are climate-related targets representative of a crisis of accountability, as pillars in a bureaucratic apparatus of governance that gives the appearance of climate action while little substantive change happens? Or are there mechanisms at work that translate abstract and arbitrary targets into concrete policy implementation? Most likely, a mix of these outcomes is at play. But the case of Norway's Zero Growth Objective illustrates some of the processes that legitimate and normalise an ambitious climate-related target. This involved soft mechanisms—inserting itself in the discourse on urban policy and moving its goal posts—and hard mechanisms—the conditioning of funding flows from national to local levels. To enable a sustainable energy transition, we need practices to legitimate the interventions that advance this transition. Under certain conditions, metrics and targets can play a constructive role in this.

References

Bulkeley, H. (2006). Urban sustainability: Learning from best practice? *Environment and Planning A, 38*, 1029–1044.

Foucault, M. (1991). Governmentality. In G. Burchell, C. Gordon, & P. Miller (Eds.), *The Foucault effect: Studies in governmentality* (pp. 87–104). London: Harvester Wheatsheaf.

Grandin, J., & Sareen, S. (forthcoming). What sticks? Ephemerality, permanence and urban transformation pathways. *In review*.

Jasanoff, S. (2010). A new climate for society. *Theory, Culture & Society, 27*, 233–253.

Jonas, A. E. G., Gibbs, D., & While, A. (2011). The new urban politics as a politics of carbon control. *Urban Studies, 48*, 2537–2554.

Kramers, A., Wangel, J., Johansson, S., Höjer, M., Finnveden, G., & Brandt, N. (2013). Towards a comprehensive system of methodological considerations for cities' climate targets. *Energy Policy, 62*, 1276–1287.

Leal, V., & Azevedo, I. (2016). Setting targets for local energy planning: Critical assessment and a new approach. *Sustainable Cities and Society, 26,* 421–428.

McCann, E. (2011). Urban policy mobilities and global circuits of knowledge: Towards a research agenda. *Annals of the Association of American Geographers, 101,* 107–130.

Methmann, C. P. (2010). 'Climate protection' as empty signifier: A discourse theoretical perspective on climate mainstreaming in world politics. *Millennium: Journal of International Studies, 39,* 345–372.

Miller, C. (2005). New civic epistemologies of quantification: Making sense of indicators of local and global sustainability. *Science, Technology and Human Values, 30,* 403–432.

Randalls, S. (2010). History of the 2°C climate target. *WIREs Climate Change, 1,* 598–605.

Rosenzweig, C, Solecki, W, Hammer, S. A., & Mehrotra, S. (2010) Cities lead the way in climate-change action [Comment]. *Nature, 467,* 909–911.

Strand, A. (2016, August 24). Nullvekstmålet—tiljublet, men mangelfullt utredet. *Samferdsel.*

Swyngedouw, E. (2010). Apocalypse forever? Post-political populism and the spectre of climate change. *Theory, Culture & Society, 27,* 213–232.

Tennøy, A., & Øksenholt, K. V. (2018). The impact of changed structural conditions on regional sustainable mobility planning in Norway. *Planning Theory & Practice, 19,* 93–113.

While, A., Jonas, A., & Gibbs, D. (2010). From sustainable development to carbon control: Eco-state restructuring and the politics of urban and regional development. *Transactions of the Institute of British Geographers, 35,* 76–93.

Open Access This chapter is licensed under the terms of the Creative Commons Attribution 4.0 International License (http://creativecommons.org/licenses/by/4.0/), which permits use, sharing, adaptation, distribution and reproduction in any medium or format, as long as you give appropriate credit to the original author(s) and the source, provide a link to the Creative Commons licence and indicate if changes were made.

The images or other third party material in this chapter are included in the chapter's Creative Commons licence, unless indicated otherwise in a credit line to the material. If material is not included in the chapter's Creative Commons licence and your intended use is not permitted by statutory regulation or exceeds the permitted use, you will need to obtain permission directly from the copyright holder.

CHAPTER 7

Governance and Legitimation in the Transition to Nordic Electric Mobility

Benjamin Sovacool

Abstract The chapter draws from empirical data collected across Denmark, Finland, Iceland, Norway, and Sweden to examine some of the differing policy regimes and electric mobility pathways in the Nordic region, especially for electric vehicles (EVs). The chapter identifies emerging crises of contestation, accountability, and participation, and it considers whether electric mobility entrenches or challenges automobility. This last point is not a given, with EVs in some situations leading to greater amounts of driving and shifting mobility practices towards automobility, yet in others, EVs seem to promote more sustainable patterns of transport as well as shifts in values. The chapter lastly offers possible policy suggestions for a more just and equitable transition.

Keywords Electric vehicles • Electric mobility • Sociotechnical transitions • Social acceptance • Automobility

B. Sovacool (✉)
Science Policy Research Unit, University of Sussex, Falmer, UK
e-mail: b.sovacool@sussex.ac.uk

© The Author(s) 2020
S. Sareen (ed.), *Enabling Sustainable Energy Transitions*,
https://doi.org/10.1007/978-3-030-26891-6_7

7.1 Introduction

Conventional forms of automobility, with their dependence on privately-owned, petroleum-powered vehicles used primarily by single occupants, are a significant source of major social ills including traffic jams and accidents, climate change, air pollution, and negative impacts on land use (Urry 2004). For example, the World Health Organization (2018a) estimates that every year 1.25 million people are killed and 20–50 million injured in traffic road crashes involving cars or motorcycles; globally, road traffic injuries are also the leading cause of death for those between the age of 15 and 29 years. In the realm of climate change, the Intergovernmental Panel on Climate Change (IPCC) notes that the transport sector produces about 7 billion tonnes of direct greenhouse gas emissions each year, making it responsible for almost one-quarter (23%) of total energy-related carbon dioxide equivalent emissions (Sims et al. 2014). With regard to ambient air pollution, emissions of particulate matter and other hazardous pollutants from road traffic contribute to hundreds of thousands of premature deaths each year (World Health Organization 2018b). Even in Europe, some 40 million people across 115 of the largest cities in the European Union are exposed to air exceeding health guidelines (for at least one pollutant); in particular, children who reside close to roads with heavy-duty vehicle traffic have twice the risk of respiratory problems as those living near less congested streets (World Health Organization 2018b).

The race for more sustainable forms of passenger mobility has, therefore, commenced, with innumerable policymakers and other stakeholders exploring electric mobility and electric vehicles (EVs) as a promising pathway. This chapter draws on extensive empirical research in the five Nordic countries—Denmark, Finland, Iceland, Norway, and Sweden—looking at the transition to electric mobility there, as part of a project known as Nordic Vehicle-to-Grid, or NV2G (Noel et al. 2019b). This data includes:

- 257 expert interview participants across 17 cities in Denmark, Finland, Iceland, Norway, and Sweden (almost one million words of transcribed text) (Sovacool et al. 2018b, c);
- Eight focus groups in Aarhus, Bergen, Copenhagen, Gothenburg, Helsinki, Reykjavik, Stockholm, and Tampere (Noel et al. 2019c);
- A representative survey of 5000+ adult participants (Sovacool et al. 2018a) as well as an online choice experiment of preferences (Noel et al. 2019a);

- 126 visits to car dealerships across the Nordic region (Zarazua de Rubens et al. 2018);
- Scenarios and simulations to capture co-benefits and determine systems optimisation (Noel 2017; Noel et al. 2017, 2018);
- Content analysis of standards for charging and grid interaction (Kester et al. 2019).

The chapter draws from this data to examine some of the differing policy regimes and electric mobility pathways in the Nordic region; identify emerging crises of contestation, accountability, and participation; consider whether electric mobility entrenches or challenges automobility; and offer possible policy suggestions for a more just and equitable transition.

7.2 Differing Policy Regimes and Sociotechnical Pathways in the Nordic Region

Within the transport studies literature, an abundance of terms are often used to describe electric mobility, including eco-mobility, electric vehicles, and micro-mobility (when referring to smaller cars or e-bikes and scooters). For the purposes of our project, we defined electric mobility as any form of mobility that uses energy drawn from the electric power grid, storing it on board for propulsion (She et al. 2017). This definition encompasses electric vehicles of all varieties—battery electric vehicles, plug-in hybrid electric vehicles, fuel-cell electric vehicles, and so on—but also electric bikes and scooters as well as the occasional trucks for freight or buses.

Despite this broad definition, the most popular form of electric mobility in the Nordic region remains the passenger electric vehicle, or EV. According to Kester et al. (2018), the Nordic countries do indeed have very different regimes for automobility and thus EVs and electric mobility. As Table 7.1 overviews, these differences begin with electricity markets, with Iceland not belonging to Nord Pool and great variation in the other four countries for consumers in terms of various fixed and flexible schemes, including an increasing number of *hourly* flexible plans based on the Nord Pool spot market. These differences on the electricity side continue on the respective car markets. The geography and differing income levels seems to lead to different car turnover rates ranging from 8.5 to almost 13 years. Regarding EVs, the countries have radically distinct levels of EV incentive programmes and markets. The all-inclusive

Table 7.1 An overview of the electricity and mobility regimes in the Nordic region

	Iceland	Sweden	Denmark	Finland	Norway
Population (Min.)	0.35	9.9	5.73	5.49	5.2
Sq. km (thousand)	103.0	447.4	42.9	338.4	385.2
Population density (thousand p/sq km)	3.3	24.3	135.6	18.1	14.3
Gross National Income (GNI) per capita (Atlas—US$)	56.990	54.630	56.730	44.730	82.330
CO_2 emissions (metric tonnes per capita)	6.08	4.62	6.78	8.51	11.74
Geography	Low population density outside of the capital; harsh weather conditions; bad road conditions	Low population density in the North; harsh weather conditions;	Flat, connecting islands, two separate electricity grids	Low population density outside the capital region; harsh weather conditions;	Low population density outside cities, difficult terrain between cities; harsh weather conditions
Non-CO_2 electricity production	99% (hydro 73%, geothermal 27%)	98% (nuclear 35%, hydro 46%, wind 10%, and bio and waste 7%)	>60% (wind 49%, bio and waste 12%)	78% (nuclear 34%, hydro 24%, bio and waste 16%, wind 3%)	98% (hydro 96%, wind 2%)
Non-CO_2 heat production	100% (geothermal 97%, electricity/heat pumps 3%)	89% (bioenergy/waste 81%)	61% (bioenergy/waste 60%)	48% (bioenergy/waste 47%)	83% (bioenergy/waste 67%, electricity/heat pumps 16%)

(*continued*)

Table 7.1 (continued)

	Iceland	Sweden	Denmark	Finland	Norway
% Renewable Energy Supply (RES) of primary energy supply	88.5%	45.9%	28.4%	32.3%	44.6%
Relation to EU	European Economic Area (EEA)	EU	EU	EU (EURO)	EEA
Climate targets (in relation to Transport)	• 2020: 10% RES share in transport. • 2050: 50–70% reduction in greenhouse gas (GHG) (comp. to 1990 levels)	• 2030: 63% reduction (to 1990 levels). • 2040: 75% reduction. • 2045: complete carbon neutrality (= 85% reduction to 1990 levels). • Transport: 70% reduction by 2030 compared to 2010.	• 2020: 20% (comp. to 1990 levels) in non-Emissions Trading Scheme (ETS) sector (incl. transport), 40% ETS sector. • 2030: 50% renewable energy • 2050: complete carbon neutrality. Copenhagen's target = 2025.	• 2030: Reduce transport GHG emissions by ±50% (compared to 2005). First replacing current fuels (with biofuels), then alternative technologies and services, targeting 250.000 plug-in electric vehicle (PEVs)/50.000 gas-fueled vehicles. • 2050: 80–95% reduction in GHG (compared to 1990).	• 2025: No new traffic growth in cities and all new passenger vehicles Zero-Emission • 2030: over 50% of heavy/commercial transport zero-emission and 50% reduction of GHG emissions (Oslo = 95%) • 2050: 100% reduction

(continued)

Table 7.1 (continued)

	Iceland	Sweden	Denmark	Finland	Norway
Average age of passenger car fleet	10.6 years	9.6 years	8.5 years	12.7 years	10.6 years
Passenger car taxation:	• Excise duty and weight differentiated registration tax. • Annual ownership tax based on weight	• Primarily CO_2 and weight differentiated yearly ownership tax (no registration tax)	• Primarily one-time value-added registration tax • Annual ownership tax based on fuel consumption	• Annual vehicle tax based on CO_2 emissions and weight	• Registration tax based on weight, engine, and emissions. • Fixed annual ownership tax.
EV incentives	• Purchase, Value Added Tax (VAT), Annual Ownership tax exemptions • Support for charging infrastructure	• Subsidy on new Battery Electric Vehicle (BEV) (4000e) and plug-in hybrid electric vehicle (PHEV) (2000e) • Company car reduction • Five-year exemption of annual ownership tax	• 20% purchase tax until 5000 cars or 2019 (revising the phase out of tax exemptions (up at 40%) • Differentiated parking. • Tax rebates for chargers	• EVs pay minimal technical purchase tax and ownership tax, no other special arrangements. • As of Jan 2017 5 mln for chargers	• Purchase tax, VAT exemptions; • 50% company car tax • Since 2015 local authorities decide on pricing level of PEV parking, toll roads, ferries, and High Occupancy Vehicle (HOV) lanes (max 50% of the highest price). • Infrastructure support on the national and local level.

Source: Kester et al. (2018)

programmes of Norway are well known, but Iceland is also offering strong tax reductions, Sweden offers a cash subsidy (as it has fewer car taxes to reduce), Denmark recently halted the phase out of its earlier strong tax reductions for EVs (currently at 40% instead of 150%) in an attempt to reinvigorate its EV sales and consumer trust in EVs, and in the case of Finland the EV incentives are fairly recent, in part due to Finnish comparative advantage in biofuels.

As Fig. 7.1 shows, these different support schemes are reflected in a different uptake of EVs as they lead to lower—in some cases competitive—consumer prices and time savings. And while Denmark stands out with its wind energy production, Norway stands out with its generous EV incentives, Finland has a large biofuel industry, and Sweden is the only country with a domestic automobile industry. All in all, the Nordic countries are different enough so that many of the major questions around electric mobility and vehicle-to-grid (V2G) come up, while they simultaneously offer flexible and modern electricity systems and a serious political concern about smog (Norway), oil imports (Iceland), and climate change (all of them) to take these developments seriously.

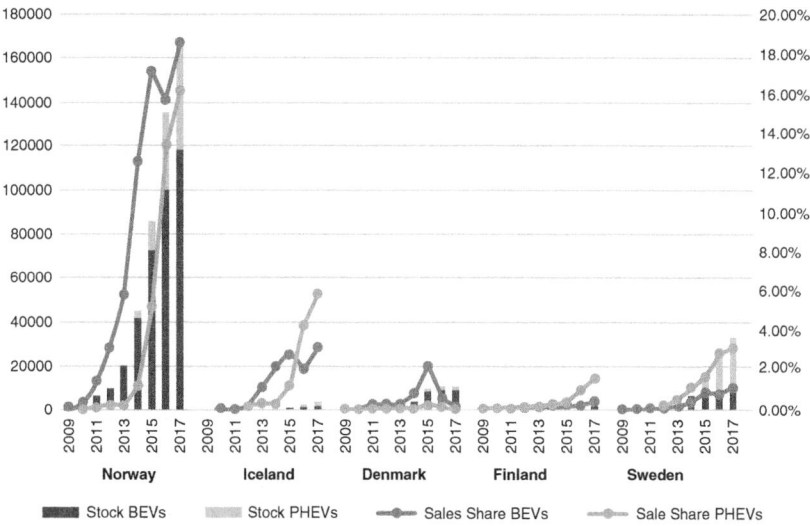

Fig. 7.1 Diffusion of electric vehicles in the five Nordic countries, 2009 to 2017. (Source: Kester et al. 2018)

The Nordic region is thus a clear-cut example of where the transition to electric mobility is underway. For example, the International Energy Agency (2018) notes that across the five Nordic countries, the total stock of EVs reached 250,000 cars at the end of 2017 and accounted for 8% of the global total, the third-largest share after China and the United States. The per capita diffusion of EVs across the Nordic region is *highest* in the world at 10.6%; the growth rate the highest in the world (up 57% from the previous year); and Norway in particular features a 39% market share of electric cars sales.

7.3 Contests over Fairness, Participation, Environmental Governance, and Vulnerability

However, even though the Nordic transition is underway, it has not been without its crises and contestations. Drawing from the empirical data from the NV2G project presented in Sovacool et al. (2019), this section explores these four challenges: inequitable access to EVs, exclusion and elitism in national planning, the creation of global externalities, and the worsening of some social vulnerabilities.

By far the most frequently mentioned injustice attribute across the entire sample of interview statements was that access to electric mobility technologies are not distributed evenly across Nordic society. As one respondent put it succinctly:

> *The most common EV in the Nordic Region is a Tesla. That's only for rich people and companies. It is not a mainstream car, it is not for everyone. It is a beautiful car, cool to have. But almost nobody can afford to.*

Another was more elaborate in their reflection and highlighted the equity and justice challenge with electric mobility:

> *Tesla owners in Norway on average have a quite high income. The Tesla is not their only car, they can have it as maybe their second or third or fourth or fifth car. It's the wealthy getting in front of the common people so they can just pass them in the queue in the morning, and that's irritating ... A recent newspaper found that the typical, single Tesla Model X owner received subsidies in 2016 worth the same amount you can hand out to provide 30,000 trips on the buses and the subway system of Oslo.*

If accurate, such a statement even quantifies the equity issues, placing a single EV adopter above the needs of thousands of public transport users—it privileges one "wealthy" person over 30,000 potential "common people."

In the domain of energy democracy and public participation, respondents raised concerns that EVs only created (or were backed by) exclusionary policies and reflected elitism in national planning and policymaking. Essentially, these comments draw on or connect with some of the distributive justice issues mentioned above, such as equity, but relate it back to procedures and the regulatory process. In this way, issues of unfair access and elitism become reflected and entrenched in policy, which then further perpetuate inequity across mobility systems. For instance, one respondent suggested that:

> *In the beginning, I thought the negative reactions to Teslas was related to envy or jealousy. But after thinking more about it, it's a rational and emotional reaction. Why should we lose a lot of money for rich people getting a cheap, expensive, luxury car? The politicians ...are [being] controlled.*

Another framed this as a procedural justice issue about policy, rather than one purely of distributive justice:

> *People see EVs as only for the upper class. They find them very unfair. To the politicians, electric mobility sounds very good and they remain convinced that EVs can help store energy, decarbonize transport, and balance the grid.*

Yet another elaborated that:

> *In Finland, government policy for EVs has been socially catastrophic, because only rich people buy new Teslas (laughs).*

Other respondents mentioned the problem as one of "*politicians prioritising between hundreds of goals*," and perhaps lacking the "*political will*" to make controversial decisions or challenge entrenched interest.

At another level, respondents mentioned that the widespread adoption of electric mobility systems, especially in a vehicle-to-grid (V2G) configuration, could potentially erode democratic processes, and undermine people's autonomy or liberty. One respondent, for example, noticed a reluctance among consumers to "*become dependent on some distant infrastructure for their daily travel.*" Another illustrated another part of the logic of this vision when noting *"people are afraid that the batteries will not last long enough and it is very costly to get new ones."* This last statement underscores the potential for a V2G system to become more easily controlled by profiteering companies—creating an exclusionary innovation system or policy regime.

The global externality issues connected to electric mobility largely touch on externalities—in various domains (environmental, community, market) and scales (local, national, global). In the environmental domain, some literature has noted that EVs, in particular, can lead to externalities such as greenhouse gas emissions from electricity use, toxic pollution from battery manufacturing and disposal, and water consumption. In terms of climate change, for EVs to actually deliver well-to-wheels carbon reductions, the carbon content of electric power generation must be low. Otherwise, EVs will simply shift the exposure to air pollution away from urban areas and towards rural populations located closer to the power plants that provide electricity for recharging EV batteries in the city. One respondent offered an illustrative statement underscoring environmental concerns in the context of plug-in hybrid EVs. They noted:

> *The problem with plug-in hybrid EVs in the region is that they can switch between fossil fuels (gasoline or diesel) and all electric mode. Many of such cars are bought by rich people not bothering to plug it in, driving it in pure fossil mode all the time only to save 100,000 to 200,000 kroner in taxes. They buy the car but never intend to use the environmental package, so that's obvious that you need some scheme to stimulate the real zero emission driving.*

In addition, some research has suggested that EVs shift pollution from local places and make it more regional; it also depends on local fuel mixes whether a net benefit to health or greenhouse gas emissions occur. Furthermore, the production of EVs requires equipment and material inputs that raise concerns about toxicity and recycling. Electric drivetrains, motors, and batteries need lithium, nickel, copper, and aluminium, as well as critical materials, somewhat harder to find, such as cobalt and indium. In this context, the possible environmental benefits of an electric mobility transition—fewer greenhouse gas emissions and improved air quality in urban environments—may come at the cost of greater pollution from factories making components and the landfills and junkyards where obsolete models end up. A final issue falls in the community domain, where externalities to greater electric mobility adoption include greater risk of accidents and traffic congestion, given that vehicles and e-bikes can still promote an automobility paradigm that transportation should be private, rather than public, and motorised rather than human-powered.

A final area of contestation relates to vulnerability, especially jobs (notably small and independent fuel providers and maintenance firms) and impacts on rural residents. In the Nordic region, many petrol and fuel stations would need to instal electric charging infrastructure, a prohibitively costly endeavour. Automotive dealerships and maintenance firms would also see a potentially large loss of revenue, as well as those selling alternatives to electric vehicles such as small-scale biofuel or hydrogen companies, a growing industrial segment at least in Denmark. Within Nordic automotive dealerships specifically, Zarazua de Rubens et al. (2018) found that salespersons generally articulate that EVs take a longer time to sell, take more effort to sell, and result in less revenue for maintenance—which can all result in negative impacts on profitability for automotive companies and dealerships, and consequently jobs, in the short term.

7.4 Legitimating or Challenging Automobility?

A deeper concern, separate from contests and challenges to accountability or equality, concerns whether EVs are in fact a radical, transformative innovation that challenges automobility, or an incremental, supportive innovation that only further entrenches it. In Table 7.2, for example, we show all of the positive *and* negative synergies electric mobility can have with sustainability. As that table highlights, electric mobility can potentially displace large amounts of carbon for passenger vehicles and even fleets, but also run the risk of further embedding motorised, private automobility as well as increased driving. Graham-Rowe et al. (2012) note for example that because adopters perceived their EVs to be more "environmentally-friendly," they drove them 1.64 times further than cars they did not see as "eco-cars." Some drivers even attempted to recharge their vehicles not by plugging in at home or at work, but by running the internal combustion engine and then using the re-generative braking system to "charge" their vehicle—"thereby negating the carbon savings" (Graham-Rowe et al. 2012: 148). This underscores that EVs can entrench automobility without necessarily decarbonising.

Part of this tension stems from the material, discursive and cultural elements that re-perform the core elements of the automobility regime. On

Table 7.2 Positive and negative synergies with electric mobility and sustainability

Dimension	Reinforces sustainable automobility	Reinforces unsustainable mobility
Intermodality	Use of EV within systems of intermodality, in combination with measures to discourage car use	Use of EV in systems that encourage excessive driving and EVs as second or third (luxury) cars
Desire for motorised transport	Substitution of cars and scooters	Increase in car-based mobility
Organised car sharing	Use of EVs in car sharing/ride-sharing schemes	Increase in preferences for private, single-occupancy driving practices
Increases in mobility	Implemented in tandem with active transport planning (walking, cycling)	Extra car trips, multiple car ownership, displaces enthusiasm for cycling
Zero-carbon and low carbon electricity	Use of EV in countries with decarbonised electricity grids	Use of EV in countries with coal-based electricity
Smart grids	Charging at off-peak times and storage for peak demand	Charging at peak times with no storage
Critical materials scarcity	Efficient manufacturing techniques with an appreciation for externalities with battery recycling	Inefficient and polluting manufacturing techniques with no battery recycling
Employment, competitiveness, and growth	Designed and promoted by sustainable firms with a focus on innovation and entrepreneurship	Coopted and marginalised by transnational conglomerates with little desire for social change

Source: Sovacool (2017)

Note: EV = Electric vehicle

both landscape and regime level, for example, the system locks itself in through constructed infrastructure, traffic rules and regulations, expertise (in terms of personnel and beliefs), travel routines, cultural values around enjoyment, status and freedom, and incumbent industries.

7.5 Policy Suggestions for a More Just and Sustainable Transition

Nonetheless, the sustainability credentials of EVs can be captured by an aggressive and proactive policy. If EVs are determined by policymakers to play an essential role in national climate change mitigation plans, our data suggests several policies to prevent or at least minimise injustice in Table 7.3. Thus, our justice framework shows that policymakers need to think broadly when implementing EVs in order to avoid half-measures of energy justice.

In addition, many of the areas of contestation, or the issues of equity and vulnerability that arise, are not "new" to EVs or V2G—they likely exist with other low carbon technologies and also conventional cars and other forms of mobility. However, a lesson here is perhaps that changing the perfor-

Table 7.3 Policy mechanisms for more sustainable and just Nordic electric mobility

Area of contestation	Example(s)	Policy response
Unfair access	EVs only accessible by higher socioeconomic consumers	Avoid regressive EV subsidies, encourage lower-cost EV development, increase consumer knowledge of cheaper EVs
Elitism in planning and policymaking	EV policy determined in scope of higher socioeconomic consumers Exclusion of other subsets of the population (low income, users of other mobility)	Better inclusion of the entire population in EV policies (e.g. public charging infrastructure coverage), Broader electrification of public transport, more comprehensive transport policy, progressive EV, and V2G subsidies
Lifecycle externalities	EVs exacerbate other externalities (congestion, electricity-related externalities) Global south excluded from EVs, instead get cheap petrol/diesel	Deployment of EVs requires deployment of other renewable electricity, transportation planning policies, internalising externalities, carefully managing battery and lifecycle waste streams Shift international focus of EVs beyond global North, international mechanisms to shift technology and support small EV initiatives present in those countries (clean development mechanism policy)
Vulnerable groups	Conventional car industry job loss, particularly maintenance Dealership resistance to selling new technologies	Implement job training programmes for new EV industry (e.g. battery specialisation, EVSE repair, V2G aggregation) similar to coal-to-solar transition Consistent EV and V2G policy signals, allowing industry preparation and investment for EV transition

Source: Sovacool et al. (2019)

Note: EV = Electric vehicle, V2G = Vehicle-to-grid, EVSE = Electric vehicle supply equipment

mance or engine of a vehicle, or introducing a new type of car such as an EV or an innovation such as V2G, does not necessarily change the underlying political economy or power dynamics behind mobility or automobility. Systems of mobility themselves—involving multiple, competing and overlapping technologies, modes of mobility, and transport infrastructures—can also be just or unjust, even if they utilise innovations such as EVs or V2G that have material potential to reduce environmental and social harms. There may be situations, practices, or socio-material configurations where V2G EVs meet principles of justice, sustainability, or sustainable development, but also areas where they may not (such as when an EV reinforces automobility and merely represents an additional car, and thus becomes a net environmental burden, or increases the demand for motorised mobility at the expense of more active walking and cycling). The sociotechnical potential of electric mobility is, therefore, situational, relational, and contingent. The answer to the question "Is it good?" will invariably be "It depends." The chapter has aimed to provide an overview of what it depends on, to inform an accountable and sustainable energy transition.

7.6 Conclusion

To conclude, the inherent promise embodied in electric mobility is just that, potential not yet fully realised. Its regional and perhaps even global deployment pathways, its future potential or vision, will differ considerably depending on context and policy. Electric mobility is at a pivotal moment in its development where it could merely reinforce aspects of conventional mobility—where society instead adopts more efficient conventional cars, or other alternative modes and fuels such as biofuel or hydrogen. Or, electric mobility could remain trapped as a niche, an important but by no means dominant system of mobility. Alternatively, perhaps electric mobility will reach high penetrations across a dirty grid, a decarbonised grid, or a super-smart high-tech digitised grid. Which of these pathways becomes a reality is contingent and context-specific—which reveals the promise, but also the peril, of electric mobility.

References

Graham-Rowe, E., Gardner, B., Abraham, C., Skippon, S., Dittmar, H., Hutchins, R., & Stannard, J. (2012). Mainstream consumers driving plug-in battery-electric and plug-in hybrid electric cars: A qualitative analysis of responses and evaluations. *Transportation Research Part A: Policy and Practice, 46*, 140–153.

International Energy Agency. (2018). *Nordic EV outlook 2018: Insights from leaders in electric mobility*. Paris: OECD.
Kester, J., Noel, L., Lin, X., Zarazua de Rubens, G., & Sovacool, B. K. (2019, January). The coproduction of electric mobility: Selectivity, conformity and fragmentation in the sociotechnical acceptance of vehicle-to-grid (V2G). *Journal of Cleaner Production, 207*, 400–410.
Kester, J., Noel, L., Zarazua de Rubens, G., & Sovacool, B. K. (2018, May). Promoting vehicle to grid (V2G) in the Nordic region: Expert advice on policy mechanisms for accelerated diffusion. *Energy Policy, 116*, 422–432.
Noel, L. (2017). The hidden economic benefits of large-scale renewable energy deployment: Integrating heat, electricity and vehicle systems. *Energy Research & Social Science, 26*, 54–59.
Noel, L., Brodie, J., Kempton, W., Archer, C., & Budischak, C. (2017). A cost minimization model of electricity production and transportation with considerations of externalities. *Applied Energy, 189*, 110–121.
Noel, L., Zarazua de Rubens, G., & Sovacool, B. K. (2018, June). Optimizing innovation, carbon and health in transport: Assessing socially optimal electric mobility and vehicle-to-grid (V2G) pathways in Denmark. *Energy, 153*, 628–637.
Noel, L. D., Carrone, A. P., Jensen, A. F., Zarazua, G. D. R., Kester, J., & Sovacool, B. K. (2019a, February). Willingness to pay for electric vehicles and vehicle-to-grid applications: A Nordic choice experiment. *Energy Economics, 78*, 525–534.
Noel, L., Kester, J., Zarazua de Rubens, G., & Sovacool, B. K. (2019b). *Vehicle-to-grid: A sociotechnical transition beyond electric mobility*. Basingstoke: Palgrave Macmillan.
Noel, L. D., Zarazua de Rubens, G., Sovacool, B. K., & Kester, J. (2019c, February). Fear and loathing of electric vehicles: The reactionary rhetoric of range anxiety. *Energy Research & Social Science, 48*, 96–107.
She, Z.-Y., Sun, Q., Ma, J.-J., & Xie, B.-C. (2017). What are the barriers to widespread adoption of battery electric vehicles? A survey of public perception in Tianjin, China. *Transport Policy, 56*, 29–40.
Sims, R., Schaeffer, R., Creutzig, F., Cruz-Núñez, X., D'Agosto, M., Dimitriu, D., … Tiwari, G. (2014). Transport. In O. Edenhofer, R. Pichs-Madruga, Y. Sokona, E. Farahani, S. Kadner, K. Seyboth, A. Adler, I. Baum, S. Brunner, P. Eickemeier, B. Kriemann, J. Savolainen, S. Schlömer, C. von Stechow, T. Zwickel, & J. C. Minx (Eds.), *Climate change 2014: Mitigation of climate change. Contribution of Working Group III to the Fifth Assessment Report of the Intergovernmental Panel on Climate Change*. Cambridge, UK and New York, NY: Cambridge University Press.
Sovacool, B. K. (2017, May). Experts, theories, and electric mobility transitions: Toward an integrated conceptual framework for the adoption of electric vehicles. *Energy Research & Social Science, 27*, 78–95.

Sovacool, B. K., Kester, J., Noel, L., & Zarazua de Rubens, G. (2018a, September). The demographics of decarbonizing transport: The influence of gender, education, occupation, age, and household size on electric mobility preferences in the Nordic region. *Global Environmental Change, 52*, 86–100.

Sovacool, B. K., Kester, J., Zarazua de Rubens, G., & Noel, L. (2018b, April). Expert perceptions of low-carbon transitions: Investigating the challenges of electricity decarbonisation in the Nordic region. *Energy, 148*, 1162–1172.

Sovacool, B. K., Noel, L., Zarazua de Rubens, G., & Kester, J. (2018c, December). Reviewing Nordic transport challenges and climate policy priorities: Expert perceptions of decarbonisation in Denmark, Finland, Iceland, Norway, Sweden. *Energy, 165*, 532–542.

Sovacool, B. K., Noel, L. D., Zarazua de Rubens, G., & Kester, J. (2019, March). Energy injustice and Nordic electric mobility: Inequality, elitism, and externalities in the electrification of vehicle-to-grid (V2G) transport. *Ecological Economics, 157*, 205–217.

Urry, J. (2004). The 'system' of automobility. *Theory, Culture & Society, 21*, 25–39.

World Health Organization. (2018a). Road traffic injuries: Key facts, February 19. Retrieved from http://www.who.int/news-room/fact-sheets/detail/road-traffic-injuries

World Health Organization. (2018b). Air pollution and climate change. Retrieved from http://www.euro.who.int/en/health-topics/environment-and-health/Transport-and-health/data-and-statistics/air-pollution-and-climate-change2

Zarazua de Rubens, G., Noel, L., & Sovacool, B. K. (2018, June). Dismissive and deceptive car dealerships create barriers to electric vehicle adoption at the point of sale. *Nature Energy, 3*, 501–507.

Open Access This chapter is licensed under the terms of the Creative Commons Attribution 4.0 International License (http://creativecommons.org/licenses/by/4.0/), which permits use, sharing, adaptation, distribution and reproduction in any medium or format, as long as you give appropriate credit to the original author(s) and the source, provide a link to the Creative Commons licence and indicate if changes were made.

The images or other third party material in this chapter are included in the chapter's Creative Commons licence, unless indicated otherwise in a credit line to the material. If material is not included in the chapter's Creative Commons licence and your intended use is not permitted by statutory regulation or exceeds the permitted use, you will need to obtain permission directly from the copyright holder.

CHAPTER 8

Accountability and the Regulation of Legitimacy: Biodiversity Conservation and Energy Extraction in the American West

Steven Wolf

Abstract Energy extraction in the western United States poses existential risks to sage-grouse, a charismatic ground-nesting bird. Study of how this concern is integrated into the governance of the sector can inform a broader analysis of sustainability transitions. I introduce a model of co-evolution of standards of legitimacy and material practices that highlights how emergence of new accountability 'tests' can potentially drive socio-ecological transformation. This evolutionary model emphasises accountability and legitimacy as mechanisms of selection (demographic/behavioural change). Because accountability mechanisms and selection pressures do not exist to transform the Colorado energy sector in a manner that benefits sage-grouse, the assessment reveals that there is no sustainability transition underway. As we focus on the broader analytical and practical challenges presented by sustainability transitions, attention to accountability, legitimacy, and selection mechanisms will be essential.

Keywords Sustainable transitions • Accountability • Legitimacy • Biodiversity conservation • Environmental governance

S. Wolf (✉)
Department of Natural Resources, Cornell University, Ithaca, NY, USA
e-mail: saw44@cornell.edu

© The Author(s) 2020
S. Sareen (ed.), *Enabling Sustainable Energy Transitions*,
https://doi.org/10.1007/978-3-030-26891-6_8

8.1 Energy Production and Loss of Biodiversity

The sage-grouse (*Centrocercus urophasianus*) is a ground-nesting bird dependent on sagebrush steppe habitat in 11 western states in the United States. The population is in marked decline, with the current range of the species reduced to 56% its historic distribution (Schroeder et al. 2004). Following formal petitions, US Fish and Wildlife Service concluded an assessment in 2010 (USFWS 2010) to determine if the sage-grouse should be protected under the Endangered Species Act (ESA). In 2010, the federal government determined that protections were warranted based on population estimates and ecological modelling, but that it was not practical to implement protections under the law due to competing demands on the agency. The federal government invited the relevant states to develop conservation plans that would protect the habitat (and ostensibly the population) of sage-grouse. Inducing the creation of these conservation plans can be understood as a means of fulfilling obligations that flow from the Endangered Species Act.

In Colorado, oil and gas development is the leading cause of sage-grouse habitat degradation (Copeland et al. 2009). A leading environmental non-governmental organisation (NGO), Environmental Defense Fund (EDF), organised relevant stakeholders to develop the Colorado Habitat Exchange, a *compensatory mitigation* programme through which the oil and gas industry could purchase habitat credits to offset habitat degradation associated with their operations. The credits would be supplied by farmers and ranchers who commit to conservation or restoration of land, thereby producing positive gains in habitat. In this way, energy development could be rendered compatible with a commitment to no-net loss of sage-grouse habitat.

In terms of socioecological interplay and feedbacks, energy demand/supply causes land use disturbance, resulting in sage-grouse population declines and awareness of risks of ecological disturbance. This has the potential to drive social regulation (i.e., the introduction of accountability mechanisms that encourage firms to avoid destroying valuable habitat and to offset habitat loss when avoidance is not practical), which can, in turn, change land use patterns to stabilise populations of sage-grouse. As depicted, this dynamic can be understood as a transition from a situation in which the energy industry contributes in a significant way to risk of sage-grouse extinction to a situation in which the energy industry responds to social demand for biodiversity protection and contributes positively to sage-grouse conservation success.

While energy transitions are generally understood to involve a shift from fossil fuels to renewable energy supply, it is useful to consider other challenges. Adaptations that address protection of wildlife, water quality, air quality, workers, and communities where extraction and processing occur all represent important challenges to the industry, the economy, and to social capacity for regulation. Studying the integration of biodiversity concerns into energy development can inform understanding of prospects for sustainability, broadly defined. More generally, this work can demonstrate how attention to accountability and legitimacy can support analysis of environmental governance.

8.2 Legitimation Crisis, Regulation, and Socioenvironmental Change: An Evolutionary Model of Environmental Governance

The framing of this volume places accountability and legitimation processes at the centre of environmental governance (see Kraft and Wolf 2018). Accountability mechanisms provide assurance against unacceptable behaviour and serve to regulate flows of legitimacy. Legitimacy is understood to be a socially mediated resource that shapes the prospects of actors, rewards and constrains behaviour, and channels socioeconomic development (e.g., industrial organisation) and material practices (e.g., techniques for producing energy). As contributing authors to this volume, we are asked to analyse practices of legitimation that serve to disrupt—as well as conserve—business as usual in order to advance scholarship on sustainability transitions. At the same time, we are encouraged to identify opportunities to challenge and to change practices/relations of accountability and flows of legitimacy in order to advance sustainability transitions.

Habermas' (1975) analysis of the legitimation crisis draws our attention to systemic dimensions of technical and institutional change within imagined sustainability transitions. For Habermas, the crisis is a state in which there are no problem-solving pathways available to incumbent decision makers. The control/regulatory apparatus is perceived as not being capable of repair or renewal. The anticipated outcome is disruptive innovation, qualitative change; a shift to a different state. 'To the extent that (ecological) scarcity is a technical problem, this does not necessarily constitute a crisis. The crisis stems from lack of institutional alternatives. What is scarce is coordination capacity. We do not have proven, practical institutional responses to what ails us, or at minimum, the switching costs and the learning challenges make transition frightening' (Wolf and Bonanno 2014: 287). In these terms, a crisis of legitimacy has the potential to catalyse a transition, some forms of which might be called sustainable.[1] This transition will entail both technical and institutional state variables. We have not advanced very far in some imagined transition towards sustainability (e.g., reduced reliance on fossil fuels and reduced CO_2 flux and reductions in economic stratification), and so it is possible to suggest that there is no legitimation crisis. In other words, people do not interpret the situation in terms of institutional failure. Consumer capitalism appears quite sustainable, and core debates are framed in technical (i.e., post-political (Swyngedouw 2009)) terms. Dominant institutions, dominant actors, and dominant material practices are able to reproduce their legitimacy despite social and ecological contradictions (Piketty 2013; Rockström et al. 2009). For this reason, this book is focused on questions about how this legitimacy is maintained and how new accountability practices might alter flows of legitimacy and advance a sustainability transition.

Science and technology studies has developed the concept of sociotechnical systems, highlighting the mutual embeddedness of social processes and technology. This integrated perspective is rather central to the sustainability transitions literature. In trying to make sense of sociotechnical change and processes of regulation, I identify flows of legitimacy and accountability 'tests' as essential considerations (see top right in Fig. 8.1). Such tests can take the form of laws, administrative rules, professional best practices, technical standards, cultural conventions, investment and consumption behaviours, and other social processes that structure discrimination routines (i.e., processes of selection within an ecological model). Processes of selection, or regulation, are central to an analysis of mechanisms that might produce a sociotechnical transition or rapid 'flip' (i.e., state change) into something we might identify as sustainability. They are also central to the analysis of how sustainability imperatives are blunted and co-opted. Blühdorn (2007) has emphasised the need to analyse how we 'sustain the unsustainable'. The reproduction of selection mechanisms/environments—that is, standards of legitimacy and mechanisms of

---

[1] Authoritarianism is a possible outcome, and the relationship between authoritarianism and sustainability requires reflection.

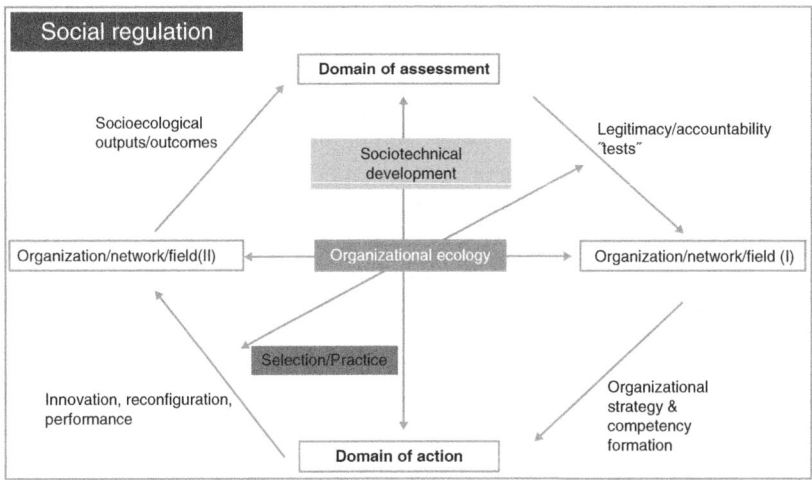

Fig. 8.1 Co-evolution of nature and society mediated by accountability mechanisms and legitimacy tests

accountability—that fail to change the distribution of relevant behaviours and outputs are a central mechanism for path dependence in socioecological systems.

Selection is the process that drives demographic change and demographic stability (i.e., organisational ecology). Here, we can imagine a population of oil and gas firms with variable capacity to respond to new regulations, new eco-audits, or new consumer sensibilities (Wolf and Primmer 2006). In addition to demographic change, selection can alter the distribution of behaviours. Firms adapt more frequently than they disappear. We can imagine the costs of offsetting the degradation of sage-grouse habitat as driving some firms out of business (i.e., churn in the population), and we can imagine such costs as shifting firms' drilling operations to geographic zones outside of prime sage-grouse habitat (an adaptation of technical practices and outputs).

The co-evolutionary model sketched in Fig. 8.1 can help us make sense of incremental processes of socioecological change (adaptation) as well as rapid flips (punctuated equilibrium). Regardless of the pace of change, the analysis presented here emphasises linkages between socially mediated assessments, economic and technical development, and socioecological change (see Norgaard 1994).

As represented in the model, standards of assessment emerge from culture, politics, and scientific interpretations of socioecological status and trajectory (e.g., changes in biodiversity and the stakes attached to it). Accountability represents a series of relational ties that position some actors to make judgements of others and impose sanctions when appropriate (Bovens 2007). Judgements are based on assessments of how well a given practice or organisation conforms to norms that derive from deep structures of society (i.e., institutions such as family, community, market, state, etc.) (Kraft and Wolf 2018). Sanctions—penalties, taxes, withdrawal of subsidies, consumer boycott, investor flight—hinder performance and reduce competitiveness, by definition, and in this sense, they are an element of selection processes (i.e., organisational ecology). At the same time, shifting standards of accountability and shifts in how legitimacy is produced/accessed gives rise to new organisational strategies and new competencies tied to emerging competitive strategies (Wolf and Primmer 2006). Out of this adaptation dynamic, we observe innovation and reconfiguration of material practices.

Changes in the institutional environment and the competitive landscape also give rise to gestures or performances that communicate engagement with norms, but amount to little material change that can be linked back in any direct way to the new accountability tests mentioned earlier.[2] Note that these performances—for example, ways of talking about sustainability concerns—can be an element of a new competitive landscape, and in this sense, they are not empty. This dynamic of adaptation—substantive and gestural—produces a newly configured population (i.e., organisation/network/field II), which is characterised by a different distribution of behaviours as well as the introduction of new material practices. These developments constitute socioecological change, and outcomes include changes in ecology and distributional shifts in the wellbeing of people and ecosystems. These outcomes give rise to new ecological risks and opportunities and new social values and politics. In this shifting cognitive and sociomaterial landscape, the stage is set for a new round of assessments and evaluations that constitute accountability practices and structure flows of legitimacy.

---

[2] In addition to disappearing from the population and adaptation, actors also have the potential to shape the selection environment. Lobbying, constructing political coalitions, public relations, and efforts to reshape culture are active strategies relevant for understanding the co-evolution of sociotechnical systems.

8.3 Accountability Tests and Legitimacy Flows of the Colorado Sage-Grouse Habitat Exchange

Accountability relations are socially mediated assessments that structure flows of legitimacy and channel sociotechnical development. In reflecting on how declining populations of sage-grouse might give rise to changes in the Colorado energy sector, we can identify a set of important actions that allow us to reflect on how accountability relations and practices of legitimation are implicated in processes of social regulation. The analysis presented here is symmetrical. The aim is to highlight the potential for accountability relations to advance a sociotechnical dynamic that supports the sustainability of sage-grouse populations, and to highlight the potential for these same relations to legitimate and reproduce the sociotechnical dynamic responsible for the existing risk of extinction.

8.3.1 Construction of a Market-based Habitat Exchange

Applied to oil and gas extraction in Colorado and the fate of the sage-grouse, the construction of the habitat exchange is an important effort to introduce accountability for habitat loss and it is a key site of production of legitimacy for a range of actors. The exchange is promoted as capable of producing no-net loss of sage-grouse habitat. By quantifying the habitat losses associated with specific oil and gas development projects and the habitat gains associated with conservation actions by Colorado landowners interested in selling habitat credits, the exchange is a platform buying and selling sage-grouse habitat offsets. These offsets are a form of compensatory mitigation. As imagined by designers of the exchange, firms seeking drilling permits from the state purchase the appropriate volume of habitat credits through the exchange, and this makes it possible to advance oil and gas production while safeguarding sage-grouse populations. Compensatory mitigation of habitat loss is the final element of the mitigation hierarchy—avoid, minimise, and offset. The design and administration of the exchange emphasises offsetting as a fallback option. Avoiding development projects that degrade habitat and altering projects to minimise disturbance to habitat advance conservation directly, while offsetting can be understood as providing a more diffuse benefit to sage-grouse.

The Colorado Exchange was created by the Environmental Defense Fund (EDF), a New York-based NGO. EDF partnered with the Colorado

Cattlemen's Association (representing landowners positioned to sell credits to oil and gas firms) and co-solicited relevant Colorado state agencies, and firms in the energy industry to participate in the creation and governance of the exchange (Large and Wolf 2018). The prospect of the sage-grouse gaining protection from the federal Fish and Wildlife Service through the ESA—and the political and economic fallout of regulation under the ESA—is generally understood as motivating this state-level cooperation. As a market-based approach to environmental management, habitat offsetting is linked to experience with the Clean Air Act, stream bank and wetlands mitigation banking, and the Clean Development Mechanism under the Kyoto Protocol. Reliance on market exchange to structure environmental management grants flexibility to individual firms, responds to criticisms of coercive bureaucratic controls, and ostensibly produces conservation at least aggregate cost. These traits lend habitat offsetting a modern and practical sensibility, which resonates positively with a broad range of relevant actors and varied logics of coordination.

Despite the elegance of the concept, after seven years of design and consultation, the exchange has not generated any habitat offsets. To repeat, the exchange has not supported any transactions that advanced conservation. Regardless of the capacity of the exchange to function, however, the concept of the exchange has produced a sustained dialogue among the central public and private sector policy actors in Colorado and nationwide.

Prospects for further development of the exchange were damaged in the summer of 2018 when the oil and gas industry formally announced that they were resigning from the exchange governance board and that they were not willing to play a further role in its development unless the expectations for offsetting were ratcheted downward. This announcement was followed by EDF shifting their personnel away from development of the exchange. The timing of this rupture was tightly linked to an announcement by the US Secretary of Interior ending mandates that supported compensatory mitigation under ESA. This policy decision was explicitly tied to ambitions to promote 'energy independence'. Over the past year, the Trump administration has continued to roll back legal protections for sage-grouse and, more broadly, to weaken ESA (Davenport/ NY Times 2019).

The habitat exchange was created to serve as a primary vehicle for holding the oil and gas industry accountable for sage-grouse habitat degradation, and it is a primary vehicle for demonstrating to federal regulators—and a wide variety of other parties—that ESA protections for sage-grouse are not necessary. The exchange continues to be represented as relevant and vibrant,[3] despite the fact that zero offsets have been created under this governance mechanism and the buyer of offsets has publicly announced their unwillingness to participate. Therefore, it seems reasonable to argue that the exchange serves to legitimate business as usual. The exchange functions to sustain the cognitive dissonance—that is, capacity to reconcile contradictions—attached to existing socioecological relations (Walker et al. 2009). The capacity of the exchange to organise and sustain dialogue in the policy field appears to be sufficient to maintain the legitimacy of existing socioecological relations. According to the co-evolutionary model sketched above (Fig. 8.1), there are no accountability tests and no selection pressure to advance structural or technical changes that could be recognised as a sustainability transition. That said, if a significant political bloc were to commit to conservation, and federal and state regulators were to reverse their position and require firms to purchase offsets (Green 2018), the exchange would be a critical element of the infrastructure supporting governance and sage-grouse conservation. In this sense, it is possible to interpret the exchange as all of the following: a failure, a distraction, and an accomplishment.

8.3.2 Quantification Tools

The technical core of the Colorado sage-grouse habitat exchange is the Habitat Quantification Tool (HQT) sage-grouse exchange. This habitat suitability model produces an integrated assessment of how site-specific land use/land cover changes affect the productivity of land for sage-grouse feeding, reproduction, nesting and fledging. HQT scores specify the magnitude of the habitat degradation (debits) associated with direct (e.g., oil and gas well pad and road and electricity service to the well) and indirect effects (e.g., spill overs from disturbed sites that degrade surrounding habitat values, measured through a distance-decay function) sage-grouse. The HQT also scores the positive contributions (credits) associated with conservation activities (e.g., ecological restoration, habitat enhancements,

---

[3] See, for instance, https://www.thepwc.org/habitat-exchangeexchange/ and https://brianallmerradionetwork.wordpress.com/2018/12/21/12-21-18-co-governor-hickenlooper-signs-executive-order-furthering-conservation-and-clarifying-mitigation-of-the-greater-sage-grouse/.

transfer of development rights). This quantification is the basis for asserting equivalencies across sites and projects, and it makes it possible to assign value and to conduct transactions through the exchange.

EDF convened a panel of scientific experts to produce the HQT, and there was an active effort to shield this process from political and economic considerations. The HQT was peer-reviewed by a committee under the auspices of the Ecological Society of America, as well as by a 3rd-party reviewer selected by the oil and gas industry. The process of creating a science-based routine for accounting of habitat values and to assign rights (credits) and responsibilities (debits) are key practices of accountability advanced by the exchange. The elaborate process through which debits and credits are assigned, and the performances of rigour associated with the algorithm, legitimates the exchange. In fact, habitat exchanges were developed in response to perceived shortcomings of existing models of offsetting based on 'conservation banking' (Toombs et al. 2018; Barral 2019). In conservation banking schemes, offsets are typically assigned based on ad hoc negotiations between administrators and buyers and sellers of credits/debits. There is typically no standardised biological modelling, and rights and responsibilities are not specified *a priori*. Additionally, offsets in habitat banking programmes have largely been financed by institutional investors engaged in a form of speculation, and there have been limited opportunities for local landowners to participate as suppliers of credits. The HQT responds to concerns about transparency, consistency, and access, which bolsters its legitimacy as a conservation mechanism. In terms of accountability, the HQT is a technical standard that quantifies rights and responsibilities. In terms of legitimacy, this standard presents opportunities for efficient assessment of the extent to which an energy project or firm has internalised a commitment to no-net loss of habitat.

In reflecting on the development and the current status of the exchange, it is worthwhile to note that mobilising science and making significant investments in a standardised, transparent, quantitative approach to assigning habitat values have not succeeded in advancing accountability applied to oil and gas firms' degradation of sage-grouse habitat. From a biological perspective, the sage-grouse does not cope well with disturbance, and this is reflected in the debits assigned by the HQT. A firm building a four-acre well pad in sage-grouse habitat can be assigned as much as 800 acres of offsetting responsibility. Since the HQT was unveiled, the oil and gas industry has consistently raised critical questions about the magnitude of the debits assigned to specific projects. The oil and gas industry has stated that they were willing to engage in offsetting, but not according to the terms embedded in the HQT. Ecological discipline can be transmitted through metrics, but power lies elsewhere.

8.4 ADVANCING A SUSTAINABLE ENERGY TRANSITION THAT SUPPORTS SAGE-GROUSE

In reflecting on the Colorado Habitat Exchange as a vehicle to address conservation, it is worthwhile to reflect critically on the conflation of habitat conservation and security of the population of sage-grouse. It is quite possible for the population to collapse without a net loss of habitat. Climate change, invasive species, wildfire, and cumulative impacts from home building, road construction, infrastructure, recreation and other human activities, combined with questions about the fungibility of habitats, raise questions about the coherence of this approach to conservation. Bracketing these issues, these concluding remarks focus on exploring the value of a co-evolutionary perspective for institutional analysis and design.

According to the co-evolutionary model presented here, a transition to a state in which energy supply does not undermine the security of the sage-grouse population requires new accountability tests that derive from new conceptions and new practices of legitimacy. These tests must channel selection in a manner that drives change over time in the distribution of relevant land use behaviours. The change in behaviours derives from a shift in the population of actors and the operational procedures, competencies, and strategies of those actors. Under existing political–economic relations, the exchange is not capable of introducing the required discipline and/or rewarding relevant innovations.

Based on this analysis, research and practical interventions should focus on the potential for new politics and new dynamics in civil, market, and cultural domains that are capable of shifting how legitimacy is produced and accessed. With respect to accountability, there is a need to focus on sanctions (i.e., the imposition of costs and risks capable of reorienting behaviour and strategy). At present, the exchange does not work because there are no mechanisms to create demand for offsets through the exchange, premised on the HQT. Oil and gas firms are able to access drilling permits from the state through other, less stringent regulatory pathways.[4] In the absence of leadership by the state—that is, willingness to impose sanctions on oil and gas firms that are heavy enough to change the extent of land use disturbance and sufficient to conserve sufficient and appropriately configured habitats—the exchange cannot function to conserve sage-grouse. Voluntary commitments by firms are insufficient and consumer preferences are not expressed in a manner capable of producing significant changes. Habitat offsetting, and perhaps most analogous market-based conservation strategies, rest on the existence or creation of demand for offsets. This demand rests on the legislative and judicial redefinition of rights and responsibilities. Unless consumers, investors, voters, and regulators hold these expectations and impose these duties, this environmental governance strategy cannot sustain sage-grouse in Colorado and advance a sustainable transition.

References

Barral, S. (2019). Ecological and management dimensions of metric production in conservation banking. *Journal of Rural Studies* (In review).

Blühdorn, I. (2007). Sustaining the unsustainable: Symbolic politics and the politics of simulation. *Environmental Politics, 16*, 251–275.

Bovens, M. (2007). Analysing and assessing accountability: A conceptual framework. *European Law Journal, 13*(4), 447–468.

Copeland, H. E., Doherty, K. E., Naugle, D. E., Pocewicz, A., & Kiesecker, J. M. (2009). Mapping oil and gas development potential in the US Intermountain West and estimating impacts to species. *PloS one, 4*(10), e7400.

Davenport/NY Times. (2019, March 15). Trump administration loosens sage grouse protections, benefiting oil companies. *NY Times*.

Green, M. (2018, July 27). *The Hill*. Retrieved May 2019, from https://thehill.com/policy/energy-environment/399262-administration-ending-rule-that-made-industry-pay-for-damages-to

Habermas, J. (1975). *Legitimation crisis*. Boston: Beacon Press.

Kraft, B., & Wolf, S. (2018). Through the lens of accountability: Analyzing legitimacy in environmental governance. *Organization & Environment, 31*, 70–92. https://doi.org/10.1177/1086026616680682

Large, D., & Wolf, S. (2018). How the endangered state acts: Reverse regulatory threat and market-based conservation policy (In preparation).

---

[4] Permits are awarded by the state through a process that involves attention to avoidance, minimisation and offsetting. Champions of the exchange argue that the terms of offsetting in these alternative forums are too generous to commercial interests, and this leads to underinvestment at all levels of the mitigation hierarchy.

Norgaard, R. B. (1994). *Development betrayed: The end of progress and a coevolutionary revisioning of the future*. London and New York: Routledge.

Piketty, T. (2013). *Capital in the twenty-first century*. Boston: Harvard University Press.

Rockström, J., Steffen, W., Noone, K., Persson, A., Chapin, F. S., Lambin, E. F., ... Foley, J. A. (2009). A safe operating space for humanity. *Nature, 461*, 472–475.

Schroeder, M. A., Aldridge, C. L., Apa, A. D., Bohne, J. R., Braun, C. E., Bunnell, S. D., ... Hilliard, M. A. (2004). Distribution of sage-grouse in North America. *The Condor, 106*(2), 363–376.

Swyngedouw, E. (2009). The antinomies of the postpolitical: In search of a democratic politics of environmental protection. *International Journal of Urban and Regional Research, 33* (3): 601–620(609).

Toombs, T. P., Sokulsky, J., & Wolfe, D. W. (2018). Habitat exchanges: A case study of biodiversity offset design in the U.S. (In preparation).

USFWS. (2010). Endangered and threatened wildlife and plants; 12-month findings for petitions to list the greater sage-grouse (Centrocercus urophasianus). Washington, DC.

Walker, S., Brower, A., Stephens, R., & Lee, W. (2009). Why bartering biodiversity fails. *Conservation Letters, 2*, 149–157.

Wolf, S., & Bonanno, A. (Eds.). (2014). *The Neoliberal regime in agri-food: Crisis, resilience and restructuring*. London: Routledge/Earthscan.

Wolf, S. A., & Primmer, E. (2006). Between incentives and action: A pilot study of biodiversity conservation competencies for multifunctional forest management in Finland. *Society and Natural Resources, 19*(9), 845–861.

Open Access This chapter is licensed under the terms of the Creative Commons Attribution 4.0 International License (http://creativecommons.org/licenses/by/4.0/), which permits use, sharing, adaptation, distribution and reproduction in any medium or format, as long as you give appropriate credit to the original author(s) and the source, provide a link to the Creative Commons licence and indicate if changes were made.

The images or other third party material in this chapter are included in the chapter's Creative Commons licence, unless indicated otherwise in a credit line to the material. If material is not included in the chapter's Creative Commons licence and your intended use is not permitted by statutory regulation or exceeds the permitted use, you will need to obtain permission directly from the copyright holder.

PART III

Conclusion

CHAPTER 9

Practices of Legitimation and Accountability Crises in a Range of Energy Transitions

Siddharth Sareen

Abstract This chapter draws together five wide-ranging cases related to energy transitions. It articulates how practices of legitimation along four registers (discursive, bureaucratic, technocratic and financial) are present in each case to extents that differ based on how each author's choice of sector and focus modulates their relevance. This chapter summarises the ways in which these practices uphold and challenge accountability crises in each energy transition case. Such juxtaposition and consolidation allow discernment of cross-cutting dimensions along which practices of legitimation play out. These dimensions include spatiality, temporality, opportunism, prefiguration, performativity, power-play and normalisation or routinisation. The specification of practices of legitimation across cases sets up a concluding synthesis which links legitimation and energy transitions with broader environmental governance scholarship on accountability.

Keywords Legitimation • Energy transitions • Discursive • Bureaucratic • Technocratic • Financial

S. Sareen (✉)
Department of Geography, Centre for Climate and Energy Transformation, University of Bergen, Bergen, Norway
e-mail: Siddharth.Sareen@uib.no

9.1 The Cross-cutting Dimensions Where Legitimation Is Practised in Each Case

What can be learned from summarising and consolidating the practices of legitimation encountered in the unpacking of five diverse energy transition cases? This chapter employs an abductive reasoning approach. The practices of legitimation that constitute the empirically informed point of departure in Chap. 2 are treated as an example of deductive reasoning here: it is possible to categorise practices along four registers (discursive, bureaucratic, technocratic and financial) that are overlapping (not mutually exclusive) and comprehensive (all practices of legitimation fit within their remit). These practices move from the general to the specific. The five cases that make up Chaps. 4, 5, 6, 7 and 8 hold examples of inductive reasoning. In each chapter, the author chooses a point of entry to offer a fine-grained analysis of accountability relations within their case of energy transition, moving from the specific to the general by means of analytical abstraction. Part III acknowledges that these analyses are limited by degrees of uncertainty—their knowledge base is necessarily incomplete. It seeks a pragmatic approach to characterise and inform decision-making despite uncertainty, and therefore applies abductive reasoning to settle upon the likeliest possible explanation in any given case.

In short, this concluding part works towards ways to characterise energy transitions as accountable to concerns of sustainability or not in disaggregated, case-specific instances of decision-making that affect decarbonisation and social equity enhancement outcomes. Accountability relations are rarely fully legible since they comprise both formal and informal practices of legitimation that require empirical study with varying data access, hence any approach that analyses accountability must address uncertainty within its design. An abductive approach to accountability analysis opens up for empirical investigation, accommodates uncertainty, and retains focus on practical applicability and real-world relevance.

Part III proceeds step-wise. This chapter articulates how practices of legitimation along four registers (discursive, bureaucratic, technocratic and financial) are present in each case to extents that differ based on how each author's choice of sector and focus modulates their relevance. It summarises the wide range of ways in which these practices uphold and challenge accountability crises in each energy transition case. Such juxtaposition and consolidation allow discernment of cross-cutting dimensions along which practices of legitimation play out. Proceeding sequentially through the five cases, it draws out seven dimensions: spatiality, temporality, opportunism, prefiguration, performativity, power-play, political economy, and normalisation or routinisation. This sets up the concluding Chap. 10, which links the four registers of practices of legitimation and the structuring set of cross-cutting dimensions with broader environmental governance scholarship on accountability.

While each case treatment can be read in multiple lights, certain dimensions stand out in each: spatiality and temporality in Timothy Moss' historical analysis of Berlin's energy transitions over the past century; opportunism in Christian Lund's study of attempts at the scalar reconstitution of authority during land conflicts in Indonesia; prefiguration and performativity in Håvard Haarstad's account of the role of target-setting in urban climate change mitigation efforts; power-play in the form of automobile incumbency, regime persistence and path dependence in Benjamin Sovacool's unpacking of electric mobility in the Nordic countries; and political economy and normalisation or routinisation in Steven Wolf's problematisation of the construction of a habitat exchange for biodiversity offsetting by energy extractive industries. The latter part of this chapter, Sect. 9.2, draws out these aspects case by case. It offers reflections in relation to which practices of legitimation play out within these dimensions and in what way.

9.2 The Registers Along Which Legitimation Is Practised in Each Case

9.2.1 For Timothy Moss

The case is three contrasting energy transitions at different historical moments in Berlin, each driven by the situated urges of a specific politics that evolves over time. Moss points out that there are different crises of accountability at each historical point, as the urban fabric of Berlin itself cannot be understood as the same space over the past century. In the 1920s, this concerned who should supply energy to Berlin; during post-war division, it concerned self-sufficiency for West Berlin's energy provision within city borders; and today it concerns ownership and control of the urban energy infrastructure. Each of these accountability crises features corresponding practices of legitimation, and this historical contextualisation (cf. Lockwood et al. 2017) serves to caution against any easy assumption of interventions that can render energy transitions accountable towards sustainable outcomes. Moss reminds us that sustainability itself is a relatively new concern in its current form, which came about during the 1970s. Drawing on earlier histories, he argues, requires acknowledgement of this limitation, but can generate a deeper appreciation of where sustainability thinking comes from, what echoes can be detected in the past, and how energy infrastructure legacies can frame current visions and enactments of sustainability. He points out the danger of committing to a certain configuration of accountability that over the course of evolving politics and institutional structures might come to constitute what Kramarz and Park (2017) call an accountability trap.

This case features a host of examples of discursive legitimation, for instance the local Communist Party's criticism of the regressive effects of tariff increases in the early 1930s, the protest camp against the planned power plant in the Spandau Forest in 1976 (Fig. 4.2), the campaign poster of the Berlin Energy Roundtable for a referendum in 2013 (Fig. 4.3), and energy security arguments used during the Cold War. It also draws out legitimation practices along the bureaucratic register, for instance through the municipal imposition of city-wide unitary utility tariffs and uniform service standards in the 1920s, and the Allies' insistence on high security standards for West Berlin's urban energy system, including three months' worth of primary energy reserves. Technocratic practices of legitimation are also in evidence in the large incumbent utility Vattenfall's contemporary emphasis on technical expertise and track record for managing the electricity and gas networks, and in cascading generating capacity requirements mandated during the security-oriented strategy during the Cold War. Finally, financial legitimation is visible in the pursuit of fair wages for employees at the city's utilities and improvements to service quality used to justify massive urban infrastructure investment (partly based on foreign debt finance) in the 1920s. It is, however, notable that the need for financial legitimation at the urban scale is absent during the Cold War years of high-cost energy security and West German government subsidies to Berlin.

Moss' historical analysis with its *spatial and temporal* purchase, then, offers rich insights into practices of legitimation along all four registers. Yet what is its import for interventions today in support of sustainable outcomes under transition? His analysis points to the articulation of demands for accountable remunicipalisation of energy infrastructure by contemporary social movements campaigning to prioritise decarbonisation and reduction in energy use over traditional criteria for urban energy management. This deconstruction and historical contextualisation of current trends that have brought about shifts in urban policy (in favour of a municipal utility and decarbonisation) is a demonstrably constructive outcome of accountability analysis, in that it provides an evidenced basis to inform in situ decision-making as well as to discuss and debate Berlin's energy transition at the present moment.

9.2.2 For Christian Lund

The case is changes in land use and in who has authority over land. This concern inevitably accompanies debates about energy transitions, as all energy sources have a land footprint, and most land use (in this case forestry or agriculture) has direct or indirect implications for greenhouse gas emissions or carbon sequestration. The questions of accountability that Lund unpacks, however, are chiefly concerned with power and social equity, and competition over the legitimation of power by institutions at different scales and with various degrees of formality. The accountability crises at play in Indonesia's hinterland are interrelated. On the one hand, there is the crisis of villagers who are being dispossessed of their land being hard put to hold a top-down state to account. The form of this state varies, as in 1978 when formal authority over large parts of land in West Java that was *de facto* used by agrarian villages shifted from the Provincial Forestry Service to the State Forest Corporation with uniformed parastatal police as part of an authoritarian regime. On the other hand, there is the crisis of what constitutes the state itself, with tussles over the scale at which authority is held. This surfaces in the villagers' recognition of the Sundanese Peasant's Movement in 2006, and more recently of the Village Office as the official local territorial administrative institution with authority over land, in order to counter the efforts of national institutions that sought to take over the land for forestry. Lund points out that the power to define subjecthood for oneself or to impose subjecthood on others is an integral part of accountability, and that this power is bidirectional (Fox 2018). Not only subjecthood, but also authority, can thus be re-purposed; making them visible in a given configuration here becomes the relational work of politics over land.

This case features instances of discursive legitimation such as the State Forest Corporation's announcement of a planting ceremony of 1,000 mahogany seedlings in rows named after government institutions (which the villagers promptly uprooted overnight), and its invocation of military terms such as 'illegal loggers' and 'subversive' to draw equivalence between the villagers' land occupation and organised crime. It also brings out specific bureaucratic legitimation practices, most notably the villagers' request (which was granted) for new ID cards from the Village Office as the official local territorial administration, which rendered their settlements official sub-villages within the territorial area claimed by the State Forest Corporation. Technocratic legitimation is also in evidence in the 1978 transfer of nearly one million hectares of official forestland in West Java to the State Forest Corporation—centralising authority away from the province—and in the latter's formal use of the language and protocols associated with national security to evict villagers as 'forest security disturbances'. Finally, practices of financial legitimation surface in the provisory system of payment (10,000 Rupiah per month) by villagers to the Sundanese Peasant's Movement instead of paying a third of their rice production as rent illegally demanded by the State Forest Corporation. They are also visible in the annual contributions of a million Rupiah by each sub-village to the Village Office, in essence a tax which established the villagers' claim as landholders.

Lund's fine-grained study of conflicts over land in remote tracts not only offers striking instances of practices of legitimation along all four registers, but also points to clear arenas that require attention for sustainable energy transitions. These arenas include the relations between people and institutions at multiple scales, and the necessity to allow for the desire for change to express itself in democratic politics. In his case, both the top-down use of force and popular resistance are *opportunistic*. Each seeks to recognise and establish specific relations between people and institutions in order to cement land claims in their favour. This reading of the shaping of accountability relations casts new light on the social contract and on authority and subjecthood.

9.2.3 For Håvard Haarstad

The case is how Norwegian cities set climate mitigation targets construed as reductions in carbon emissions at the urban scale. While these targets are seemingly ambitious and commendable, they encounter challenges of commensurability across cities, and often lack concrete strategies for operationalisation. Haarstad identifies an accountability crisis that the very presence of decarbonisation targets can serve to justify prolonged delay on actual climate mitigation, as targets allow cities to channel the discursive power of the promise of laudable action at the expense of diffusing political pressure over the urgency of substantive action to achieve these goals which remains both slow and insufficient. Yet he flips this to point out that target-setting itself is not only performative but can also be regarded as a form of prefigurative politics, whereby the apparent failure to meet targets that increasingly come to be seen as desirable can spark another accountability crisis, one that can drive necessary climate mitigation at the urban scale. The Zero Growth Objective for urban transport in Norway, argues Haarstad, has resulted in concrete agreements signed by its largest cities in 2016 and 2017 that have not only committed to limit traffic but also delivered results by way of a reduction in private car traffic during 2018. Contra the techno-managerial apparatus of the post-political condition (Swyngedouw 2010) that simply supports the status quo, the carrying power of numbers may motivate action by working targets into routinised repertoires.

This case offers a slew of examples of discursive legitimation, starting with the White Paper on Norwegian Climate Policy from 2006 which articulated the need for a shift to public and non-motorised transport, the White Paper on Norwegian Climate Policy from 2012 which formulated this as a 'goal' or target, and the very statement of the Zero Growth Objective. This posits that all growth in personal traffic in Norway's largest cities must be covered by public or non-motorised transport. Bureaucratic legitimation is also at play given that these and other government policies (such as the Climate Accord of 2008 in the Norwegian parliament) consistently reference a 2 °C target to limit global warming and have worked this into a broad range of national policy documents and strategies, including for urban transport in this specific case. The use of technocratic practices of legitimation is evident in the National Transport Plan Working Group's reasoning that 'zero' is a very easy target to measure and thus useful in holding cities to account, and the subsequent agreements signed by the country's largest cities with specific indicators to measure performance on urban car traffic. Crucially, financial legitimation accompanies the Zero Growth Objective through these Urban Environment Agreements, which tie the amount of central funding allocated to cities for local transport infrastructure with their prowess in meeting the target.

Haarstad thus constructs the use of metrics as more than simply a bureaucratic apparatus of governance that perpetuates accountability crises in the shiny guise of new mitigation targets. He argues that targets perform work that helps enable sustainable energy transitions by working their way into specific policies and indicators within sectors such as transport. They drive future priorities by linking them to concrete objectives that can be measured (zero growth) and punished or rewarded (through urban transport infrastructure budget allocation). This relational analysis of policy-making and the operationalisation of targets highlights the value of *prefigurative* politics. Accountability analysis of this case contributes a valuable reconsideration of the role of targets in legitimating gradual but incremental climate mitigation action. Rather than challenging the existing sectoral configuration outright, targets work *performatively* to reorient its workings through the very routine, normalised structures and processes that shape sectoral futures.

9.2.4   For Benjamin Sovacool

The case is the advent of electric mobility in the five Nordic countries. As power from the electric grid is based on renewable energy to large extents in these contexts, this shift from fossil fuel powered vehicles to grid charged ones constitutes a prima facie energy transition. But Sovacool's analysis of electric vehicle roll-out problematises this assumption, and flags four crises of accountability. The first concerns inequitable access to electric vehicles, which so far largely remain the preserve of privileged people even in these relatively wealthy countries. The second points out that exclusion is reflected in national planning around electric mobility, which risks making people dependent on distant infrastructures (like electric charging stations) on terms beyond their democratic control. The third crisis is on multiple spatial scales and pertains to the creation of externalities at remote sites of material extraction to build electric vehicles, as well as the risk of relocating pollution from cities to regional sites of electric power production. The fourth crisis features the burden on some sectoral stakeholders such as fuelling stations that might have to invest in costly charging station infrastructure or risk job loss and vehicle dealerships that might have to invest more time and effort into electric vehicle sales. Sovacool argues that these crises, while perhaps inevitable components of shifting sectoral regimes, stem from the uneven effects of transition dynamics on different actors, and from inequities that are deeply embedded within existing systems of mobility.

This case draws out a host of instances of discursive legitimation, most notably from people challenging the roll-out of electric vehicles in terms of its sustainability effects. These interviewees critique subsidies accorded to Teslas as luxury electric vehicles; equate this to 30,000 public transport tickets per beneficiary; are sceptical of hybrid vehicles as allowing owners to cash in on incentives without affording any means to monitor their actual usage of electricity rather than internal combustion engines; and are critical of political tokenism in public discourse around electric vehicles. Bureaucratic legitimation is evident to varying extents across Nordic countries, from Norway's all-inclusive packages to incentivise electric vehicles (which are so far mainly cars) to Denmark's reluctant extension of lower duties (40% instead of 150%) on electric cars, but by comparison comes far less into play in relation to the electrification of public transport. Practices of technocratic legitimation are presented generically to promote sustainable mobility through charging at off-peak times, mandating battery recycling to reduce externalities, emphasising the decarbonisation of electric grids and coordinating roll-out with planning that prioritises non-motorised transport forms and intermodal electric transport. Finally, financial legitimation is notable in the enormous support provided for private electric cars which has been used by relatively rich people, and in the absence of similarly strong support to rapidly build out public electric transport infrastructure or cushion vulnerable groups against regressive effects of national fiscal policies on electric mobility (for instance through free public transport).

Sovacool thus illustrates practices of legitimation along all four registers, drawing on a large body of empirical material to characterise the multi-sited, multi-scalar and polycentric nature of accountability relations in mobility systems under transition. His case surfaces instructive principles (Tables 7.2 and 7.3) across comparative country contexts (Table 7.1) for how to work towards sustainable energy transitions in electrifying mobility systems. Treatment underscores the importance of unpacking *power-play* to fathom automobile incumbency, regime persistence and path dependence. By studying the practices of legitimation that accompany shifts to electric mobility, accountability analysis brings several crises to the fore. It provides a means to point out specific measures that can be undertaken in each context to overcome these crises.

9.2.5 For Steven Wolf

The case is the construction of a habitat exchange market that could enable habitat replacement for biodiversity conservation of the sage-grouse (an endangered ground nesting bird that depends on sage brush steppe habitat) in Colorado while permitting the expansion of energy extractive industries. On the one hand, this can be regarded as a complete non-starter, as Wolf points out that over the course of seven years, the habitat exchange failed to record a single transaction—an apparent accountability crisis in that it fails to address sage-grouse population decline. He attributes this to the lack of appetite of the oil and gas companies to stump up the expenses for the amount of scientifically requisite land to compensate for the loss of biodiversity habitat, and inadequate political will to force their hand. On the other hand, as the process unfolds, it does construct the numerical model informed by cross-sectoral concerns (land costs and requirements for the fossil fuel majors and sage-grouse habitats respectively). Wolf argues that this is a step in the direction of accountable socio-ecological regulation, as it has brought into being an accountability test. Given a different future political economic context, the very existence of this data infrastructure (the Habitat Quantification Tool) and market infrastructure (the Colorado Habitat Exchange) increases its likelihood of eventual insertion into pertinent bureaucratic routines, and normalisation into decision-making around land allocation and habitat exchange.

This case draws out numerous instances of discursive legitimation, including the United States federal administration's explicit linkage of 'energy independence' with its ending of mandatory compensatory mitigation under the Endangered Species Act in 2018, and the continued representation of the habitat exchange as relevant and vibrant despite its never having executed a single transaction. Ironically, the habitat exchange was instrumental in arguments against protecting sage-grouse populations under the Endangered Species Act. Practices of bureaucratic legitimation are visible in the non-governmental organisation Environmental Defense's efforts to set up the Colorado Habitat Exchange and orchestrate participation in its creation and governance by various relevant actors (including a cattlemen association, state agencies and energy extractive industries), layering this effort on experience with habitat offsetting under the Clean Air Act and the Kyoto Protocol's Clean Development Mechanism. Technocratic legitimation in this case pertains to the strategy of championing a market mechanism to avoid critique of coercive bureaucracy and to benefit from efficiencies such as low transaction costs, and to associated innovations such as the Habitat Quantification Tool to calculate compensation amounts for replacement of sage-grouse habitats. Financial legitimation, while present in the very logic of a market mechanism for carbon offsetting of habitat loss, remained absent in practice. As the subject of controversy when the oil and gas industry protested the debits assigned to them based on the modelled cost calculations, as also when it resigned from the exchange's governance board, questions of finance were used to delegitimate the whole exercise.

Wolf articulates accountability relations as a hollow performance in his case, where practices of legitimation along the four registers serve to perpetuate a crisis of accountability. He emphasises that what remains missing is sanction, an imposition of requirements that would drive demand for offsets, even when the calculation and market infrastructure are put in place. These latter developments represent the innovation of mechanisms that can be used to *routinise* and normalise accountability if society manifests the *political economic* will to demand a sustainable energy transition that must necessarily support sage-grouse as well. Thus, accountability analysis enables a clear account of what remains lacking to render this energy transition case sustainable.

REFERENCES

Fox, J. (2018). The political construction of accountability keywords. *IDS Bulletin*, *49*(2), 65–80.

Kramarz, T., & Park, S. (2017). Introduction: The politics of environmental accountability. *Review of Policy Research, 34*(1), 1–4.

Lockwood, M., Kuzemko, C., Mitchell, C., & Hoggett, R. (2017). Historical institutionalism and the politics of sustainable energy transitions: A research agenda. *Environment and Planning C: Politics and Space, 35*(2), 312–333.

Swyngedouw, E. (2010). Apocalypse forever? Post-political populism and the spectre of climate change. *Theory, Culture & Society, 27*, 213–232.

Open Access This chapter is licensed under the terms of the Creative Commons Attribution 4.0 International License (http://creativecommons.org/licenses/by/4.0/), which permits use, sharing, adaptation, distribution and reproduction in any medium or format, as long as you give appropriate credit to the original author(s) and the source, provide a link to the Creative Commons licence and indicate if changes were made.

The images or other third party material in this chapter are included in the chapter's Creative Commons licence, unless indicated otherwise in a credit line to the material. If material is not included in the chapter's Creative Commons licence and your intended use is not permitted by statutory regulation or exceeds the permitted use, you will need to obtain permission directly from the copyright holder.

CHAPTER 10

Conclusion: Legitimation and Accountability in Energy Transitions Research

Siddharth Sareen, Timothy Moss, Christian Lund, Håvard Haarstad, Benjamin Sovacool, and Steven Wolf

Abstract This concluding synthesis argues that practices of legitimation can empirically deconstruct any given energy transitions case to identify

S. Sareen (✉) • H. Haarstad
Department of Geography, Centre for Climate and Energy Transformation,
University of Bergen, Bergen, Norway
e-mail: Siddharth.Sareen@uib.no; Havard.Haarstad@uib.no

T. Moss
Integrative Research Institute on Transformations of Human-Environment
Systems (IRI THESys), Humboldt University of Berlin, Berlin, Germany
e-mail: timothy.moss@hu-berlin.de

C. Lund
Department of Food and Resource Economics, University of Copenhagen,
Copenhagen, Denmark
e-mail: clund@ifro.ku.dk

B. Sovacool
Science Policy Research Unit, University of Sussex, Falmer, UK
e-mail: b.sovacool@sussex.ac.uk

S. Wolf
Department of Natural Resources, Cornell University, Ithaca, NY, USA
e-mail: saw44@cornell.edu

© The Author(s) 2020
S. Sareen (ed.), *Enabling Sustainable Energy Transitions*,
https://doi.org/10.1007/978-3-030-26891-6_10

mechanisms that constrain or enable accountability to decarbonisation with social equity enhancement. The versatile analytical application of these practices can advance environmental governance research on steering energy transitions towards sustainability. This chapter explicates seven cross-cutting dimensions and indicates how practices of legitimation play out within them in five cases related to energy transitions, drawing on contextualised examples from two cases for each dimension. This illustrates how practices of legitimation (discursive, bureaucratic, technocratic and financial) can reframe wide-ranging cases from diverse perspectives, fields and disciplines. Applied researchers can choose customised dimensions and enlarge this indicative set to identify situated mechanisms that modulate accountable energy transitions.

Keywords Accountability • Governance • Legitimacy • Energy transitions • Sustainability

What is the collective takeaway from our exploratory analysis centred on accountability? Defined as accountability to decarbonisation with enhanced social equity, the concept is analytically generative for characterising components of any given energy transition as contributing to sustainability or not. Operationalised as four registers of practices of legitimation, accountability can be profitably applied across a wide range of cases. This application can emphasise specific cross-cutting dimensions based on which accountability relations are of contextual interest. The five cases highlight grounded practices of legitimation, whether discursive, bureaucratic, technocratic or financial, that relationally produce accountability. The dimensions that surface in these cases link accountability with other environmental governance concepts that are useful for advancing critical analyses of energy transitions. While provisional, this synthesis constitutes a basis that future research is invited to adapt and employ.

Section 10.1 furnishes a brief description of each of the seven indicative dimensions that are embodied in the five cases related to energy transitions in this book. Using illustrative examples from two cases for each of these dimensions, Sect. 10.2 demonstrates how practices of legitimation can be applied within each dimension. Finally, Sect. 10.3 summarises the significance of the five cases for future environmental governance scholarship on accountability in energy transitions.

10.1 Accountability, Registers, Cross-cutting Dimensions and Practices of Legitimation

Analyses focused on accountability relations can demonstrably construe a wide variety of cases in energy transition terms and pinpoint a range of accountability crises. Such reframing can help articulate how specific accountability crises are being maintained or challenged through practices of legitimation along registers of discourse, bureaucracy, technocracy and finance. This book has presented and consolidated a variety of case treatments—historical, conflict-centred, comparative, multi-scalar and cross-sectoral. This foray has surfaced a number of cross-cutting dimensions. Sareen (2019a) argues in Chap. 9 that our case studies span and equip us to discern seven indicative dimensions that can serve to structure our insights and guide future application. Within each such dimension, it is possible to identify practices of legitimation that are at work to contest, uphold or produce new specific outcomes in relation to accountable energy transitions.

Table 10.1 plots the registers along which the practices of legitimation play out against each of the cross-cutting dimensions that come up due to case selection and approach, which are choices guided by analysts' contextual knowledge. This makes the practices of legitimation pliable and oriented at situated analyses of accountability. They can inform interdisciplinary analysis and identify interventions that can enable sustainable outcomes

Table 10.1 Practices of legitimation with indicative dimensions for five wide-ranging cases

Registers/Dimensions	Discursive	Bureaucratic	Technocratic	Financial
Spatiality	Berlin's historical energy transitions, Nordic electric mobility transitions			
Temporality	Berlin's historical energy transitions, Indonesian land conflict			
Opportunism	Indonesian land conflict, Norwegian zero growth target-setting			
Prefiguration	Norwegian zero growth target-setting, Colorado habitat exchange			
Performativity	Norwegian zero growth target-setting, Colorado habitat exchange			
Power-play	Nordic electric mobility transitions, Indonesian land conflict			
Routinisation	Colorado habitat exchange, Nordic electric mobility transitions			

during energy transitions in a given context. The four registers along which legitimation is practised—discursive, bureaucratic, technocratic and financial—play out within each dimension represented in the rows. These dimensions include spatiality, temporality, opportunism, prefiguration, performativity, power-play and routinisation (or normalisation). The table indicates two main cases which concern each dimension, but aspects certainly surface in other cases as well. The dimensions structure our description of how practices of legitimation can be applied to analyse accountability in energy transitions governance. Despite the wide range of these five cases, future work along these lines will doubtless generate additional dimensions. Whereas the four registers along which legitimation is practised are elaborated in Chap. 2 (Sareen 2019b), the cross-cutting dimensions are explicated below with summary reflections on how each one manifests in two of the five cases.

10.1.1 Spatiality

Legitimation plays out simultaneously at and across multiple spatial scales during an energy transition. At stake are questions of distribution—where are benefits and burdens relocated from any sectoral changes, where are winners and losers based—and of the locus of decision-making and the sites that it affects across the spatial scale. In Berlin's historical energy transitions case, the spatial dimension appears pertaining to where energy is generated, where energy infrastructure is financed and where energy infrastructure is controlled and owned. This varies in relation to Berlin's territorial boundaries as well as the political economy of its geographical context. In the Nordic electric mobility transitions case, the spatial dimension relates to material decoupling in terms of where energy is produced to power the electric grid and where vehicles are manufactured. It also relates to where energy infrastructure like charging stations comes up, which jobs this creates and displaces, and what siting implies for which actors control electric mobility. Similar multi-scalar issues come up concerning material inputs (such as cobalt and lithium) as well as waste flows (especially electronic waste).

10.1.2 Temporality

Legitimation plays out differently over time, both during the same energy transition and during sequential ones. The temporal dimension directs attention to how sociotechnical and political economic configurations evolve within the same spatial context. This concentrates power at different spatial scales and makes different societal choices politically viable. It opens up new technological possibilities through arenas of innovation where timing and concomitant infrastructural investment dynamically determine energy futures. In Berlin's historical energy transitions case, these transitions are refracted by changing mores of political pressure interwoven with societal expectations and the material evolution of energy infrastructure. This includes the intergenerational equity aspects that underpin current campaigns to climate-proof Berlin's energy infrastructure. In the Indonesian land conflict case, citizens squeezed off their land by an authoritarian regime are forced to adopt new tactics to retain land control over time. This brings about new competing recognition of institutional authority by subjects. They seek to strengthen the state at the local scale where it is more responsive to their needs, creating new governmental configurations over time.

10.1.3 Opportunism

Legitimation plays out in powerful ways at specific conjunctures that can be definitive for a given energy transition. These moments of rupture or leverage points can be understood through the cross-cutting dimension of opportunism. Opportunistic or ad hoc legitimation capitalises on a circumstantial opening to wrest control of new possibilities and establish them in sociomaterial form through informal but rapidly formalised means rather than through existing formulae or behavioural patterns. It thus constitutes a quantum change in how society is configured with regard to a particular energy transition. In the Indonesian land conflict case, West Javanese villagers exercise their right to pay rent with discretion, recognising a local authority in the form of the Village Office rather than the central government. This in turn shapes relations of authority in favour of their recognition as landholders. In the Norwegian zero growth target-setting case, a global 2 °C climate mitigation target is translated into a Zero Growth Objective to limit car traffic.

10.1.4 Prefiguration

Legitimation plays out in premeditated ways, where actors strategically manoeuvre energy transitions to secure advantageous new sectoral configurations. In contrast to opportunism, the dimension of prefiguration highlights how particular choices are orchestrated and made seemingly inevitable, despite having been initiated in a circumstance where they were highly contingent. This dimension enables us to trace how specific pathways are brought into being out of a wide array of possibilities. In the Norwegian zero growth target-setting case, setting a highly ambitious target that curbs any future increase in car traffic in Norway's largest cities puts a literal brake on this hitherto growing sectoral segment within a short span. In the Colorado case, the failed attempt to secure habitat replacement for the sage-grouse from land takeover by energy extractive industries nevertheless creates infrastructures for data (Habitat Quantification Tool) and markets (Colorado Habitat Exchange) for future habitat exchange.

10.1.5 *Performativity*

Legitimation plays out as farce that can risk perpetuating the status quo and supporting energy transitions that lead to unsustainable outcomes, for instance decarbonising without enhancing social equity. The dimension of performativity draws attention to this tendency of employing rhetoric to obfuscate the absence of sufficient substantive action. Legitimation can thus become a clever and attractive but ultimately hollow performance, where new accountability relations to transition in a sustainable manner are not shaped for a different energy future, despite fanfare. In the Norwegian zero growth target-setting case, the Zero Growth Objective can be read as an ambitious target that, without a slew of accompanying sectoral policies, would simply remain unattainable; more critically, it could be argued as a means of distracting attention away from the carbon-emitting aviation sector which continues to grow. In the Colorado case, the expectation that a habitat exchange market would work (despite its subsequent failure) is implicated in the removal of compensatory mitigation mandates stemming from the Endangered Species Act.

10.1.6 *Power-play*

Legitimation plays out in uneven topographies of power, where outcomes are not shaped in a vacuum of fair decision-making processes, but socially modulated by influential actors within evolving institutional structures with specific historical legacies. The dimension of power-play highlights the role of both inequitable power relations and more structural factors such as path dependency and regime persistence during energy transitions. It directs attention not only to overt confrontation and contestation but also to the absence of important deliberations where power grabs or incumbency prematurely close particular energy futures. In the Nordic electric mobility transitions case, the automobility regime and existing biases of systems of mobility are reproduced in the roll-out of electric mobility to a greater extent than the adoption of public and non-motorised transport solutions. In the Indonesian land conflict case, West Javanese villagers are unable to even consider recourse to authority at the national scale for their marginalised concerns and resort to the local scale.

10.1.7 Routinisation

Legitimation plays out through enactment within the existing sociopolitical fabric, at times achieving incremental change with greater ease and effectiveness than through more disruptive attempts at energy transitions. Through routinisation or normalisation, practices of legitimation work their way into the bureaucratic and banal decision-making apparatus of existing, often powerful institutions. Rather than subjecting these institutions themselves to scrutiny, such legitimation reorients and repurposes their internal functioning. In the Colorado case, the choice of a habitat exchange is seen as a workable middle ground that can plausibly bring energy extractive industries on board in a politically feasible and efficient manner to replace sage-grouse habitats and conserve the declining population; Environmental Defense focuses its efforts not on protesting fossil fuels but on assembling requisite data and market infrastructure. In the Nordic electric mobility transitions case, while the roll-out of electric mobility might suffer from existing problems of mobility systems, policies to encourage and coordinate it have made the Nordic countries global front-runners in electric mobility adoption.

10.2 Applying Practices of Legitimation Across Registers and Dimensions

Having defined the dimensions, the next section illustrates how the registers along which legitimation is practised can be applied within each dimension. We draw on the five cases whose practices of legitimation have been deconstructed and consolidated in Chap. 9 (Sareen 2019a). As illustrated above, multiple cases feature legitimation within each dimension; for clarity, we only present practices from two cases for each dimension.

10.2.1   The Spatiality Dimension

Within this dimension, discursive legitimation plays out at specific sites in situated ways, with consequences for what kind of energy transition is legitimated. In Berlin's historical energy transitions case, discursive legitimation appears spatially in the use of energy security arguments during the Cold War to push for self-sufficient energy production within city limit. It is also illustrated by the protest camp against the planned power plant in the Spandau Forest in 1976 (Fig. 4.2), which signifies contested territorialisation under energy transition. In the Nordic electric mobility transitions case, spatiality is implicit in people's critique of subsidies for luxury electric cars, which are equated with 30,000 transport tickets for each beneficiary, drawing attention to the spatial concentration of privilege and elitism, and its equity effects during transitioning mobility systems.

Bureaucratic legitimation is spatially expressed in the Berlin case as the municipal imposition of city-wide unitary tariffs across utilities and uniform service standards in the 1920s. This constitutes a smoothening and unification of urban territory for energy service delivery. Technocratic legitimation manifests spatially in the same case: the large incumbent utility Vattenfall's contemporary emphasis on technical expertise and track record for managing electricity and gas networks is a mode of ensuring continued relevance for actors with large spatial coverage, despite sectoral shifts towards openness to new small-scale actors. Financial legitimation also operates spatially in this case, as revealed in the adoption of city-wide fair and equal sectoral employee wages and service quality improvements to justify massive urban infrastructure investment (partly financed through foreign debt) in 1920s Berlin.

10.2.2   The Temporality Dimension

Here, discursive legitimation shows temporal significance in the Berlin case, pinpointed as discursive shifts from criticism of the regressive effects of tariff increases (by the local Communist Party during the 1920s) to a distinct emphasis on ownership in the campaign poster of the Berlin Energy Roundtable in 2013 (Fig. 4.3 shows this proclaiming 'Our municipal utility, our power grid, our Berlin' for a referendum). Priorities and their discursive justification change over time in ways that reveal an evolving basis for accountability claims. Bureaucratic legitimation also makes sense of temporal patterns such as in the Berlin case with high security standards built into the urban energy system in the 1970s, including three months' worth of primary energy reserves. This artefact of geopolitics has temporal legacies that shape subsequent energy infrastructure.

Technocratic legitimation exhibits a temporal dimension in the same case with Berlin's requirements for cascading generating capacity during the security-oriented strategy of the 1970s. These embed particular protocols into energy infrastructure that extend into current sectoral standards. In the Indonesian land conflict case, the transfer of nearly one million hectares of official forestland in West Java to the State Forest Corporation in 1978 centralises authority away from the province in a manner that gains significance during land ownership conflicts three decades later. Financial legitimation expresses temporally as a highlighted singularity in the Berlin case where, in contrast to urban politics shaping energy infrastructure investments, financing simply did not require validation at the urban scale during the Cold War years of prioritised energy security and West German government subsidies to Berlin.

10.2.3 The Opportunism Dimension

Within this dimension, discursive legitimation comes into play in the Indonesian land conflict case when the State Forest Corporation announces a planting ceremony of 1000 mahogany seedlings in rows named after government institutions, as well as when the villagers promptly uproot them overnight, both channelling the occasion into the purposive reframing of where authority rests, through imposition and resistance. Bureaucratic legitimation is notable within this dimension in the same case when the villagers request (and are granted) new ID cards from the Village Office as the local territorial administration, which renders their settlements official sub-villages in the territorial area claimed by the State Forest Corporation.

Technocratic legitimation exhibits an opportunistic dimension in the Norwegian zero growth target-setting case, when the National Transport Plan Working Group reasons that 'zero' is a very easy target to measure and thus useful in holding cities to account, and in subsequent agreements signed by Norway's largest cities with indicators to track performance on urban car traffic. Financial legitimation comes up in the Indonesian land conflict case by way of the provisory system of payment by villagers to the Sundanese Peasant's Movement, rather than paying rent illegally demanded by the State Forest Corporation. It is also present in each sub-village's annual contributions to the Village Office, in essence embodying a land tax to establish the villagers' claim as landholders.

10.2.4 The Prefiguration Dimension

Here, discursive legitimation is apparent in the Norwegian zero growth target-setting case, where the White Paper on Norwegian Climate Policy 2006 articulates the need for a shift to public and non-motorised transport, the White Paper on Norwegian Climate Policy 2012 formulates this as a 'goal' or target, and the Zero Growth Objective states that all growth in personal traffic in Norway's largest cities must come through public or non-motorised transport. Bureaucratic legitimation also takes on a prefigurative dimension in the same case, where Norway's policies (such as the Climate Accord of 2008) consistently reference a 2 °C target to limit global warming and work this into a range of national documents and strategies, including for urban transport. This imbrication of a broad goal into concrete policies firms up the possibility of a stronger basis for ambitious energy transitions in urban mobility.

Technocratic legitimation is instantiated as prefigurative in the Colorado habitat exchange case in the innovation of the Habitat Quantification Tool, which can calculate compensation amounts for replacement of sage-grouse habitats. This paves the path for biodiversity conservation mechanisms in circumstances of greater political will. Financial legitimation is evidently prefigurative in the Norwegian target-setting case, where the Urban Environment Agreements under the Zero Growth Objective tie the central funding allocated to cities for local transport infrastructure with their prowess in meeting the target. This linkage moves future incentives for the sectoral evolution of urban mobility into closer alignment with accountability to sustainable energy transition targets.

10.2.5 The Performativity Dimension

Within this dimension, discursive legitimation is evident in the Colorado case, where the state habitat exchange was represented as relevant and vibrant despite never recording any transactions, and was used to argue against protecting the sage-grouse under a federal Endangered Species Act. The habitat exchange served as a mechanism to perform and uphold hollow accountability without changing substantive relations on the ground. Bureaucratic legitimation plays a performative role in the Norwegian case, where Norway's policies consistently reference a 2 °C target to limit global warming and have worked this into a range of national documents and strategies; this can also be seen as prefigurative in Sub-Sect. 10.2.4.

Technocratic legitimation is at work within the performative dimension in the Colorado case in terms of the strategy of championing a market mechanism to circumvent critique of coercive bureaucracy and benefit from efficiencies like low transaction costs. This strategy brings the Habitat Exchange and Habitat Quantification Tool into being. Financial legitimation is performative in the same case: questions of finance are used to delegitimate the whole exercise as the subject of controversy when the oil and gas industry protests the debits assigned to them based on the modelled cost calculations, as well as when it resigns from the governance board of the habitat exchange.

10.2.6 The Power-play Dimension

Here, discursive legitimation is in evidence in the Nordic electric mobility transition case. People's scepticism about hybrid vehicles surfaces in concerns that these allow their owners to cash in on incentives (for adopting low-emission vehicles) without affording the means to monitor their actual usage of electricity rather than the internal combustion engines. In the Indonesian land conflict case, the State Forest Corporation invokes military terms such as 'illegal loggers' and 'subversive' to draw equivalence between the villagers' land occupation and organised crime, another instance of power-play through discursive delegitimation. Bureaucratic legitimation operates as power-play in the Nordic case, when Norway offers all-inclusive incentive packages and Denmark maintains lower duties (40% instead of 150%) for electric vehicles, but incentive schemes to electrify public transport remain far less substantial.

Technocratic legitimation manifests within the power-play dimension in the Indonesian land conflict case, where the State Forest Corporation uses the formal characterisation and protocols associated with national security to evict villagers as 'forest security disturbances'. This legitimation allows the state to levy its might against claim-making subjects. Financial legitimation embodies power-play in the Nordic electric mobility transitions case. Enormous support is provided for private electric cars used by relatively rich people, without similarly strong support to rapidly build out public electric transport infrastructure or cushion vulnerable groups against the regressive effects of fiscal policies on electric mobility.

10.2.7 The Routinisation Dimension

Within this dimension, discursive legitimation is in evidence in the Colorado habitat exchange case. The federal administration puts an end to mandatory compensatory mitigation by drawing explicit links with energy independence to make energy extraction an issue of national security. In the Nordic electric mobility transition case, protest against discursive legitimation to routinise inequitable transition surfaces as people's critique of political tokenism in public discourse around electric vehicles. Bureaucratic legitimation is expressed as routinisation in the Colorado case, where efforts by Environmental Defense, layered upon prior experiences with habitat offsets, orchestrate participation in the creation and governance of the Colorado Habitat Exchange by various relevant actors.

Technocratic legitimation appears as routinisation in the Nordic case, which identifies dynamics such as promoting off-peak charging, mandating battery recycling to reduce externalities, emphasising the decarbonisation of electric grids and coordinating electric vehicle roll-out with prioritised non-motorised and intermodal electric transport. Financial legitimation manifests as routinisation in the Colorado habitat exchange case. Finance remains absent in practice, but present in the very logic of markets as mechanisms for the efficient implementation of accountability on which the market-based offsetting of habitat loss is premised.

10.3 Environmental Governance Research on Accountability in Energy Transitions

Not all cases of energy transition necessarily feature practices of legitimation across all dimensions. The dimensions are partly an artefact of each author's strategically chosen focus and partly reflect data availability. Thinking in terms of accountability and legitimation does not supplant other methods and common sense, but rather offers diagnostic value. It is purposely pliable; the dimensions are overlapping, not mutually exclusive, nor comprehensive. Applied researchers and analytically oriented practitioners can apply the practices of legitimation to fit situated needs, mobilising the four registers within strategic dimensions of their choice. This analytical approach to accountability is based in abductive reasoning to settle upon the likeliest possible explanation in any given case of energy transition and pragmatically inform decision-making despite uncertainty. Such analysis can characterise disaggregated components of any energy transition case as accountable to concerns of sustainability or not. Scientifically evidencing both the formal and informal practices of legitimation that are at work during energy transitions can aid decision-making towards outcomes that decarbonise and enhance social equity. This approach can thus combine analytical rigour with practical applicability and real-world relevance.

The five cases in this book show that energy transitions are many things and involve not only changing energy sectors but also cognate sectors such as land, forest, transport, biodiversity, markets and political economies of multi-scalar contexts. Our practically oriented vision of enabling accountable governance for sustainable energy transitions represents a programmatic task across many sectors. To inform practical decision-making of various energy transitions and their constituent parts in contextually informed and responsive ways, applied researchers can operationalise an accountability-based approach in their respective fields within broader environmental governance scholarship. Their domain knowledge and disciplinary sensibilities will help them customise this approach to suit their purposes.

The illustrations in this book aim to aid such intellectual uptake and cross-fertilisation, and thus pave the path for situated efforts to study practices of legitimation. To demonstrate the generative potential of an accountability-based analytical approach to energy transitions governance, we offer closing reflections by working sequentially outward from the five cases.

In the Berlin case, Timothy Moss shows the relevance of historical accounts focused on accountability analysis to inform our understanding of energy transitions today by deconstructing assumptions along spatial and temporal axes. His overarching point is that histories of energy provision and use can be instructive sources of inspiration. The issue of accountability is not the preserve of present-day energy governance. It has been invoked in myriad ways in the past to justify energy solutions in certain places at certain times. History helps us understand accountability, therefore, as a situated political construct. This sensitises scholars not only to the variety of justifications that have been mobilised in the name of particular purposes and beneficiaries in the past but also to the ephemeral nature of accountability criteria. What today may seem self-explanatory, may tomorrow be questioned.

History can point us to times and places when crises of accountability did challenge prevalent logics, policies or practices of energy provision. Such critical junctures can reveal past attempts to delegitimate a hegemonic sociotechnical configuration and assess their achievements with the benefit of hindsight. At the same time, history can generate an appreciation of the obduracy of argumentative tropes enrolled to legitimate the predominant system. As the Berlin case illustrated, institutional norms can prove just as path dependent as the material structures they regulate. The fixation on energy security—and the capacity reserves this engendered—in West Berlin during the Cold War era created a legacy of insularity with which the city is still struggling to cope even 30 years after reunification.

Finally, history can direct attention to the roots of sustainability thinking in a particular space-time context. Sustainability as we know it was not a term in use before the 1970s, but its origins can be instructive, such as past efforts to save energy, use renewables or challenge supply-driven logics of supply. The social movements pioneering novel modes of accountable energy governance in Berlin today cannot be comprehended fully, Moss argues, without reference to their forebearers and the historically constructed sociotechnical regimes they challenged in bygone decades.

Christian Lund employs a conflict-centred approach anchored in a reading of classic texts within development studies, political science and political ecology to show how empirical examination of accountability is linked with the constitution of authority and subjecthood. Lund's (2016) overall argument is that to treat the 'state' (or any other institution) as a finished product gets in the way of understanding it. It is always in the making. Political authority is (re)produced through its successful exercise; especially when exercised over important issues in relation to the social actors concerned.

Arguably, when institutions recognise claims to rights, they themselves become recognised by the claimants of these rights. That is to say, rights and authority are mutually and simultaneously established. Claims therefore invoke public authority and governing capacity in different institutions, be they statutory or not. And, conversely, those who can claim to authorise people's claims to rights acquire and exercise political authority.

This dynamic is garnered with attempts at legitimating the claims to rights and authority. However, just as the institutions are never truly settled but are, in fact, processes, the repertoires of legitimation are also contingent. To understand these dynamics of institutional formation requires grounded, empirical research allowing us to go beyond state theories modelled after ahistorical ideal types.

Lund's argument thus points to directions where fieldwork-based analyses of accountability can attend to indirect and under-attended aspects of energy transitions.

Håvard Haarstad brings a human geography and urban planning lens to bear on accountability along with a science and technology studies concern with metrics, revealing the relational modulation of energy transitions across multiple scales. His chapter deals with the question of whether climate targets matter for actual policy implementation. He observes that climate-related targets are all around—countries have them, regions have them, cities have them. Does this have any effects on how practical politics proceed, on what happens in practice? Much of the social sciences would take a sceptical view. Swyngedouw's (2010) popular rendering of the 'post-political condition', for example, describes climate targets as part of a techno-managerial apparatus that shifts rhetoric towards climate change but at the same time makes sure that nothing actually happens. While recognising the merits of a sceptical view, Haarstad aims to look at the other side of this coin. Is it possible that targets, even seemingly overly ambitious ones, may have real and substantive effects contributing to a sustainable transition?

He starts from the basic idea that there is power in numbers. As many social scientists have pointed out, quantification makes nature knowable and controllable (Miller 2005). This could mean that reducing a sustainable transition—a messy, complicated and multifaceted process—to a quantifiable target can have powerful effects. In fact, While et al. (2010) argue that, by lending itself to quantification, climate change becomes a potentially powerful target of political action and regulation. Haarstad points to one instance of how a quantified goal (zero) becomes enrolled and legitimated in political practice and, arguably, effects substantive change. Since 2006, the goal of having 'zero growth' in private car traffic has worked its way into Norwegian policy-making across a range of areas, particularly transport and urban development. It affects flows of funding from the national government to the major cities. It has become a major condition for urban policy-making.

This illustrates how a quantified target has the potential to work its way into the 'techno-managerial apparatus' (Swyngedouw 2010) and inflect material change. This particular case entailed a combination of involved soft mechanisms, as the target gradually inserted itself in the discourse on urban policy and moved its goal posts, and hard mechanisms, namely national-to-urban funding flows. The takeaway message is that climate-related targets can play an important role in legitimating practices that advance sustainable energy transitions.

Benjamin Sovacool demonstrates how a political economic, multi-sited comparative deconstruction of sectoral change from a public policy and social justice perspective can surface uneasy questions about accountability even in progressive energy transitions. Such an analysis offers a compelling antidote to the optimism inherent in much current discussion and debate about the desirability of electric mobility as a pathway for environmental sustainability. In this context, due to the transportation sector's dependence on fossil fuel energy sources and the monumental negative consequences for climate change, air pollution and other social impacts, countless researchers, policymakers and other stakeholders view a widespread transition to electric mobility as both feasible and socially desirable (Mitchell et al. 2010; Tran et al. 2012). The International Energy Agency (2017) projects under the 'Sustainable Development Scenario' that 875 million electric vehicles (EVs) will need to be adopted by 2040. Mitchell et al. (2010) call EVs nothing short of 'transformative' and 'revolutionary' for their potential effects on mobility patterns. Turton and Moura (2008, p. 1091) add that when EVs are placed in a vehicle-to-grid configuration, their transformative potential multiplies, representing 'a paradigm shift in how the energy and mobility markets are related'.

However, the Nordic transition to electric mobility when viewed from a framing of sector-wide multi-scalar linkages, questions this so-called revolution. It underscores how wedding accountability to analyses of vulnerability and justice in energy transitions can fruitfully change the frame and criteria by which we examine mobility transitions. In addition, many of the injustices identified, or the issues of equity and vulnerability that arise, are not 'new' to electric mobility—they likely exist with other low-carbon technologies and also conventional cars and other forms of mobility. However, a lesson here is perhaps that changing the performance or engine of a vehicle, or introducing a new type of car such as battery electric vehicle, does not necessarily change the underlying political economy or power dynamics behind mobility or automobility. Systems of mobility themselves—involving multiple, competing and overlapping technologies, modes of mobility and transport infrastructures—can also be just or unjust, even if they utilise innovations such as electric vehicles. The justice potential of electric mobility is therefore situational, relational and contingent.

Steven Wolf develops an environmental sociology framework to address dynamics in biodiversity conservation. The case of the sage-grouse, a ground-nesting bird imperilled by energy development in Colorado, USA, offers a window onto broader challenges of energy transitions and socio-ecological regulation. The chapter pursues a general, abstract analysis of accountability within environmental governance. Accountability mechanisms are identified as 'tests' of conformity with institutionalised norms. These tests mediate access to legitimacy and other resources that structure competition and organisational ecology dynamics (i.e., shifts in the population of actors and behaviours) (Kraft and Wolf 2018). The co-evolutionary model of socioecological regulation that is presented seeks to offer an integrated, dynamic treatment of accountability (e.g., social controls developed to regulate land use changes that reduce sage-grouse habitat), standards of legitimacy (e.g., prevailing norms regarding the appropriateness of accountability mechanisms), sociotechnical practices (e.g., oil and gas drilling activities) and environmental quality (e.g., health of sage-grouse populations). This theoretical treatment highlights opportunities for research on accountability to inform general analyses of governance and regulation.

The empirical analysis highlights how efforts to advance habitat offsetting (i.e., market-based approaches to conserving land in order to compensate for degradation of sage-grouse habitat) have served to maintain the legitimacy of existing models of oil and gas development. More specifically, Wolf's analysis highlights how multi-stakeholder dialogue around construction of habitat offsetting mechanisms and mobilisation of scientific expertise and quantification routines are implicated in performing conservation without producing measurable protections for sage-grouse. To date, after seven years of engagement, no habitat has been conserved in Colorado through the habitat exchange. Yet the public construction of elaborate new accountability routines and promises of future capacity to achieve 'no-net loss' of habitat seems to function adequately to legitimate existing socioecological relations. In this sense, accountability processes are a central mechanism through which we sustain the unsustainable (Blühdorn 2007).

To conclude, we come full circle to the urgency of the climate change challenge, the need for sustainable energy transitions, and the conundrum that such sociotechnical transitions are feasible and desperately needed despite which they are held back in a wide variety of ways. The response unpacked by means of an accountability-centred analytical approach is that a dynamic configuration of legitimation practices that constrain and enable sustainable energy transitions manifest this conundrum. Identifying and evidencing these practices as applied researchers and analytically oriented practitioners, we can unravel the present conundrum and advance accountable governance for sustainable energy transitions. We trust that the pointers and reflections offered in this book will motivate and equip colleagues to support this endeavour.

REFERENCES

Blühdorn, I. (2007). Sustaining the unsustainable: Symbolic politics and the politics of simulation. *Environmental Politics, 16*, 251–275.

International Energy Agency. (2017). *World energy outlook 2017.* Paris: OECD.

Kraft, B., & Wolf, S. (2018). Through the lens of accountability: Analyzing legitimacy in environmental governance. *Organization & Environment, 31*, 70–92. https://doi.org/10.1177/1086026616680682

Lund, C. (2016). Rule and rupture. State formation through the production of property and citizenship. *Development and Change, 47*(6), 1199–1228.

Miller, C. (2005). New civic epistemologies of quantification: Making sense of indicators of local and global sustainability. *Science, Technology and Human Values, 30*, 403–432.

Mitchell, W. J., Borroni-Bird, C. E., & Burns, L. D. (2010). *Reinventing the automobile personal urban mobility for the 21st century.* Cambridge, MA: MIT Press.

Sareen, S. (2019a). Practices of legitimation and accountability crises in a range of energy transitions. In *Enabling sustainable energy transitions: Practices of legitimation and accountable governance.* London: Palgrave Macmillan.

Sareen, S. (2019b). A typology of practices of legitimation to categorise accountability relations. In *Enabling sustainable energy transitions: Practices of legitimation and accountable governance.* London: Palgrave Macmillan.

Swyngedouw, E. (2010). Apocalypse forever? Post-political populism and the spectre of climate change. *Theory, Culture & Society, 27*, 213–232.

Tran, M., Banister, D., Bishop, J. D. K., & McCulloch, M. D. (2012). Realizing the electric-vehicle revolution. *Nature Climate Change, 2*, 328–333.

Turton, H., & Moura, F. (2008). Vehicle-to-grid systems for sustainable development: An integrated energy analysis. *Technological Forecasting and Social Change, 75*, 1091–1108.

While, A., Jonas, A., & Gibbs, D. (2010). From sustainable development to carbon control: Eco-state restructuring and the politics of urban and regional development. *Transactions of the Institute of British Geographers, 35*, 76–93.

Open Access This chapter is licensed under the terms of the Creative Commons Attribution 4.0 International License (http://creativecommons.org/licenses/by/4.0/), which permits use, sharing, adaptation, distribution and reproduction in any medium or format, as long as you give appropriate credit to the original author(s) and the source, provide a link to the Creative Commons licence and indicate if changes were made.

The images or other third party material in this chapter are included in the chapter's Creative Commons licence, unless indicated otherwise in a credit line to the material. If material is not included in the chapter's Creative Commons licence and your intended use is not permitted by statutory regulation or exceeds the permitted use, you will need to obtain permission directly from the copyright holder.

Correction to: Enabling Sustainable Energy Transitions

Correction to:
Siddharth Sareen, Enabling Sustainable Energy Transitions, https://doi.org/10.1007/978-3-030-26891-6

This book was inadvertently published with the incorrect copyright holder "The Editor(s) (if applicable) and The Author(s), under exclusive licence to Springer Nature Switzerland AG". This has now been amended throughout the book to the correct copyright holder "The Editor(s) (if applicable) and The Author(s)".

The following sentence has been included in the Acknowledgment section.

Siddharth Sareen: "The author gratefully acknowledges funding from a University of Bergen postdoctoral research fellowship (financed by Bergen Research Foundation and University of Bergen-Equinor Akademia Agreement), the Open Access publication fund at the University of Bergen, the Strategic Programme for International Research Collaboration and the Faculty of Social Sciences at the University of Bergen."

Timothy Moss: "Gerda Henkel Foundation"

The updated version of the book can be found at
https://doi.org/10.1007/978-3-030-26891-6

Christian Lund: "The research for this paper has benefitted from generous funding from the Danish Research Council and the European Research Council (ERC). ERC Grant: State Formation Through the Local Production of Property and Citizenship (Ares (2015)2785650 – ERC-2014-AdG – 662770-Local State)."

Appendix A

A WORKSHOP, PARALLEL EXHIBITIONS AND ASSOCIATED EVENTS

Several factors ensured a productive and convivial writing process, and made this book possible. The conditions of its production also served a further purpose through their own ontology, embodying its intent of being accessible to a wider audience. This appendix tells the story of much of what went into the making of this book and the collaborations that inform it.

Stemming from concerns of social and environmental equity and justice, my interest in accountability has been informed by instruction from and engagement with the co-authors. Christian Lund's work on how authority is produced in reflexive relation with claims over rights motivated a focus on relational practices. Steven Wolf's work, drawing together accountability, legitimation and empirical artefacts—captured in Kraft and Wolf (2018)—shaped thinking around practices of legitimation as an entry point to the empirical study of accountability. Håvard Haarstad's work on relational ontology and the networked governance of efforts to decarbonise informed the development of a relational approach. Benjamin Sovacool's work on energy justice was instructive in determining how to engage decarbonisation and social equity enhancement as twin aspects of accountability in governing energy transitions to sustainability. Timothy Moss' work, deepening historical understandings of energy transition drivers, nuanced views on the basis for and implications of contemporary energy sector accountability relations.

These scholars generously agreed to engage and contribute insights based on their empirical work to collectively consider an analytical approach centred on the study of practices of legitimation. Featuring their work from fields as varied as human and economic geography, development studies, energy studies, environmental sociology and history enables the book to speak to colleagues across wide-ranging disciplines and applied research traditions. This aims to catalyse a greater analytical focus on accountable energy transitions within environmental governance scholarship.

In addition, vibrant fields of social science research on the governance of energy transitions and cognate subjects furnished arguments to engage with and concepts to inspire and direct critical thinking. A workshop grant enabled the co-authors to come together in Bergen during 14–17 May 2019, along with authors of 15 manuscripts prepared for a special issue of the Global Transitions journal on a closely related theme, for two days of discussions amongst over 20 scholars. For this opportunity, I am grateful to the Strategic Programme for International Research Collaboration, and to the Faculty of Social Sciences at the University of Bergen. In parallel with this workshop, I co-organised two public exhibitions. The first was built around the concept of an 'Idea box for energy transitions', and the second was a collaboration within a show titled 'Potential exceeds the demand' by textile artist Margrethe Brekke.

The idea box for energy transitions was a physical invitation to the public to contribute their solutions for energy transitions by putting sheets with their writing into a slot in a box painted in the yellow colour of the Sustainable Development Goal (SDG) 7. This SDG aims to achieve clean energy for all. I designed the idea box largely from upcycled materials, and with the assistance of several colleagues, curated workshops to collect solutions. The idea box was launched at the opening weekend of the European Green Capital 2019 in Oslo, from where people posted ideas to Bergen. It was then installed at the Bergen Public Library from January to March 2019, and carried around to workshops during this period. These included a workshop on the accountable governance of sustainable energy transitions during the National SDG Conference 2019, workshops with teachers and citizens interested in energy, and an event integrated into the Klimathon (an annual national event on climate adaptation). A group of colleagues at the Centre for Climate and Energy Transformation built an exhibition around the ideas that came in, which ran during 10–20 May 2019 at the Bergen Public Library. This included a selection of books related to energy transitions as well as prints of 17 motifs from a 6.25 square metre textile art from the other exhibition, alongside the idea box itself.

The collaboration with Margrethe Brekke's exhibition emerged organically during late 2018. Hosted at the Hordaland Kunstsenter art gallery during May–July 2019, this exhibition provided visual portrayals of existing possibilities for energy transitions. We discussed ways of depicting a future energy system powered largely by renewable energy, with her visualisations and my technical inputs. This resulted in her textile piece titled 'Rhythmic energy mixes: Days and years with Dr. Siddharth Sareen', which emphasised flexible daily and annual cycles of such energy systems. Details of the motifs she developed for this large piece were part of the parallel idea box exhibition. The Hordaland Kunstsenter exhibition also featured a poem I wrote and performed during an event called 'Fest for Fesken' (party for the fish) organised by the people's campaign for a fossil-free Arctic (Folkeaksjonen oljefritt Lofoten, Vesterålen og Senja) at Bergen's Café Opera on 14 November 2018, reflecting on my time spent engaging with climate activism in the sister city of Seattle during September–October 2018. This poem, 'The case for hope amidst climate change catastrophe', was recorded and displayed on headphones with accompanying visuals that featured Brekke's textile art, and the book concludes with it.

During the mid-May workshop, I anchored a discussion between Margrethe Brekke and Benjamin Sovacool on the 'Imaginaries of energy transition: Public, artistic and academic' at the art gallery. Judith Dalsgård developed this into a podcast as part of a series at the Centre for Climate and Energy Transformation. Workshop participants and interested local residents toured Brekke's exhibition and were also given a tour of the idea box exhibition. These activities constituted a form of engagement with various publics beyond academia, including Bergen's cultural and artistic community. They also enabled two-way engagement rather than outreach, providing a window of insight into what people think about energy transitions and inviting them into a sustained exchange with energy scholars. The exhibitions built a basis for collaboration with public institutions such as Bergen Public Library and Hordaland Kunstsenter. Opening and closing sessions as well as six keynote talks (five of them based on the case chapters and a sixth by Sunila Kale) during the mid-May workshop were livestreamed and made permanently available on the Youtube channel of Bergen Public Library. Children from the International School of Bergen, directed by Annie Sareen, contributed short thematic theatrical performances during the workshop.

As with many things, it is possible to say that 'it takes a village' to govern energy transitions to be accountable to public interests like decarbonising while enhancing social equity. The ontology of producing the content of this book, by way of the workshop and these parallel events, took many parts of the city of Bergen. Along with any influence it might have on wider audiences, this local effect of connecting people and institutions constitutes a key outcome of the book project. Such efforts are vital for building a platform to nurture greater public awareness regarding the accountable governance of energy transitions. Documenting them as part of this book closes the circle and hopes to encourage others to undertake similar efforts customised to their local contexts. Appendix B complements this textual narrative with a photographic essay that captures some key details of the events that took place in Bergen during May 2019.

Reference

Kraft, B., & Wolf, S. (2018). Through the lens of accountability: Analyzing legitimacy in environmental governance. *Organization & Environment*, *31*(1), 70–92.

Appendix B

Photos from the Events in Bergen, May 2019

This appendix, a photo essay, documents visual details from two exhibitions that ran in parallel with the mid-May workshop in Bergen, and from the workshop itself.[1] It is divided into four sections: photos from the 'Idea box for energy transitions' exhibition at Bergen Public Library, photos from the 'Potential exceeds the demand' exhibition at the Hordaland Kunstsenter art gallery, photos from the workshop titled 'Accountability analysis: Enabling sustainability under energy sector transitions' and a poem that was part of the art gallery exhibition. All photos were taken during 9–17 May 2019 in Bergen.

The Idea Box for Energy Transitions—An Exhibition at Bergen Public Library
Several colleagues associated with the Centre for Climate and Energy Transformation at the University of Bergen helped me curate the 'Idea box for energy transitions' exhibition—Judith Dalsgård, Thea Gregersen, Tshin Ilya Chardayre, Gregory Ferguson-Cradler and Amber Nordholm— along with collaborating artist Margrethe Brekke and the director of Hordaland Kunstsenter, Mathijs van Geest. Several of us are pictured here,

---

[1] Except Figs. B1.2, B1.3 and B1.7 where the Hordaland Kunstsenter art gallery is duly credited, all photos used were taken or arranged by the author.

Fig. B1.1 Setting up the exhibition at Bergen Public Library

right after having finished installing the exhibition a day prior to its opening on 10 May 2019 at Bergen Public Library.

The exhibition featured a selection of solutions for energy transitions submitted by the public through various workshops, as well as an assortment of thematically pertinent books, and motifs from a large textile piece at the parallel exhibition at Hordaland Kunstsenter. It was placed in a central room at the Bergen Public Library to share the crowd-sourced social imaginary with people in Bergen.

APPENDIX B   143

Fig. B1.2 The 'Idea box for energy transitions' exhibition. (Photo credit: Hordaland Kunstsenter)

The exhibition was installed in a manner that invited engagement, and designed to be approachable from any direction. People could leaf through folders with ideas, take a brochure with background information about the initiative with them, and pick up a flyer of the workshop held in the same building during the exhibition. The idea box itself, which collected ideas during January–March 2019, is also visible as part of the exhibition. The exhibition was listed as an Energy Days event and associated with the European Union Sustainable Energy Week.

144 APPENDIX B

Fig. B1.3 The idea box as part of the exhibition at Bergen Public Library. (Photo credit: Hordaland Kunstsenter)

During the workshop, 20 researchers from abroad spent three days discussing analytical approaches centred around accountability for the governance of energy transitions towards sustainability. On the afternoon of 15 May, they stepped out of the auditorium at Bergen Public Library to take a look at the exhibition in the main space of this century old institution.

APPENDIX B   145

Fig. B1.4 Workshop participants browse the idea box for energy transitions exhibition

Those associated with the exhibition, including collaborating artist Margrethe Brekke, shared reflections on the process with workshop participants. Here, the art gallery director is explicating connections between the two exhibitions.

Fig. B1.5 Bridging the exhibitions at Bergen Public Library and Hordaland Kunstsenter

Potential Exceeds the Demand—An Exhibition at Hordaland Kunstsenter Art Gallery
The title of Margrethe Brekke's art exhibition emphasised the fact that we already have technological potential for low-carbon transitions far in excess of what is currently taking place. Our collaboration on one of her textile pieces revolved around visualising a future renewable energy system. The circular pattern with motifs representing many energy generating technologies highlights possibilities for flexibility, both daily and annually, in future energy systems with high levels of penetration of renewable sources of energy. It depicts the potential of technologies like agri-photovoltaics, concentrating solar power and reverse hydro pumping for a sustainable energy transition.

APPENDIX B   147

Fig. B1.6 'Rhythmic energy mixes: Days and years with Dr. Siddharth Sareen' by Margrethe Brekke

Margrethe Brekke's exhibition at Hordaland Kunstsenter featured three textile pieces of 6.25 square metres each, accompanied by some smaller works and two audio recordings with videos. The three large pieces dominated the art gallery space and conversed with each other. Each spoke to a wider audience based on scientific understandings of potential energy transitions, with basic shapes, colours and patterns representing specific volumes, proportions and time.

Fig. B1.7 Margrethe Brekke's 'Potential exceeds the demand' exhibition at Hordaland Kunstsenter

Margrethe Brekke gave a guided tour of her art exhibition to workshop participants and interested people in Bergen to kick off a collaborative art and academia evening event on 14 May 2019. This brought together those familiar with the city's cultural scene and several international visitors with insights from research on environmental governance and energy transitions.

APPENDIX B 149

Fig. B1.8 Margrethe Brekke reflects on her art exhibition while giving a guided tour

Margrethe Brekke after giving a guided tour of her exhibition, with Annie Sareen, who directed a thematic performance by the children of the International School of Bergen the next day. In the background is Kristin Frøya, energy director at the University of Bergen, who also collaborated with Brekke for the exhibition with an audio recording that connected energy transitions with lived experience in Norway, and Timothy Moss, a keynote speaker at the workshop the rest of the week. The headphones on the wall featured an audio recording of my poem 'The case for hope amidst climate change catastrophe', whose text is included at the end of this appendix.

Fig. B1.9 The forces behind the artistic events

A large, engaged audience filled Hordaland Kunstsenter for the collaborative evening event. Here, they listen attentively to Magrethe Brekke's reflections on the role of the arts in enabling energy transitions, and experiences during her own journey from engaging utopian ideals to channelling scientific knowledge in her textile art. Benjamin Sovacool, a keynote speaker during the workshop and photographed here, followed Brekke's presentation by drawing from his research on energy justice and humanising energy transitions along lines of gender, labour and geographical topographies of power. Their talks and a discussion I moderated between them is available as an hour-long podcast, the sixth episode in the CET Climate Talks series.[2]

---

[2] Available online at https://www.uib.no/en/cet/124342/podcast-cet-climate-talks.

Fig. B1.10 'Imaginaries of energy transition: Public, artistic and academic' with Margrethe Brekke and Benjamin Sovacool

The discussion between Brekke and Sovacool was followed by a social evening and continued discussions on the theme amongst the audience, which included residents of Bergen and workshop participants who had just arrived in the city.

Fig. B1.11 Exchanges between the arts, academia and the public

Workshop on 'Accountability Analysis: Enabling Sustainability Under Energy Sector Transitions'
During the opening session of the workshop on accountability analysis and sustainable energy transitions in the main auditorium of Bergen Public Library, children from the International School of Bergen did theatrical performances on related themes, including climate change, deforestation and biodiversity, which they spent months preparing for as part of their classes on performing arts.

Fig. B1.12 Theatrical performances by International School of Bergen students directed by Annie Sareen

The workshop participants and other interested people in Bergen joined two intensive days packed with six keynote talks, 15 paper discussions and opening and closing sessions about practices of legitimation and accountability analysis for energy transitions governance towards sustainability. These discussions, which included all the co-authors of this book, were invaluable towards finalising this manuscript, as well as airing and providing feedback on articles that were subsequently submitted to a special issue of the Global Transitions journal on the same theme.

Fig. B1.13 The accountability analysis workshop at Bergen Public Library

The five case chapter authors of this book gave keynote talks during the workshop, as did Sunila Kale of the University of Washington-Seattle. Here, Timothy Moss gives the first of these keynotes, historicising accountability through Berlin's energy transitions, based on his argument in Chap. 4 of this book. These talks as well as the opening and closing sessions of the workshop were live-streamed and are available on the Youtube channel of Bergen Public Library.[3]

---

[3] Available online at https://www.youtube.com/user/bergenpubliclibrary/videos (dated 15–16 May 2019).

APPENDIX B   155

Fig. B1.14 Timothy Moss gives a keynote talk at the workshop on accountability analysis

The workshop keynote talks were followed by lively discussions where participants took the stage along with the speakers. The 15 paper presentations were presented by discussants based on pre-circulated manuscripts, with authors subsequently responding to these interpretations and leading into a discussion with the workshop participants. Here, Christian Lund poses a question to Håvard Haarstad about his analysis of target-setting for climate mitigation, which comprises Chap. 6 of this book.

156   APPENDIX B

Fig. B1.15 Christian Lund and Håvard Haarstad during a workshop keynote session

The workshop also served as an occasion for researchers in many countries to become better acquainted and discuss their work on the governance of energy transitions and cognate themes in a relaxed social setting outside the academic sessions. At the end of the first of two days packed with sessions, participants gathered at the Bergen Public Library restaurant, Amalies Hage, for a long meal.

Fig. B1.16 Discussions among the workshop participants continued over dinner

At the end of two days of sessions, the workshop keynote speakers and some accompanying family members gathered over a closing dinner at the local restaurant Colonialen 44. Pictured from left to right are Steven Wolf, Annie Sareen, myself, Peter Andersen (head of the Department of Geography at University of Bergen), Christian Lund, Håvard Haarstad, Timothy Moss and his wife Ulrike, and Shobha succeeded by her daughter Sunila Kale.

Fig. B1.17 Closing workshop dinner with keynote speakers

The workshop was planned to end with Norwegian Constitution Day, the national day of Norway, on Friday, 17 May 2019. This started with a traditional breakfast at the hotel where the keynotes stayed, by Bergen's central lake. Visible in the window is a passerby in her national dress, a bunad. Later in the day, workshop participants joined in the traditional parade through the city streets and spent a day enjoying Bergen at its best in glorious spring weather with happy people out and about.

APPENDIX B 159

Fig. B1.18 Starting festivities on the national day of Norway

Some workshop participants joined the traditional closing procession, carrying torches from the thirteenth-century Bergenhus fortress past the famous Bryggen harbour and into the centre of Bergen where many residents had gathered for the annual public fireworks show to close the celebrations. In the middle is Lakin Anderson, a doctoral candidate at Uppsala University who participated in the workshop as part of his fieldwork to research the practices of climate and energy scientists at the Centre for Climate and Energy Transformation as a case study for his dissertation.

Fig. B1.19 A traditional torchlight procession through Bergen

The workshop ended with a bang with the annual fireworks show at the central lake in Bergen, called Lille Lungegårdsvannet (or Smålungeren in the Bergensk dialect). A viking boat mock-up is visible, and behind the fireworks one can discern the tallest of Bergen's seven mountains, Ulriken. With that, three intense and productive days of academic and wider collaboration drew to a close.

Fig. B1.20 The annual fireworks on 17 May in Bergen

The final section of the appendix ends this book with a poem that makes the case for hope amidst climate change catastrophe. The poem embodies an extension of the book's main line of argument. It gently but firmly states that, while enabling sustainable energy transitions is hard and prospects can at times look bleak, the stakes to ensure accountability are high, and we do have the tools and means at our disposal.

The Case for Hope Amidst Climate Change Catastrophe

Is hope apocalyptic after all?
Does it let us wait, twiddling our thumbs,
In between bursts
Of furious
Activity?

Do we find kindred spirits
In our search for salvation and think
We are closer
To accomplishment?

When in fact, loss follows loss,
Wildfires burn,
Countries drown,
Species disappear.

Or would that be an unkind misconstrual?

Do times like this
Render us in need
Of friends, now more than ever?

Is compassion our mast
Hope our guiding star
And empathy born of friendship
The wind in our gutsy sails?

Who loses? What prevails?

We fought for Initiative sixteen thirty-one
The Pacific Northwest
The first frontier
Of hope for change to a politics of trying
Of recognising
What times call on us to do.

To make polluters pay, to compensate
Victims of fossil fuels and give a chance
To an energy sector powered by renewables

In the here and now
Rather than
A decade hence.

But Big Oil poured in millions
Money talked and people listened
The Initiative took a beating.

Opportunities are fleeting
And it's already
Out of sight, out of mind,
All that we must leave behind.

No time to mope, the only way
To cope is to return to hope.

Or is it? Does hope motivate
Here in Seattle's sister city
Connected by a totem pole
Down at Nordnes in Bergen?

Or does remoteness obfuscate
While hope simply distracts,
Sustaining the unsustainable
Regurgitating facts
About one point five degrees
While delaying acts
That would keep it all in the ground,
Firmly under the sea
Out around Lofoten
Where our politics are floundering
Much like Pacific island states?

What scope is there for hope
When murder merely agitates
Blinded by greed? A world that's rigged
To keep expanding drilling.
Pumped by oil, we grease the wheels
And keep the coffers filling.
Softly we murmur "We are better
Than others at not spilling."

The most majestic icebergs thaw
Glaciers are melting
New trade routes emerge
As opportunity.
That submerges hope.
It is a more powerful motivator.

What about the opportunity
To save hundreds of millions,
Entire coastal cultures from submergence?

When debate is anchored in opportunism
Hope is reduced to a spectacle.

We must defy and contest such
Imaginaries. Call them out
Consistently
As misleading hopemongers.

Hope is not Janus-faced, it does not look away
When counter-arguments are deposited.
Hope rests in respectful judgement,
In rooting for measured deliberation.

With no respect, no room for basic dignity,
No recognition of the right to life
In all its fullness
And diversity
It is apocalypse now.

Channel hope
To resist the dislocation
That perpetuates fossil fuel hegemony
And paves the way
For regulation to depoliticise
What is the most political thing of all:
Our future, our here and now,
The right to echo the call
Championed by Greta Thunberg.

Hope is a tool to levy
Reasonable demands in unreasonable times
Expecting power to yield to truth.

We live in an apocalyptic moment
That empathy and friendship help us recognise.
Solidarity is our vessel of choice
And on these tumultuous waters under
Cloudy skies, hope is our guiding star.

Index

A
Access, 4, 6, 18, 19, 21, 25, 27, 38, 48, 55, 56, 80, 81, 98, 99, 106, 112, 133
Accountability analysis, 106, 109, 112, 113, 115, 129, 141, 152–155
Accountability crisis, vii, 4–11, 110, 111, 114
Automobility, 74, 75, 83–84, 86, 123, 132

B
Berlin, 36, 37, 42–50, 107–109, 120, 121, 124, 125, 129, 130, 154
Bureaucratic, 16, 19–22, 24, 54, 71, 96, 106, 108, 111, 113, 114, 118, 120, 123–128

C
Colorado, 38, 90, 95, 99, 100, 114, 122, 123, 126–128, 133
Conflict, 37, 55, 65, 66, 107, 110, 121, 123, 125–127

D
Discursive, 6, 16–19, 37, 66, 83, 106, 108, 109, 111, 112, 114, 118, 120, 124–128

E
Empirical, ix, 4, 16, 18, 25, 36, 38, 43, 48–50, 80, 106, 113, 130, 131, 133, 137, 138
Energy governance, 43, 45, 48, 129, 130
Energy infrastructure, 4, 5, 21, 27, 36, 38, 42, 48, 49, 107, 108, 120, 121, 125
Environmental governance, vi, viii, 8, 16, 28, 36, 39, 47–48, 80–83, 91–94, 100, 107, 118, 119, 128–134, 138, 148

F
Financial, 9, 16, 20, 25–27, 49, 106, 108, 110, 111, 113, 114, 118, 120, 124–128

H

Habitat exchange, 38, 90, 95, 99, 107, 113, 114, 122, 123, 126–128, 133
Historical, 36, 37, 42, 43, 50, 107–109, 119–122, 124, 129, 137

I

Indonesia, 55–59, 107, 109
Institutional authority, 8–10, 18, 37, 121

M

Mobility transitions, 82, 120, 123, 124, 127, 128, 132

N

Nordic, 38, 74–86, 107, 112, 113, 120, 123, 124, 127, 128, 132
Norway, v, 37, 69–71, 74, 79, 80, 111, 113, 122, 125–127, 158, 159

O

Opportunistic/opportunism, 107, 110, 120–122, 125–126

P

Performative/performativity, 37, 107, 111, 120, 126–127
Portugal, 4–7, 16
Power-play, 107, 113, 120, 127–128

Practical, 9, 65, 90, 92, 96, 99, 106, 129, 131
Practices of legitimation, vii–ix, 7–11, 16–28, 36, 39, 42, 43, 48–50, 91, 95, 106–115, 118, 123–129, 137, 138, 153
Prefigurative/prefiguration, 107, 111, 112, 120, 126, 127

R

Routinisation, 107, 120, 123, 128

S

Sage-grouse, 38, 90, 91, 93, 99–100, 113–115, 122, 123, 126, 127, 133
Spatial/spatiality, 25, 27, 42, 47, 107, 112, 120, 121, 124, 129
Sustainability transition, 67–68, 91, 92, 97

T

Target-setting, 37, 64–71, 107, 111, 121, 122, 125, 126, 155
Technocratic, 16, 22–25, 106, 108, 110, 111, 113, 114, 118, 120, 124–128
Temporal/temporality, 24, 50, 107, 108, 120, 124–125, 129

Z

Zero Growth Objective, 68–71, 111, 121, 122, 126